When Con~~flict~~

For Meredith, Herwald, Ben and Zand

Start where conflict parties are, not where third parties want them to be.

When Conflict Resolution Fails

An Alternative to Negotiation and Dialogue:
Engaging Radical Disagreement
in Intractable Conflicts

Oliver Ramsbotham

polity

First published in 2017 by Polity Press

Polity Press
65 Bridge Street
Cambridge CB2 1UR, UK

Polity Press
350 Main Street
Malden, MA 02148, USA

ISBN-13: 978-0-7456-8798-8
ISBN-13: 978-0-7456-8799-5 (pb)

A catalogue record for this book is available from the British Library.

Library of Congress Cataloging-in-Publication Data

Names: Ramsbotham, Oliver, author.
Title: When conflict resolution fails : an alternative to negotiation and
   dialogue / Oliver Ramsbotham.
Description: Malden, MA : Polity Press, 2016. | Includes bibliographical
   references and index.
Identifiers: LCCN 2016011436 (print) | LCCN 2016023136 (ebook) | ISBN
   9780745687988 (hardback) | ISBN 9780745687995 (pbk.) | ISBN 9780745688015
   (Mobi) | ISBN 9780745688022 (Epub)
Subjects: LCSH: Conflict management. | Arab-Israeli conflict.
Classification: LCC JZ6010 .R263 2016 (print) | LCC JZ6010 (ebook) | DDC
   303.6/9--dc23
LC record available at https://lccn.loc.gov/2016011436

Typeset in 10.5 on 12pt Sabon by Servis Filmsetting Ltd, Stockport, Cheshire
Printed and bound in the UK by CPI Group (UK) Ltd, Croydon

For further information on Polity, visit our website: politybooks.com

CONTENTS

ILLUSTRATIONS

Figures

Tables

Boxes

Maps

PREFACE

Two factors have shaped the way this book is written. First, it is a short book about a large subject. Second, it is intended for readers some of whom will have no previous knowledge of conflict resolution or of the Israel–Palestine conflict that is taken as a case study. So the emphasis is on conveying main points clearly without too many qualifications which might obscure the argument. After a somewhat academic opening chapter to set the scene, the text is thereafter kept clear of jargon, acronyms and unnecessary references. Instead of lengthy literature reviews, wherever possible ideas are illustrated in the most simple way by direct quotation and then tested by concrete examples. Under pressure of space, preference has been given to the case study (chapters 5 to 8) over what precedes and follows it. So in chapter 3, for example, there is no attempt to do justice to the rich literatures on dialogue, problem-solving and negotiation. Instead, the main effort is to illustrate how classic conflict resolution sets aside or ignores the radical disagreements at the heart of intractable conflict and why, as a result, there may be no further recourse when that proves premature. Chapter 4 is then able to focus on what might be done to remedy this.

It should be made clear that this book is not a criticism of conflict resolution, which is my own topic and the field I have spent my professional life studying, teaching and writing about. But, however many successes there are, particular attention always needs to be paid to failure, because, as argued in chapter 1, this is where growth and development most readily occur. So the key question is: What can be done when, so far, conflict resolution approaches do not work? The book is intended not as a *replacement* of conflict resolution but – as made clear in chapter 9 – as an *extension* of it.

In relation to the case study, this preface is being written in early June 2016. In Israel the Labor Party in 2016 adopted a new Comprehensive Diplomatic Security Plan that affirms renewed commitment to a 'two-state solution', as noted in chapter 7, but Avigdor Lieberman's virulently rejectionist party has recently joined the ruling coalition government. In line with the 'two-track' strategy set out in chapter 6, Palestinians plan a major international campaign focused around 5 June 2017, the fiftieth anniversary of the Israeli takeover, demanding an end to the ambiguity of the status quo and a stark choice for Israel: either end the occupation and deliver two states for two nations or give equal rights to all throughout the area subject to Israeli control until a political solution is found. Palestinians feel ambivalent about the nature of a renewed emphasis on a 'regional setting' for final agreement, which includes an Egyptian focus on intra-Palestinian reconciliation between Fatah and Hamas and Saudi Arabian intimations about adapting the 2002/2007 Arab Peace Initiative, possibly as part of a 'Sunni' Arab/Israeli front against Iran. There is great uncertainty about the succession to President Abbas. At wider international level there is a continually shifting 'French initiative', promise of a future 'Quartet Report' to rekindle international involvement, talk of a possible 'swansong' of 'Obama parameters' (perhaps in the form of a UN Security Council Resolution), and uncertainty about the new regional role of Russia. The impact of the outcome of the US presidential election is another imponderable.

Readers who would like to acquaint themselves further with the academic dimension of analysis can consult *Contemporary Conflict Resolution* (Ramsbotham, Woodhouse and Miall 2016), which provides a comprehensive overview of the conflict resolution field, and my book *Transforming Violent Conflict: Radical Disagreement, Dialogue and Survival* (2010), for more on the particular phenomenon of radical disagreement.

Kevin Avruch gives a characteristically accurate and succinct summary of the central argument in the book, from which the extract on the back cover is taken. I can do no better than to end this preface by reproducing the full version here:

In his earlier *Transforming Violent Conflict* (2010) Ramsbotham introduced the ideas of 'radical disagreement' (the main linguistic manifestation of intractable conflict) and its communicative counterpart 'linguistic intractability' to the lexicon of conflict resolution. He also demonstrated how and why, in the face of these two conditions, the usual methods in the conflict resolution 'toolkit' – principled (interest-based) negotiation, interactive problem-solving, and dialogue – so often fail. This book, using the Israeli–Palestinian conflict as its main case, begins where the earlier one leaves off. He describes a form of 'extended conflict resolution', built around ideas and practices of 'strategic engagement' that constitute the preconditions necessary for conflict resolution to have any chance of success. Along the way he challenges our ideas of the role of third parties and proposes what may be, ethically, the outer limits of conflict resolution itself.

Part I

The Argument

1

LEARNING FROM FAILURE

Bringing warring parties to the negotiating table is the aim of any peace process. But what happens when those negotiations falter and conflict resolution fails? Is everything lost, or are there prospects for meaningful change in even the most intractable of conflicts?

Introduction

This book sums up work I have done over several decades on the communicative aspect of intractable conflicts – beginning with *Choices* in 1987. Intractable conflicts are those in which attempts at peaceful containment, settlement and transformation have so far gained no purchase. In 'frozen' conflicts there is a semblance of peaceful management, but this is superficial and is likely to break down again. I say 'so far' because it is always possible that such attempts will succeed in future, as conflict resolution wants, and as has happened in many other cases. But 'so far' can go on for years, if not decades, during which time unimaginable destruction and damage to human lives and life hopes may be inflicted. The victims are overwhelmingly the most vulnerable. What, if anything, can be done in these circumstances? The focus is on how best to handle what I call *linguistic intractability* and its chief verbal manifestation *radical disagreement*.

In order to get to grips with this challenge we first need to know both what conflict resolution is trying to achieve and what aspects of prevailing patterns of large-scale conflict block the way. This is the job of chapters 1 and 2. The main argument begins in chapter 3.

It will be helpful to remember in what follows that the aim of conflict resolution is to overcome violence, not conflict. Conflict

3

cannot be overcome, because it is inherent in social and political change. And conflict should not be overcome, because without it injustice and unjust systems cannot be challenged. Mahondas Gandhi and Martin Luther King were opposed to violence. But they were not opposed to conflict. They wanted to eliminate the British occupation of India and racial discrimination in the United States. Nelson Mandela wanted to overthrow apartheid in South Africa. To do this, levels of conflict had to be *raised*, not *lowered*. Here is King in his famous address from the Washington memorial on 23 August 1963:

> We have also come to this hallowed spot to remind America of the fierce urgency of *now*. This is no time to engage in the luxury of cooling off or to take the tranquillizing drug of gradualism. *Now* is the time to make real the promises of democracy. The whirlwind of revolt will continue to shake the foundations of our nation until the bright day of justice emerges.[1]

What does this imply about peace processes in deep-rooted and intractable conflicts? First, that in peace talks between undefeated conflict parties the aim is often not to end the conflict, but to transmute it into non-violent forms of continuing struggle and change. Otherwise the conflict parties will not enter the peace process. For example, this is what happened in Northern Ireland in 1998. Here a 'post-war settlement' is a 'continuation of the conflict by other means' (which is why, for reasons explained below, I call it *Clausewitz in reverse*). Requiring an 'end of conflict' in such cases is unrealistic and self-defeating. It also follows that a further aim is to separate what I call *extremists of ends*, who are uncompromising about strategic goals, from *extremists of means*, who are uncompromising about the use of violence. This is a central distinction in dealing with terrorism, as made clear in chapter 9.

It may seem surprising in the light of this that conflict resolution regularly discounts the radical disagreement that lies at the heart of linguistic intractability as an 'all-too-familiar' dead end and a terminus to dialogue that needs from the outset to be transformed, not learnt from. In intractable conflicts this is premature. Radical disagreement turns out to be perhaps the least familiar aspect of intense political conflict. And conflict resolution fails when the conditions that it presupposes do not yet exist, the assumptions on which it rests (often drawn from the social and political sciences) do not yet apply, and conflict parties are not yet ready to behave in the way it wants. It may then find that it has no other recourse when it is confronted by the 'war of words' (the radical disagreement) that pervades intractable asymmetric conflict and blocks conflict resolution at all levels.

What is the alternative? The central argument in chapter 4 is that, when conflict resolution fails, we should turn in the opposite direction – to conflict engagement. Instead of ignoring radical disagreement, we should first try to understand what obstructs the way and then adapt practice accordingly. This means starting where conflict parties are, not where third parties want them to be. It means beginning not *between* conflict parties but *within* them. Internal disagreements are often more ferocious than external disagreements. And internal divisions can be the main blockage to external accommodation. Above all, it means promoting *collective strategic thinking* by the main identity groups: Where are they? Where do they want to be? How do they get there? Why are conflict parties prepared to do this when they are not prepared for conflict resolution? Because they want to overcome internal divisions – not in order to 'understand the other', but in order to win. So how can this nevertheless be a 'placeholder' for a possible future initiation or revival of conflict resolution? A number of reasons are given in chapter 4 and illustrated in the case study. This is the core of the book. Emphasizing strategic discourse *within* parties to a conflict is often the real key to progress when other avenues are blocked – including the regularly overlooked strategic question of how to influence the internal dynamics of the other side. Chapter 4 also offers a template for how to conduct collective strategic thinking of this kind based on the work of the strategy groups described in Part II. Practitioners may want to try this out for themselves.

Taking as its focus the long-running and seemingly irresolvable conflict between Israel and Palestine, the argument in the case study in Part II is that what is needed in these circumstances is not less radical disagreement, but more. Only by understanding what is blocking the way and by promoting collective strategic engagement within, across and between the groups involved – including third parties – can deadlock be transformed. Chapters 5 and 6 go beyond the tendency among behavioural scientists to treat 'intractable' conflicts as primarily the result of correctible subjective misunderstandings. They demonstrate how the differing narratives of the parties to the conflict come out of their 'lived experience' and are thus in a basic sense as real as the 'objective' conflicts over land and power – and inseparable from them. That is what blocks conflict resolution. In terms of strategic thinking, the case study shows how at the heart of asymmetric conflict lie the radically different requirements of *possessors* and *challengers*. The question of the dialectics of power is central here. For example, why should Israelis give up anything if the status quo continues to be better than any strategic alternative? And how can Palestinians transform the status quo when the process of bilateral negotiation brokered by the United States is itself part of what perpetuates it? It is only the promotion of strategic engagement that illuminates these critical dynamics.

Chapter 7 shows the importance of including all the main crosscutting identity groups in the strategic engagement process in complex transnational conflicts. In this case, it is the neglected constituency of Israeli Palestinians (20 per cent of the population of Israel) that needs for the first time to be fully represented as a 'core group' in strategic negotiations.

Using the example of the attempt, between July 2013 and April 2014, by US Secretary of State John Kerry to end the conflict, chapter 8 shows that third parties are not neutral, impartial or disinterested in intractable political conflicts of this kind. It also demonstrates how a conflict resolution approach to negotiation such as *principled negotiation* needs to be supplemented in times of maximum attrition by a prior *strategic negotiation* approach, which links strategic thinking *within* conflict parties to the wider (regional, international) strategic *context* where prevailing patterns of transnational conflict are now increasingly determined.

Part III looks at wider applications in terms of other phases, other levels and other conflicts. This introduces a new and as yet relatively unexplored frontier in conflict studies. It holds out rich promise for extending conflict engagement in some of the world's deadliest and most difficult hot spots. A central argument here is for linking conflict resolution to strategic studies. Turning from strategic engagement to 'heuristic engagement' (from the Greek word for 'discover'), chapter 10 explores *agonistic dialogue* (the dialogue of struggle or dialogue between enemies) and concludes that, in intractable conflicts, conflict parties are not nearer, but much further apart than was supposed. It uncovers why there is no adequate third-party theory or 'philosophy' of radical disagreement. Part III ends on a suitably humble note by asking what happens when even strategic conflict engagement and 'extended conflict resolution' fail.

Summing the whole thing up, the book argues that, during times of maximum attrition, the radical disagreements that constitute the core of linguistic intractability are best seen as an *opportunity* rather than as a *terminus*. This opens up a new dimension in conflict studies. Learning how to understand and respond to this is the central task of the as yet underdeveloped field of heuristic and strategic conflict engagement.

The rest of this chapter offers a survey of the conflict resolution field under the theme most suitable for this book – learning how to respond to failure.

Second-order social learning and conflict resolution

From the beginning social learning theory has been at the heart of conflict resolution. The founders of the field stressed the importance of understanding complex systems in the search for ways of transforming violent into non-violent conflict. Morton Deutsch, John Burton and others drew on general systems theory to explain the cooperative and competitive behaviour of social organisms[2] and on game theory to analyse the variety of options available to conflict parties.[3] Burton was particularly influenced by the idea of first-order and second-order learning.[4] It is not only individuals who need to learn adaptive responses in order to survive but socio-cultural systems in general, whose underlying assumptions and habitual patterns of behaviour tend to resist necessary change. If a system – or species – does not adapt, it is discarded. History is littered with examples of systemic obsolescence. It is a never-ending process, as previous success may prove counter-productive in a new environment. Then it is important to stop investing in what may have worked before and to discover what the altered circumstances demand. The requirement is to learn the right lessons and to adapt accordingly. What are the right lessons? It is by looking at the *frontiers of failure* – those locations where the system is malfunctioning – that second-order social learning is best achieved.

In the 1950s, when the conflict resolution field was established, the advent of nuclear weapons meant that violent human conflict now threatened the future of *Homo sapiens* as a whole. This was an existential crisis. For Kenneth Boulding (whose systemic training was in economics), 'the international system is by far the most pathological and costly segment of the whole social system.'[5] For Anatol Rapoport (biologist and mathematician), 'the illusion that increasing losses for the other side is equivalent to winning is *the* reason that the struggles are so prolonged and the conflicting parties play the game to a lose/lose end.'[6] Social systems that cling to what Rapoport called 'default values' (first-order learning) are not capable of achieving the transformation required. So the 'critical issue of peace' – the need to convert destructive into constructive conflict – demanded the 'incorporation of second order learning in social systems'. And, given the changed environment, this could only be done 'through a participative design process'.[7]

Such were the ideas that inspired the 'early church' of conflict resolvers in the 1950s and 1960s. The first issue of the *Journal of Conflict Resolution* (1957) put it like this:

> The reasons which have led us to this enterprise may be summed up in two propositions. The first is that by far the most practical problem facing the world today is that of international relations – more specifically the prevention of global war. The second is that if intellectual progress is to be made in this area, the study of international relations must be made an interdisciplinary enterprise, drawing its discourse from all the social sciences and even further.[8]

The complex systems that made war not only possible but, in some cases, likely operated in many overlapping spheres – military, political, economic, social, psychological – and at many different levels. So this must be matched by the requisite responses from conflict resolution. That is why the new field had to be interdisciplinary.

But, as they developed their programme, conflict resolution theorists and practitioners found that more and more 'frontiers of failure' needed to be taken into account and addressed if the complex system as a whole was to be transformed. What had begun as a focus on the pathology of interstate war had expanded twenty years later (*Journal of Conflict Resolution* 1973) to take in major drivers of conflict, such as both north–south socio-economic divisions and environmental constraints, which were seen as potential generators of global conflict and therefore in urgent need of systemic transformation:

> The threat of nuclear holocaust remains with us and may well continue to do so for centuries, but other problems are competing with deterrence and disarmament studies for our attention. The journal must also attend to international conflict over justice, equality and human dignity; problems of conflict resolution for ecological balance and control are within our proper scope and especially suited for interdisciplinary attention.[9]

A critical early realization among some of the most creative shapers of the new conflict resolution field was that the stipulations of second-order social learning applied as much to their own enterprise as to any others. In order to keep the field adaptive, innovative and effective, therefore, it was necessary to focus continually on the 'frontiers of failure' – those sites where conflict resolution itself did not (or did not yet) work. These were the locations where adaptation and growth were most needed, where reality checks could best be taken, and where new ways of responding were most likely to be discovered.

A brief history of the field can be seen to reflect this Popperian perspective.[10]

Lessons from the frontiers of failure: conflict resolution in its first fifty years

In the first, heroic period in the 1950s and 1960s, the existing study of international relations was seen to have been taken over by first-order realist ways of thinking which offered no solution to the main systemic threats. The pioneers of the conflict resolution field challenged realist reliance on competitive military defence preparations, balance of power theory, and deterrence as the main preventers of war, because these could no longer be relied on to work in the nuclear age and the penalty of failure would be too high. Instead they looked to a far wider study of human conflict that also embraced non-interstate wars, revolutions, insurrections, and human conflicts at other levels right down to small group and individual struggles. The statistical underpinning for this study was found in earlier analyses of 'deadly quarrels' in general by Pitirim Sorokin (1937), Lewis Fry Richardson (1960, posthumous publication) and Quincy Wright (1942). There are accounts of the excitement with which founders of the field greeted the arrival in the United States of Stephen Richardson with microfiches of his father's as yet unpublished work.

As well as being multidisciplinary and multi-level, the new field also aspired to be multicultural – drawing from non-Western Gandhian, Buddhist and other traditions – and aimed to be both analytic (polemology) and normative (eirenics) and to combine the theoretic (theoria) and the applied (praxis).[11] This manifested itself in the way innovative pre-1950 initiatives at different levels were now brought together and integrated into what it was hoped would be a decisive paradigm-shift – including Mary Parker Follett's 'mutual gains' approach in labour relations (1942), Von Neumann's and Morgenstern's game theory (1944), Kurt Lewin's work on the social psychology of group conflict (1948), Crane Brinton's 'anatomy of political revolution' (1938) and David Mitrany's argument for the 'functional development of international organisation' as the foundation of a 'working peace system' (later seen to have anticipated the European Coal and Steel Community and eventually the European Union) (1943).

At the heart of this distinctive new conflict resolution field were three conceptual nodal points that are worth bearing in mind.

9

First there was Morton Deutsch's distinction between destructive and constructive conflict.[12] We have already noted in the introduction how the aim of conflict resolution is to prevent or end violent conflict, but not 'constructive' conflict.

Second, there was Johan Galtung's contrast between direct, structural and cultural violence.[13] Direct violence is where children are murdered. Structural violence is where children die through poverty. Cultural violence is whatever blinds us to this or seeks to justify it. We end direct violence by changing conflict behaviour, structural violence by removing structural contradictions and injustices, and cultural violence by changing attitudes. These responses relate in turn to broader strategies of peacekeeping, peacebuilding and peacemaking respectively. Negative peace is defined as the cessation of direct violence, and positive peace as the overcoming of structural and cultural violence as well.

Putting Deutsch's and Galtung's ideas together, the normative aim of conflict resolution was to transform actually or potentially violent conflict into non-violent forms of struggle and change. In contrast to the determinism inherent in some forms of realism and Marxism, conflict resolution insisted that violence in all its forms is ultimately subject to the possibility of human decision, and that it can and must be overcome if future generations are to survive. Given the deep biological, psychological and institutional roots of violence, this was bound to be an uphill – indeed perpetual – struggle. The odds were not in favour of conflict resolution. There would be setbacks *en route*.

Third, there was John Burton's idea that intractable conflicts are rooted in the failure of existing institutions to satisfy non-negotiable basic human needs:

> The conclusion to which we are coming is that seemingly different and separate social problems, from street violence to industrial frictions, to ethnic and international conflicts, are symptoms of the same cause: institutional denial of needs of recognition and identity, and the sense of security provided when they are satisfied, despite losses through violent conflict.[14]

For Burton, although basic human needs – identity needs, security needs, autonomy needs, development needs – are non-negotiable, they are also non-zero sum, so that the door to resolution is always open. The term 'non-zero sum' comes from game theory and means that, unlike some conflicts over scarce resources, one side's gain does not mean another's loss – indeed, one side often cannot gain security or maximize development unless the other side does the same.

10

It seems fair to conclude that, in its first two decades, the founders of the conflict resolution field had indeed creatively explored the 'frontiers of failure' in the management of human conflict and, as a result, had put together a promising alternative paradigm. The institutional bases for the new approach had been laid, mainly in North America and Europe. A set of complementary methodologies had been formulated, encompassing the 'subjectivist' dialogue approach, the 'objectivist' rational negotiation approach, and the 'structuralist' social justice approach – tentatively corresponding to attempts to address the 'attitude', 'behaviour' and 'contradiction' vertices of Galtung's conflict triangle. And there had been the beginning of a testing out of theory in practice with the early experiments in 'controlled communication' or 'problem-solving' workshops.[15] Some internal disputes within the field were still unresolved, but this can itself be seen as a sign of potential future growth from a social learning perspective.[16]

During the next period in the 1970s and 1980s, those working in the conflict resolution field continued to labour under the constraints of the Cold War, intensified by the Soviet takeover in Afghanistan (1979) and complicated by the Iranian revolution (1979). In the early 1980s the nuclear arms race reached its zenith. This was a period of consolidation and development in conflict resolution, possibly less innovative, but still responsive to newly perceived challenges. Notable here at international level, building on Charles Osgood's 'graduated and reciprocated initiatives in tension reduction' (GRIT) approach to détente, were Robert Axelrod's associated conclusions about the 'evolution of cooperation' in game theory, together with its implications for arms control (in which Rapoport's 'tit-for-tat' strategy came out surprisingly strongly).[17] At domestic level, the whole field of Alternative Dispute Resolution began to be elaborated (covering labour relations, public policy disputes, neighbourhood conflicts, family mediation, etc.).[18] While, between the two, Burton's needs theory was applied with great prescience by Edward Azar to a host of non-interstate intractable conflicts that he called 'protracted social conflicts'. His analysis in terms of *preconditions* that made certain societies more prone to conflict, and *process dynamics* that dictated whether or not in the event major armed conflict erupted, laid a sound theoretical base for what the Carnegie Commission later called 'structural' and 'operational' prevention.[19] All of this was innovative at a time when international relations and security studies were preoccupied mainly with the Cold War confrontation.

This was a period in which negotiation studies (notably the Harvard Program on Negotiation), multi-track diplomacy and mediation studies were put on a firm analytic basis. Conflict resolution centres spread around the world, and the idea of a global civil society that transcended gender and culture barriers was articulated, notably by Elise Boulding, Secretary-General of the International Peace Research Association (IPRA), with her promotion of the idea of 'future imaging' in all social and political planning, so that decisions are taken in terms of human needs over a '200-year present', which in terms of explanation and understanding reaches back into the past but in terms of impact takes in the equal interests of future generations.[20]

In the 1990s, the conflict resolution field had reached a point of maturity where the end of the Cold War made a number of its terms and approaches, relatively marginalized in the earlier period, all at once the stock-in-trade of politicians and pundits. Peacekeeping, peacemaking and peacebuilding occupied international attention, while 'conflict prevention' moved to the centre of the UN's agenda – and the agendas of regional organizations (OSCE, African Union) and international financial institutions (World Bank, International Monetary Fund). The ending of the Cold War revealed a world that had long been familiar in conflict resolution – a plethora of protracted social conflicts in which economic struggles to control the resources of vulnerable states, ethno-national efforts to redraw the boundaries of states, and ideological attempts to change the nature of states all demanded a more sophisticated array of management, settlement and transformation approaches than had been widely familiar before. The conflict resolution field responded by elaborating ideas of 'contingency' (varying requirements in different conflict types and phases) and 'complementarity' (synchronizing a range of responses).[21] For example, aid and development agencies that had hitherto avoided conflict resolution, because they did not see their role as 'political', now acknowledged that good conflict analysis was essential for the success of their missions and that good conflict impact assessment was necessary to ensure that they 'did no harm'.[22] Most of the environments within which they now worked were intense conflict zones of the kind with which conflict resolution had long been engaged, where traditional ideas of political neutrality were compromised.

Where are the frontiers of failure today?

But greater exposure also brought greater criticism. After a honeymoon period in the early 1990s, when some hoped that the original declared purposes of the United Nations and associated international organizations might at last be realized – and the paradigm shift envisaged by the founders of conflict resolution might actually take place – the skies soon clouded over. Debacles in Bosnia and Rwanda (no doubt unfairly) discredited UN-led peacekeeping interventions. The Oslo peace process in Israel/Palestine, hailed in the conflict resolution field as a textbook example of its methodology, stalled in the second half of the decade and appeared to discredit this mode of peacemaking, while post-war peacebuilding projects in countries such as Cambodia and Haiti also ran into difficulties. The 11 September 2001 attacks on the USA ushered in the 'war on terror', to be followed by the embroilments in Afghanistan and Iraq. Much of the Islamic world was convulsed by struggles to define its ideological and political identity. Ominous echoes of the Cold War resounded around confrontation in Ukraine. The quiet voice of conflict resolution seemed to be drowned out.

At theoretical level, too, conflict resolution was assailed by critics from the right and from the left. For traditional realists, in a world where irreconcilable interests compete for power, 'soft' conflict resolution approaches were dismissed as ineffective and dangerous. What possible answer could conflict resolution have to the lethal combination of rogue states, globalized crime, the proliferation of weapons of mass destruction, and the fanatical ideologues of international terrorism? For critical theoretic inheritors of the Marxist mantle, in the structurally unequal world of late capitalism, 'problem-solving' conflict resolution approaches were seen to reinforce existing imbalances and to fail to address the need for underlying change. For poststructural theorists, conflict resolution discourse about cosmopolitan values was permeated by unwarranted universalizing assumptions about truth and reality. Beyond this lay even broader assaults such as Paul Salem's 'critique of western conflict resolution from a nonwestern perspective'.[23]

The key question for the conflict resolution field from the standpoint of second-order social learning is whether it is responding creatively to these critiques. Have theorists and practitioners from around the world acknowledged the cases in which established conflict resolution approaches have so far failed, and adapted accordingly? How are success and failure measured? Is adequate ongoing evaluation built in to the different enterprises so that they can be self-correcting? Is the field still innovative and dynamic? Are lessons being learnt from the frontiers of failure?

Conclusion

In summary, the main thing to take from this chapter is the idea from second-order learning that, when conflict resolution fails, the obstruction must not be ignored or prematurely set aside. On the contrary, what blocks the way must be actively *acknowledged, understood* and *adapted to*. We will turn to this task in chapters 3 and 4. But first we must ask how serious current failures are. How high is the mountain that those who espouse the hopes and aspirations of conflict resolution have to climb? What are the dimensions of intractable conflict that conflict resolution seeks to address?

2

CONFLICT RESOLUTION
AND ITS ENEMIES

In this chapter we survey the current situation in order to get some idea of the scale of the challenge that conflict resolution faces in its quest to reduce violence in international politics. What does the conflict and violence data tell us? How should it be interpreted? What is the conflict resolution response? And how does all of this help us to pinpoint where the impediments to conflict resolution lie?[1]

We can begin with the optimistic thesis of Steven Pinker in his influential but controversial book *The Better Angels of our Nature: Why Violence Has Declined* (2011),[2] in which he argues that measurable violence in the world has been declining for millennia and that 'we may be living in the most peaceable era in our species' existence'.[3] By 'violence', Pinker means war, homicide, genocide, domestic violence, how children, minorities, and animals are treated, and so on. His survey is based on comparative measures of violence relative to size of population. The main metric he applies for measuring violence is deaths per 100,000 per year. On Pinker's vast canvas the decline in violence is seen to have gone through five phases: the 'pacification process' from hunter-gatherers to agricultural civilizations; the 'civilizing process' from the Middle Ages to nation-states; the 'humanitarian revolution' associated with the abolition of slavery and slow reduction in torture; the 'long peace' after the Second World War; and the 'new peace' after the end of the Cold War.

For Pinker, the 'shockingly high homicide rates of pre-state societies, with 10 to 60 per cent of the men dying at the hands of other men', have been progressively tempered by the evolution of the modern democratic state with its monopoly of force; by the bringing of potential enemies 'into each other's moral circles by facilitating trade, cultural exchanges, and people-to-people activities'; by a

15

progressive 'feminization' of society; by increased cosmopolitanism brought about by mass literacy and mobility; and by the 'escalator of reason', which reframes violence as a problem to be solved rather than a contest to be won. This is a pretty good summary of the conflict resolution approach outlined in chapter 1. At the root of this for Pinker is that the human mind is a 'combinatorial, recursive system': we have not only thoughts, but thoughts about thoughts. So, in a passage reminiscent of Burton's second-order learning argument, he sees the 'advances in human conflict resolution' as 'dependent on this ability'. For Pinker, the mindsets predisposed to violence 'evolved to deal with hostilities in the ancestral past, and we must bring them into the open if we are to work around them in the present.' Anti-evolutionists avert their gaze from 'the evolutionary logic of violence', because they fear that 'acknowledging it is tantamount to accepting it or even to approving it':

> Instead they have pursued the comforting delusion of the Noble Savage, in which violence is an arbitrary product of learning or a pathogen that bores into us from outside. But denying the logic of violence makes it easy to forget how readily violence can flare up, and ignoring the parts of the mind that ignite violence makes it easy to overlook the parts that can extinguish it. With violence, as with so many other concerns, human nature is the problem, but human nature is also the solution.[4]

Not surprisingly the topic is highly disputed. Some of this relates to the huge literature on the nature and roots of aggression and violence in human society. Some concerns the evolution of warfare and the modern state. Some is to do with Pinker's statistical methodology itself. Many readers, confronted by shocking recent levels of violence in the Middle East, Africa, Ukraine and elsewhere that have erupted since Pinker's book was published, may remain unconvinced by the thesis.

But the thesis has also received quite widespread analytic support – for example, from Andrew Mack and his colleagues in the carefully argued *Human Security Report 2013: The Decline of Global Violence: Evidence, Explanation and Contestation*,[5] which also attributes much of the decline in violence to the evolution of a new 'global security governance system' since 1945 along lines advocated and supported by the founders of the conflict resolution field in the same period:

> In its current stage of development, this continually expanding system of global security remains inchoate, disputatious, inefficient, and prone to tragic mistakes. But as previous *Human Security Reports* have

argued, the evidence suggests that it has also been remarkably effective in driving down the number and deadliness of armed conflicts.[6]

In 2016 Pinker and Mack reasserted this thesis.[7]
Who is right?

The 'long peace' post-1945 and the 'new peace' post-1990

Turning to the last two of Pinker's phases, the new 'international order' after 1945 was only the latest in a series of attempts to construct what Kalevi Holsti calls a 'peace system' after previous periods of convulsion and war, such as the Thirty Years' War (Westphalia 1648), Louis XIV's wars (Utrecht 1713), the Napoleonic wars (Vienna 1815) and the First World War (Paris 1919).

Table 2.1 reproduces Holsti's comparison of post-war peace orders over the last 350 years, together with eight 'prerequisites for peace' on which his comparison is based.[8] Holsti concludes that the greater the number of criteria met, the more stable the ensuing period turned out to be. According to him there has been least success in relation to the last two criteria – developing methods of peaceful change and anticipating future conflict-generating issues. This is where the capacity for second-order social learning, discussed in chapter 1, comes in.

Although the nature of the post-1945 system was largely dictated by the victors of the Second World War, the values expressed in the Preamble to the UN Charter reflected the two main conflict resolution aims of promoting both negative peace (ending large-scale direct violence) – 'to save succeeding generations from the scourge of war, which twice in our lifetime has brought untold sorrow to mankind . . .' – and positive peace (overcoming structural and cultural violence):

> to reaffirm faith in fundamental human rights, in the dignity and worth of the human person, in the equal rights of men and women and of nations large and small; to establish conditions under which justice and respect for the obligations arising from treaties and other sources of international law can be maintained; and to promote social progress and better standards of life in larger freedom.[9]

By the time Holsti was writing, in 1989, it could be argued that, despite the fact that the political, economic, psychological and ideological forces that generate violence are deeply rooted in human

17

Table 2.1   Post-war peace orders, 1648–1945

Prerequisites for peace	Westphalia	Utrecht	Vienna	Paris	San Francisco
Governance	Yes	Yes	Yes	No*	Yes
Legitimacy	Yes	No	Yes	No	Yes
Assimilation	Yes	Yes	Yes	No	Yes
Deterrence	Yes	No	Yes	No	No**
Conflict resolution	No	No	Yes	Yes	Yes
War as problem	No	No	No	Yes	Yes
Peaceful change	No	No	No	No	No
Future issues	No	No	No	No	No
Conditions satisfied	4/8	2/8	5/8	2/8	5/8

Source: Holsti, 1991: ch.13
*short-lived governance mechanism in League of Nations
**failure to develop deterrent capacity such as proposed Military Staff Committee or UN Standing Forces

Prerequisites for peace

- *Governance* (some system of responsibility for regulating behaviour in terms of the conditions of an agreement)
- *Legitimacy* (a new order following war cannot be based on perceived injustice or repression, and principles of justice have to be embodied into the post-war settlement)
- *Assimilation* (linked to legitimacy: the gains of living within a system are greater than the potential advantages of seeking to destroy it)
- A *deterrent system* (victors should create a coalition strong enough to deter defection, by force if necessary, to protect settlement norms or to change them by peaceful means)
- *Conflict resolving procedures and institutions* (the system of governance should include provision and capacity for identifying, monitoring, managing and resolving major conflict between members of the system, and the norms of the system would include willingness to use such institutions)
- *Consensus on war* (a recognition that war is the fundamental problem, acknowledgement of the need to develop and foster strong norms against the use of force and clear guiding principles for the legitimate use of force)
- *Procedures for peaceful change* (the need to review and adapt when agreements no longer relate to the reality of particular situations: peace agreements need to have built-in mechanisms for review and adaptation)
- *Anticipation of future issues* (peacemakers need to incorporate some ability to anticipate what may constitute conflict causes in the future: institutions and system norms should include provision for identifying, monitoring and handling not just the problems that created the last conflict but future conflicts as well)

18

institutions, human historical memory and, in the view of some, human nature, remarkable gains had been made. It was extraordinary that, unlike the League of Nations, the United Nations had retained membership of all major states – even surviving the advent of Maoist China – and presided over a dramatic decline in the incidence of inter-state war. It had been equally notable that the imperial era had been brought to an end with decolonization and a fourfold increase in UN state membership (from about fifty in 1945 to nearly 200 today). The world trade system now included Russia, India and China. Regional organizations were linked actively into this global system. There had been striking gains in overall human welfare according to a number of measures, despite gross inequalities and exceptions, and there was no reason why over the next decades these would not be spread wider.

There are, of course, other explanations for the decline in inter-state war during this period, including realist balance of power and deterrence explanations (Churchill: 'safety will be the sturdy child of terror') and arguments that anti-colonial wars and civil wars were 'proxy' great power wars.

But what about the twenty-five-year period that has now elapsed since the end of the Cold War? Has there been a 'new peace' following the further reordering of the international system since 1990, as Pinker suggests?

Certainly, over this comparatively short time a sequence of successive transformations of the world scene has taken place with remarkable rapidity. For example, during this period my colleagues, Hugh Miall and Tom Woodhouse, and I have brought out four successive editions of our book *Contemporary Conflict Resolution*. Each time we thought that the update should not be too onerous. Each time we were wrong. At the risk of oversimplification, the first edition marked the transition from a *bipolar world* to what US President George Bush senior reluctantly called a *New World Order*. It seemed to many that at last the UN, unshackled from its Cold War paralysis, might be able to play the role that its founders had envisaged. By the time of the second edition, however, we were faced with the *unipolar moment*, when the US hyperpower saw itself – and was widely seen – as the main shaper of world history. The attack on the World Trade Center and the Pentagon in September 2001 ushered in a 'war on terror' in which conflict resolution approaches were marginalized or coopted. By the time of the third edition we had moved with remarkable rapidity into a much more *multipolar* world. The 2008 financial crisis indicated the moment when the US economy on its own was no longer able to sustain the world financial system, while embroilments in Afghanistan and Iraq demonstrated the limits of US military power. And now, contemplating the situation towards the end of the second decade of the twenty-first century, we are confronted by a highly complex and shifting balance of forces that has once again made analysis both difficult and controversial. China has emerged as a global challenger, and Russia refuses to accept the subordinate role that was cast for it in the 1990s. Since the third edition of our book in 2011 have come the Arab revolutions, the Ukraine conflict, rising tension between China and Japan, continuing fighting in Afghanistan, the failure of the latest attempts to broker peace between Israelis and Palestinians, and conflicts elsewhere in the world. Many who follow these events in the media are given the strong impression that earlier relatively benign international conditions are now worsening – even that the 1945 system itself is under strain and might join earlier 'peace systems' in eventually being overturned by violent challenges that it can no longer contain.

What is the evidence on trends in global violence? Conflict resolution has from the start insisted that analysis must be based on data, not impressions. What do the statistics suggest?

The statistical evidence

The data on large-scale conflict and violence has grown exponentially in recent years. It is now an ongoing flood that continually increases in size, sophistication and variety. Box 2.1 gives a simplified view of the way in which different datasets, hitherto separate, are now increasingly being brought together to give a fuller and more nuanced picture of the changing situation year by year. Using the terminology on violence introduced in chapter 1, this means that it is increasingly

---

Box 2.1 Statistics of direct and indirect violence

(A) *Measuring direct violence*	(B) *Measuring structural and cultural violence*
Political violence data (riot, atrocity, war)	Fragile states and cities data
Terrorism data	Sustainable peace data
Organized crime data (homicides)	

---

possible to measure not just 'negative peace' (the presence or absence of direct violence) but also 'positive peace' (levels of structural and cultural violence).

What does the evidence suggest?

On *armed conflict* data available in 2015, Therése Pettersson and Peter Wallensteen at Uppsala recorded forty active conflicts in the world in 2014 according to their criteria, which is an increase of six since 2013:

> The number has increased in recent years but is still substantially lower than in 1991, the peak year after the end of the Cold War. 2014 also saw an increase in battle-related deaths. An escalation of several conflicts, and the extremely violent conflict in Syria, resulted in the highest number of battle-related deaths since the end of the Cold War.[10]

Figures from the 2015 *Global Peace Index* suggest that, between 2008 and 2014, numbers of war-related fatalities per year have risen from 49,000 to 180,000, with more than half the number (90,500) coming from Syria and Iraq.[11] This certainly indicates a worsening environment, away from the situation ten years ago and back towards the 'peak years' in the early 1990s. But the early 1990s was also a period when optimism and hopes of a more peaceful 'new world order' were at their height. Some conflicts that had been fuelled by Cold War rivalry came to an end then (Cambodia, El Salvador, Mozambique, etc.) and others flared up once the superpower lid had been removed (Bosnia, Somalia, Rwanda, etc.). In other words, 'statistics of deadly conflicts' were worse when, despite the horror for those affected, general impressions of the prevalence of violence in world politics were at their lowest.

Figures for *terrorism* have also escalated. According to the *Global Terrorism Index*, which covers 162 countries, there has been a marked upswing in deaths from terrorism of 61 per cent since 2012 to a level five times what it was in 2000. But the figures also show that 80 per cent of these have come in five countries: Afghanistan/Pakistan, Syria/Iraq and Nigeria (and overwhelmingly from al-Qaeda, Islamic State, Boko Haram, and also al-Shabaab in Somalia/Kenya).[12] If figures for the rest of the world are disaggregated from these, the graphs suggest that overall global levels of deaths from terrorism between 2000 and 2013 have remained the same or even gone down. It is important to take 'swamping' into account (cases where individual 'spikes' in the data can distort the overall picture). It is also difficult to separate terrorism from war when groups such as Islamic State seize territory and are transformed into quasi-states capable of waging approximations to conventional war.

Organized crime figures are considerably higher than those for armed conflict or terrorism and are now increasingly included in overall assessments of levels of global direct violence.[13] Here the situation again varies strikingly in different parts of the world. In Latin America, for example, where levels of armed conflict as conventionally measured are relatively low, figures for violence through organized crime are in some cases extraordinarily high. There are severe problems in gathering reliable statistics on organized crime in some countries. Figures are not yet precise enough to determine whether there has been an overall rise or decline in 2013–14.

Turning to the complex challenge of assessing 'structural and cultural violence', statistical advances have also been made.

For example, we now have systematic and increasingly elaborate attempts to measure levels of *state fragility*, such as successive reports by the Organization for Economic Cooperation and Development (OECD). Statistics on state fragility suggest that numbers of fragile states in 2013 had increased by four since the previous year (fifty-three fragile states rather than forty-nine states – a quarter of the member states of the UN).[14] Linking up with the statistics on organized crime, on the issue of *fragile cities* a 2014 International Peace Institute survey noted that forty-one of the top fifty 'dangerous cities' were in Latin America, and commented:

> Alongside the unprecedented urbanization of the last decade, urban fragility has emerged as a central challenge in global security and development. Like the fragile state, fragile cities suffer from rising instability, poverty, and violence and lack the capacities needed to face the magnitude of these challenges. Some analysts believe fragile or 'failing' cities mark "a new frontier of warfare", whether situated inside a war-torn state or a largely peaceful one.[15]

To measure levels of *peacefulness*, the *Global Peace Index* uses a mixture of twenty-four quantitative and qualitative indicators to rank more than three-quarters of UN member states. Indicators are gathered under eight 'pillars': well-functioning government; a sound business environment; equitable distribution of resources; acceptance of the rights of others; good relations with neighbours; free flow of information; high levels of human capital; and low levels of corruption.[16]

Using these criteria, the 2015 *Global Peace Index* concludes that 'the societal safety and security domain improved slightly last year (2014), driven by falls in the homicide rate and the likelihood of violent demonstrations.' It reports that its overall global 'score' remained stable in 2014 compared with the year before, but that this conceals wide regional discrepancies. Four geographical regions 'experienced an improvement in peace in comparison with 2013, while five became less peaceful.' Eighty-one countries were measured to be 'more peaceful' in 2014 compared to 2013 and seventy-eight 'less peaceful'. The most dramatic change here, unsurprisingly, came in the Middle East and North Africa (MENA) region, which for the first time registered as the least peaceful region in the world. The MENA region accounted for a high proportion of the increase in terrorist-caused deaths as noted above, some 100,000 of the overall 180,000 deaths from internal conflicts in 2014, and huge increases in the figures for refugee and internally displaced persons. Once again, the regional level of analysis is becoming increasingly prominent.

Amid all this, one set of statistics stands out in terms of dramatic escalation. The most recent figures from the UN High Commissioner for Refugees (2015) show the combined figure for global refugees and internally displaced persons still climbing, and now reaching the highest number since 1945 (59.5 million compared with 51.2 million in 2013 and 37.5 million a decade earlier).[17] This shocking figure is perhaps the most alarming indicator of all, combining as it does the outcome of war, persecution, state failure and sectarian violence, as well as criminal 'people traffic' and the spreading of information through social media about a 'better life' elsewhere. This composite tsunami of human suffering is hard to analyse and harder still to manage. It now joins earlier eras of mass migration and challenges the capacity of existing international and regional institutions to cope. Around 75 to 80 per cent of forcibly displaced people are housed in developing countries.

The 2015 *Global Peace Index* estimates that, overall, 'the economic impact of violence on the global economy in 2014 was US $14.3 trillion, which represents 13.4 per cent of world GDP.'[18]

Interpreting the evidence

Conflict interpretation is overdetermined. There are too many – often contradictory – theories of conflict. All the political, sociological, psychological, anthropological, cultural and gender sciences – including evolutionary biology – are based on theories of conflict. Competing theories and interpretations lie at the very heart of intense political conflicts themselves in the form of what I call 'radical disagreement'.

For this reason, Hugh Miall, Tom Woodhouse and I, in our 2016 edition of *Contemporary Conflict Resolution*, offer not a theory of conflict, but an overall 'interpretative framework' of prevailing patterns of what we call contemporary *transnational conflict* to indicate the different levels and sectors in and across which various theoretical interpretations can be located. Table 2.2 reproduces a summary of the framework, which I will comment on only briefly here.

Table 2.2   An interpretative framework for transnational conflict

	Level	Feature
1	Global	*Global drivers* Geopolitical balance of power (great power rivalry) North–South economic divide Discrepancy between state borders and distribution of peoples Global ideological contestation *Transnational connectors* Flows of people, weapons, resources, communications, ideas
2	Regional	*Complex conflict systems* e.g., Arab world, West Africa, East Africa, Latin America, North America, Europe, former Soviet states, Central Asia, South Asia, East Asia *Intra-regional dynamics* Regional interstate rivalries, spillover, cross-border demography, contagion, diaspora, etc.
3	State	*Measures of fragility* *Social*: weak society – cultural/religious divisions, ethnic imbalance *Economic*: weak economy – poor resource base, relative deprivation, uneven development *Political*: weak polity – partisan government, regime illegitimacy, levels of repression *Geographic*: weak central control
4	Identity	*Nature of conflict parties (bases for group formation)* Ethnic/sectarian/clan/family/class (links to global drivers) *Intergroup dynamics (escalation, de-escalation)* Group actions and strategies (politicization, militarization) State actions and strategies Built-in mechanisms of conflict (reciprocal dynamics)
5	Elite/ individual	*Leadership roles* Exclusionist policies, factional interest, rapacity/greed, violent strategies

Note: It is at levels 4 and 5 in particular that group psychology and individual psychology become prominent.

Transnational conflict is global–local conflict in which conflict at global (and intermediate) level impacts at local level (where most of the suffering is experienced), and local-level conflict can have global repercussions – the self-immolation of a Tunisian fruit seller in December 2011 triggered the fall of the regime in Egypt and the collapse of the existing regional system. Transnational conflicts can rapidly change character and mutate, with *transnational connectors* – cross-border flows of people, weapons, resources, information, ideas – acting like veins and arteries in linking and animating the different parts of the system.

Many of the deep drivers of transnational conflict originate at global level, where changes in the global balance of power have led to a loss of central control in comparison with the Cold War period and a consequent 'regionalization' of international politics. Economic imbalance fuels wars to control the resources of the state. Global ideological contestation – democratic, socialist, nationalist and now, most strikingly, religious – intensifies struggles to determine the nature of the state. And discrepances between state borders – imposed during and after the colonial period – and much older and more numerous distributions of peoples breed wars of secession that challenge the very existence of the state. It is still at state level, therefore, that the critical battles are fought out. The state remains, at least formally, the main satisfier of internal needs and the most significant player on the international scene. That is why such emphasis is placed on shoring up 'fragile states'. And that is why such alarm is expressed about what is widely seen as a systemic crisis in the post-colonial state structure itself. It is into these gaps that newer players – using existing conflict formations and deploying the methodology of international terror and the communications revolution – are now able to challenge traditional political and military centres of power.

At the beginning of this section we noted how conflict theory is riven with divergent, and often competing, interpretations. Transnational conflicts themselves, as illustrated in table 2.2, are permeated by radical disagreement at all levels and across all sectors. Returning to the question of how to 'read' the resulting amalgam, this section concludes with an illustration of how radical disagreements also permeate third-party argument *about* such interpretations, together with the policy conclusions that flow from them. For example, Walter Russell Mead sums up his interpretation of the evidence like this:

> So far, the year 2014 has been a tumultuous one, as geopolitical rivalries have stormed back to the center stage. Whether it is Russian forces

seizing Crimea, China making aggressive claims in its coastal waters, Japan responding with an increasingly assertive strategy of its own, or Iran trying to use its alliances with Syria and Hezbollah to dominate the Middle East, old-fashioned power plays are back in international relations. The United States and the EU, at least, find such trends disturbing. Both would rather move past geopolitical questions of territory and military power and focus instead on ones of world order and global governance: trade liberalization, nuclear nonproliferation, human rights, the rule of law, climate change, and so on . . . All these happy convictions are about to be tested. Twenty-five years after the fall of the Berlin Wall . . . [i]n very different ways, with very different objectives, China, Iran and Russia are all pushing back against the political settlement of the Cold War . . . What binds these powers together . . . is their agreement that the status quo must be revised.[19]

To which John Ikenberry responds:

Walter Russell Mead paints a disturbing portrait of the United States' geopolitical predicament . . . But Mead's alarmism is based on a colossal misreading of modern power realities. It is a misreading of the logic and character of the existing world order, which is more stable and expansive than Mead depicts . . . [I]t is a misreading of China and Russia, which are not full-scale revisionist powers but part-time spoilers at best, as suspicious of each other as they are of the outside world. True, they look for opportunities to resist the United States' global leadership, and recently, as in the past, they have pushed against it, particularly when confronted in their own neighbourhoods. But even these conflicts are fuelled more by [the] weakness [of] their leaders and regimes than by strength. They have no appealing brand. And when it comes to their overriding interests, Russia and, especially, China are deeply integrated into the world economy and its governing institutions . . . Alliances, partnerships, multilateralism, democracy – these are the tools of U.S. leadership, and they are winning, not losing, the twenty-first century struggles over geopolitics and the world order.[20]

It can be seen that radical disagreements of this kind impact on policy responses at different levels. For example, in relation to the Western response to the Ukraine conflict in 2014–15, one line of interpretation learns the 'lessons of history' by comparing the conflict with the situation on the eve of the First World War: we must not allow great power rivalries to let us 'sleepwalk' into war. This leads to a 'liberal' policy response. A rival line of interpretation, however, learns the 'lessons of history' by comparing the conflict with the situation on the eve of the Second World War: we must confront aggression at the outset in the only language that the aggressor understands.

This leads to a 'conservative' policy response. Much hangs on the outcome of radical disagreements such as this.

Cosmopolitan conflict resolution and the challenge of intractability

Cosmopolitan conflict resolution has to engage transnational conflict at all levels and across all sectors in order to minimize direct structural and cultural violence in global politics. This is its daunting reactive task. In addition, it has to be proactive – promoting the principles of cosmopolitan conflict resolution so that they are internalized and owned across nations and cultures, not seen as features of a passing world order that have been deployed to normalize injustice and inequality in the interest of hegemons.

In taking up this challenge, conflict resolution has to address (a) possible evolutionary and cultural sources of violence, (b) the drivers of violence that make the outbreak of direct violence more or less likely at global, regional and state levels, and (c) what Edward Azar called the 'process dynamics' at conflict party and elite/individual levels that dictate whether or not in specific cases violent or non-violent options are pursued. These three levels of causation correspond to Hidemi Suganami's analysis of the causes of war into necessary causes (What are the conditions which must be present for wars to occur?), correlate causes (Under what circumstances have wars occurred most frequently?) and specific historical causes (How did this particular war come about?).[21]

It is now possible to define conflict intractability in broad terms.

There has been a great deal written about what Burton called 'deep-rooted conflict' and Azar called 'protracted social conflict', triggered latterly by Louis Kriesberg, Terrell Northrop and Stuart Thorson's 1989 book *Intractable Conflicts and their Transformations*.[22] This includes Heidi and Guy Burgess's work on 'constructive confrontation' and their website 'Beyond Intractability' (www.beyondintractability.org), 'a free knowledge base on more constructive approaches to destructive conflict', Bernard Mayer's *Staying with Conflicts: A Strategic Approach to Ongoing Disputes*,[23] and Peter Coleman's *The Five Percent: Finding Solutions to Seemingly Impossible Conflicts*.[24] Perhaps the most elaborate analysis of intractable conflict has been Chris Mitchell's *The Anatomy of Intractable Conflict*.[25] As discussed further in chapter 4 (note 2), political theorists such as Chantal Mouffe also see political conflict as unavoidable and argue that the aim should be to move from antagonistic to agonistic relations.[26] In similar vein, Adrian Little's *Enduring Conflict: Challenging the Signature of Peace and Democracy* argues that premature reconciliation may suppress conflicts that need to be pursued.[27] In the agonist's view, the aim should be to recognize the legitimacy of the opponent, to accept adversarial relations, but to avoid enmity. I hope that the suggestions made in this book will be seen as a development and reinforcement of this work – and that of other colleagues in the conflict resolution field.

In the light of all this, therefore, intractable conflict can be defined most simply as being made up those features of transnational conflict that as yet block cosmopolitan conflict resolution. Intractable conflicts are those in which attempts at peaceful containment, settlement and transformation have so far failed. Conflict intractability is a complex system of interconnecting aspects. The task of conflict resolution is to unlock it.

Conclusion

Having introduced the conflict resolution field in chapter 1 and reviewed the challenge of prevailing patterns of transnational conflict here – thereby defining the nature of conflict intractability in general – it is time to focus on *communicative approaches* in conflict resolution and the *linguistic intractability* that resists them. That is a task for the next chapter.

3

WHY CONFLICT RESOLUTION FAILS

Human beings do not struggle silently. Verbal quarrels and disputes permeate all dimensions of conflict. The previous chapter has shown how resistance to conflict resolution – intractability – is located across all the levels and sectors of transnational conflict. Within this, *linguistic intractability* is the name of those aspects of intractability where *communicative conflict resolution approaches* meet the greatest resistance. This, too, manifests itself across the system, but particularly at conflict party (identity group) and elite/individual levels. At the heart of linguistic intractability is the phenomenon of *radical disagreement*, the chief verbal aspect of the struggle, the war of words in which conflict parties exhort their supporters, confront each other, and appeal for third-party support – and third parties respond accordingly. The war of words is just as virulent – and can be just as potent – as the war of weapons.

There are many explanations for the origins and nature of wars of weapons. But, even here, a historian such as Michael Howard traces the decisive factor in whether or not wars break out to the articulations of those who make such decisions (although few in the conflict resolution field would attribute so much to conscious reason):

> Whatever may be the underlying causes of international conflict, even if we accept the role of atavistic militarism or of military-industrial complexes or of sociobiological drives or domestic tensions fuelling it, wars begin with conscious and reasoned decisions based on calculation, made by *both* parties, that they can achieve more by going to war than by remaining at peace.[1]

There are also many – perhaps too many – explanations for the origins and nature of wars of words. The term 'wars of words' here does not just mean propaganda. It refers, rather, to the deep linguistic battle that underpins all deadly struggles. It is not conscious propaganda that is lethal for conflict resolution, but the sincerity that underlies it.[2] All the historical, anthropological, cultural, sociological and psychological sciences are drawn on for explanations that account for verbal confrontation in the processes of conflict party formation and the escalation and de-escalation of the subsequent conflicts – as noted below.

The three questions that we need to address in this chapter are: What is communicative conflict resolution trying to achieve in relation to radical disagreement? What are the theoretical assumptions about radical disagreement that underpin communicative conflict resolution? And what happens when communicative conflict resolution approaches are applied to examples of radical disagreement in intractable conflicts?

What is communicative conflict resolution trying to achieve in relation to radical disagreement?

There are three main overlapping communicative approaches in conflict resolution: negotiation, problem-solving and dialogue. This includes various forms of *negotiation for political accommodation, interactive problem-solving* and *dialogue for mutual understanding* (see box 3.1).

Negotiation is associated with *conflict settlement*, mainly at elite level; dialogue is associated with *conflict transformation*, mainly at societal level; and interactive problem-solving – historically the core conflict resolution approach – bridges between the two. What are these communicative conflict resolution approaches trying to achieve?

Here is a famous account of what *principled negotiation* (interest-based negotiation) seeks to bring about taken from the original edition of *Getting to Yes* (Fisher and Ury, 1981), still by far the best-selling book in the field (over 2 million copies sold in more than twenty languages):

> The answer to the question of whether to use soft positional bargaining or hard is 'neither'. Change the game. At the Harvard Negotiation Project we have been developing an alternative to positional bargaining: a method of negotiation explicitly designed to produce wise outcomes efficiently and amicably. This method, called *principled negotiation* or *negotiation on the merits*, can be boiled down to four basic points. These four points define a straightforward method of negotiation that

30

Box 3.1 Negotiation, problem-solving and dialogue

Conflict resolution approach	Negotiation for political accommodation	Interactive problem-solving	Dialogue for mutual understanding
Example	Principled negotiation	Problem-solving workshops	Hermeneutic dialogue
Third-party role	Mediation	Training	Facilitation
Aim	Getting to yes	Transform win–lose (= lose–lose) into win–win	Fusion of horizons
Radical disagreement seen as	Positional debate	Competitive debate	Adversarial debate

can be used under almost any circumstances. Each point deals with a basic element of negotiation, and suggests what you should do about it.

- People: separate the people from the problem
- Interests: focus on interests, not positions
- Options: invent multiple options looking for mutual gains before deciding what to do
- Criteria: insist that the result is based on some objective standard

. . . Each side should come to understand the interests of the other. Both can then jointly generate options that are mutually advantageous and seek agreement on objective standards for resolving opposed interests . . . To sum up, in contrast to positional bargaining, the principled negotiation method of focusing on basic interests, mutually satisfying options, and fair standards typically results in a *wise* agreement. The method permits you to reach a gradual consensus on a joint decision *efficiently* without all the transactional costs of digging into positions only to have to dig yourself out of them. And separating the people from the problem allows you to deal directly and empathetically with the other negotiator as a human being regardless of any substantive differences, thus making possible an *amicable* outcome.[3]

It can be seen that the aim from the outset is to change the discourse of the conflict parties and, as the first move, to transform 'positional debate' (radical disagreement) into principled negotiation.

The nature and aim of *interactive problem-solving* is succinctly summed up here by one of the pioneers in the field – Morton Deutsch:

> In brief, the theory equates a constructive process of conflict resolution with an effective cooperative problem-solving process in which the conflict is the mutual problem to be resolved cooperatively. It also equates a destructive process of conflict resolution with a competitive process in which the conflict parties are involved in competition or struggle to determine who wins and who loses; often the outcome of a struggle is a loss for both parties ... At the heart of this process is reframing the conflict as a mutual problem to be resolved (or solved) through joint cooperative efforts.[4]

Here the aim once again is to transform the discourses of conflict parties into something they were not before, by discarding the destructive 'win–lose' language of 'competitive debate' (radical disagreement) and transforming it from the beginning into the constructive language of cooperative problem-solving.

Finally we turn to the aims of *dialogue for mutual understanding*. This is once again a wide field covering many forms of dialogue.[5] But here is a summary of what is common across these differences by the editors of a well-regarded review of *dialogic approaches in conflict resolution*:

> The most common dictionary definition of dialogue is simply as a conversation between two or more people. In the field of dialogue practitioners, however, it is given a much deeper and more distinct meaning. David Bohm went back to the source of the word, deriving from the Greek root of 'dia' which means 'through' and 'logos' which is 'the word' or 'meaning', and therefore saw dialogue as meaning flowing through us. Elements of this deeper understanding of the word include an emphasis on questions, inquiry, co-creation, and listening, the uncovering of one's own assumptions and those of others, a suspension of judgment and a collective search for truth ... [In contrast] a debate is a discussion, usually focused around two opposing sides, and held with the object of one side winning. The winner is the one with the best articulations, ideas and arguments.[6]

In this case the aim is to shift from 'adversarial debate' (radical disagreement) straight away into what is seen to be an entirely different communicative mode. Radical disagreement is defined as the antithesis of dialogue. So the aim from the outset is, once again, to change the discourses of the conflict parties in a fundamental way by setting radical disagreement aside and focusing on fostering mutual understanding.

As a helpful clarification here, this is how Ronald Fisher distinguishes between *problem-solving* and *dialogue*:

Unlike the more focused forms of interactive conflict resolution, such as problem-solving workshops, dialogue interventions tend to involve not influential, informal representatives of the parties, but simply ordinary members of the antagonistic groups. Furthermore, dialogue is primarily directed toward increased understanding and trust among the participants with some eventual positive effects on public opinion, rather than the creation of alternative solutions to the conflict.[7]

It can be seen from these examples that the phenomenon of radical disagreement – lying as it does at the heart of linguistic intractability – is dismissed in mainstream communicative conflict resolution as positional debate, competitive debate and adversarial debate. Radical disagreement is seen as an all-too-familiar and unproductive dead end, a terminus to dialogue. Conflict resolution wants to unravel the tangled skein of conflict. Radical disagreement pulls the knot tighter. The aim from the beginning in conflict resolution is to transform and overcome radical disagreement, not to learn from it.

To demonstrate this in detail would require a comprehensive review of the huge range of methodologies used in communicative conflict resolution. This is clearly too big a task for this book. Readers can find a fairly extensive review in my book *Transforming Violent Conflict: Radical Disagreement, Dialogue and Survival* (2010, esp. pp. 52–92); see box 3.2 for the approaches looked at there.

Box 3.2 Some communicative conflict resolution approaches reviewed

Game theoretic conflict resolution
Alternative dispute resolution (industrial, family, neighbourhood, community relations, commercial, victim–offender)
Interest-based negotiation/mediation
Controlled communication and analytic problem-solving (needs based) workshops
Psychodynamic workshops
Public decision conflict resolution
Interpersonal dialogue
Intergroup dialogue (race, religion, gender)
Intercultural/interreligious dialogue
Dialogue between civilizations

Here is another example, from the TRANSCEND methodology of one of the founders of the field – Johan Galtung:

> A debate is a fight with verbal, not physical weapons (in French *battre* = beat). The victory usually goes to he who can catch the other in more contradictions ... A dialogue, *dia logos*, through the word, by using words, is something quite different. There is no competition to win a battle of words. The parties are working together to find a solution to a problem ...[8] [The aim of dialogue] is to get under the skin of each other in a questioning way, not in the drilling way of a debate. Imagine now that instead of debating, trying to defeat each other with words, they had used their eloquence in a dialogue, with the aim of finding how their contradictions could be transcended and their perspectives combined in a higher unity ['fusion of horizons'].[9]

Galtung does at times recommend identifying the 'axioms of faith' associated with radical disagreement, but this is only in order to: 'start touching them, tinkering with them, shaking them, inserting the word "not", negating them so that everything becomes more flexible.'[10]

There are highly sophisticated attempts to accommodate *conflict asymmetry* in communicative conflict resolution, such as Vivienne Jabri's application of Jürgen Habermas's *discourse ethics* in communicative action. But what happens when conflict parties nevertheless fail to reach agreement?

> Individuals and groups involved in social relations do not always reach rational consensus. Where disagreement occurs, a variety of options are available. Groups and individuals may adopt strategic behaviour where actors may seek to influence communicative interaction through, for example, the direct manipulation of information on their intentions or the shared external world. Groups may also break off communication and resort to violence ... A process situated in discursive ethics, however, rejects these options and enters a dialogic relationship of free objection and justification.[11]

It can be seen that Jabri envisages only three alternatives when 'disagreement occurs': two of them – strategic manipulation and resort to violence – do not concern conversational interchange, while the third is a return to the pure depoliticized space of Habermasian communicative action. None of them relates to ongoing radical disagreement.

Another example of coming to terms with conflict complexity is John-Paul Lederach's work on developing the theory and practice of *dilemmatic conflict transformation*. Here he can be seen to advocate ignoring the false simplifications of radical disagreement in order to develop dilemmatic thinking:

34

We are not able to handle complexity well if we understand our choices in rigid either/or or contradictory terms. Complexity requires that we develop the capacity to identify the key energies in a situation and hold them up together as *interdependent goals*. . . The capacity to live with apparent contradictions and paradoxes lies at the heart of conflict transformation.[12]

This is an inspiring programme. But in intractable situations, where conflict parties are not yet ready to see their incompatible conflict aims as 'interdependent goals' or to reimagine their life and death struggle as a coexistence of 'apparent contradictions and paradoxes', the main suggestion in this book is that more prior work needs to be done.

Even in approaches that begin by forefronting radical disagreement, nearly always the reason for doing this is to expose its bankruptcy and to move away from it as soon as possible. For example, in Harold Saunders's five-stage *Sustained Dialogue* approach (practised effectively in Tajikistan), disagreement is addressed at the beginning of stage 2, when stories are told, grievances are expressed, and an attempt is made to 'clear the air'. By the end of stage 2: '"me" becomes "we", "what" becomes "why", and participants shift from speaking "to" each other to speaking "with" each other.'[13]

While, after the 'adversarial' phase of Jay Rothman's ARIA approach in which disagreements are aired, facilitators say:

You have now experienced a very familiar, and I am sure you will all agree, a rather unconstructive approach to dialogue. Each of you stated your position, each of you suggested why the other side is wrong or to blame for the conflict. Few of you listened to anyone else, and, frankly, very little, if anything, new was learned. This is the normal approach that all of you have experienced perhaps every time you have discussed the situation with someone who holds a very different perspective than your own. I invite you now to experiment with a new way.[14]

In short, conflict resolution approaches do not take radical disagreement seriously. The aim from the outset is to persuade the conflict parties to move from positions to interests, from win–lose to win–win exchanges, and from adversarial debate to genuine dialogue. This implies that radical disagreements are seen as relatively superficial features of conflict, generated by deeper causes and resolvable only when these causes (mutual enemy images, incompatible goals, unsatisfied human needs) are directly addressed. Before moving on to test conflict resolution approaches by applying them directly to examples of radical disagreement, let us briefly note the extensive theoretical wellsprings from which this idea of the superficiality of radical disagreement is drawn.

What are the theoretical assumptions about radical disagreement that underpin communicative conflict resolution?

Like all interpretative responses to social phenomena, communicative conflict resolution approaches rest on theoretical assumptions about the phenomena in question. We noted above how all the historical, anthropological, cultural, sociological and psychological sciences are drawn on for explanations that account for verbal confrontation in the processes of conflict party formation and the escalation and de-escalation of the subsequent conflicts.

For example, a common distinction made across a wide range of methodologies in communicative conflict resolution is between 'objective' and 'subjective' factors – realistic differences between competing interests over resources that generate goal incompatibilities, on the one hand, and contrasting preferences and perceptions linked to value differences and perceived threats to basic needs, on the other. The former can be bargained over, but the latter cannot. So, in its effort to prevent escalation and foster de-escalation, communicative conflict resolution has to address both substantive and phenomenological elements.[15] A consequent theoretical assumption behind many communicative conflict resolution approaches is that radical disagreements are somehow part of the 'subjective' penumbra that surrounds 'objective' and substantial issues and processes – and are built into social institutions accordingly. One of the main arguments in this book – to be made explicit in chapter 10 – is that radical disagreement cannot be confined to either of these two categories – subject or object. It breaks out of this straitjacket – and that is one of the main reasons why conflict resolution cannot yet control it.

Another common theoretical assumption is that radical disagreements are made up of a coexistence of equivalent 'narratives', or rationalizations of political interest, or social constructions, or psychological projections, or historico-cultural posits. This assumption – common to realists on one hand and post-structuralists on the other – is shared widely throughout the social, political and psychological sciences. In short, radical disagreements are described – and explained – as being *functional* for conflict parties. Another main argument in this book is that radical disagreements are not mere juxtapositions of functionally equivalent attributes. This is not what any of the conflict parties are saying. That they are not saying this is what makes it radical disagreement. To anticipate, radical disagreements are not an innocuous coexistence of subjectivities in some supposed neutral 'third space' but a life-and-death struggle to occupy the whole of discursive space – and act accordingly.

Because both these deep theoretical roots of communicative conflict resolution – assumptions about *reflexivity* and assumptions about *equivalence* – are dealt with more fully in chapter 10, we will not go further into them here.

What happens when communicative conflict resolution approaches are applied to examples of radical disagreement in intractable conflicts?

We are now able to apply communicative conflict resolution approaches to *examples* of radical disagreement. It is a striking feature of linguistic intractability that, uniquely, examples of the radical disagreements at the heart of intractable conflicts can be presented and disseminated on the printed page. No other feature of intense political conflict can be made publicly available in this way. No doubt key aspects of radical disagreement – such as gestures, tones, emotional behaviour – are lost. But what can be conveyed are still recognizably examples of radical disagreement itself.

This is a key point in the book. In order to clarify what is at issue, from now on *examples* of radical disagreement will be recorded between *bar lines*. For instance, in chapter 2 we looked at an example of radical disagreement between Walter Russell Mead and John Ikenberry (pp. 25–6). In that case, both extracts would be put in inverted commas, because these are *ipsissima verba* – the very words they used. That is what the conflict parties are individually saying within the context of radical disagreement. But the radical disagreement itself is everything that is contained within the bar lines. What individual conflict parties say is monological. The radical disagreement is polylogical.

We can now look at the application of conflict resolution approaches to *examples* of radical disagreement. First we will look at what happens when dialogue for mutual understanding is applied to one type of intractable conflict. Then we will investigate what occurs when all three main conflict resolution approaches are applied to another type.

Hermeneutic dialogue and Afghanistan

We have seen how, in dialogue for mutual understanding, 'adversarial debate' (radical disagreement) is seen as the opposite of dialogue. From the outset, what is wanted instead, we are told, is 'an emphasis on questions, inquiry, co-creation, and listening, the uncovering of one's own assumptions and those of others, a suspension of judgment and a collective search for truth'. This is 'hermeneutic' (interpretative) dialogue, along lines suggested in the philosophy of Hans-Georg Gadamer.[16] The ultimate goal is a 'fusion of horizons' or the 'co-creation' of a new and expanded understanding. These 'dialogic attitudes' are seen to be integral to the conflict resolution enterprise by Benjamin Broome:

> The third culture can only develop through interaction in which participants are willing to open themselves to new meanings, to engage in genuine dialogue, and to constantly respond to the new demands emanating from the situation. The emergence of this third culture [fusion of horizons] is the essence of relational empathy and is essential for successful conflict resolution.[17]

Here the Canadian philosopher Charles Taylor invokes hermeneutic dialogue in order to overcome cultural differences and to accommodate radically different ways of 'holding things true':

> For instance, we become aware that there are different ways of believing things, one of which is holding them as a 'personal opinion'. This was all that we allowed for before, but now we have space for other ways and can therefore accommodate the beliefs of a quite different culture. Our horizon is extended to take in this possibility, which was beyond its limit before. But this is better seen as a fusion rather than just an extension of horizons, because at the same time we are introducing a language to talk about their beliefs that represents an extension in relation to their language. Presumably, they had no idea of what we speak of as 'personal opinions', at least in such areas as religion, for instance. They would have had to see these as rejection, rebellion, heresy. So the new language used here, which places 'opinions' alongside other modes of believing as possible alternative ways of holding things true, opens a broader horizon, extending beyond both the original ones and in a sense combining them.[18]

But how does this apply to the radical disagreement between those wanting to impose Western-style democracy in Afghanistan and the determination of the Taliban to resist this and impose *sharia*? Can we overcome this radical disagreement by setting it aside in favour of a premature 'fusion of horizons' in the way Taylor suggests? In the first place, does 'our' realization that there are 'other ways of holding things true' than as 'personal opinions' mean that we are therefore prepared for the imposition of *sharia* that is based on these 'other ways'? If not, will 'they' not see this dialogic approach as a subterfuge in which 'our' horizon has not been expanded at all? Conversely, what does it mean to suggest that 'they' now realize that putting human 'opinions' on the same footing as the revealed word of God means that Western secular and Islamic horizons are now 'combined'? It can be seen that the idea of a fusion of horizons is premature in those cases where its own underlying assumptions are at odds with what is in contention in the as yet continuing radical disagreement:

> Democracy means sovereignty for man. Islam means sovereignty for the *sharia*. In the American form of democracy any issue is allowed to be put to a vote of the people, and the majority decision prevails upon all. Can we Muslims put an issue that has already been decided for us by Allah up for a vote and accept the will of the majority if they vote against the will of Allah? Of course we cannot, so we can never accept democracy as defined, practiced and promoted by America.[19]

This example shows how dialogue for mutual understanding can itself be seen to be based on assumptions that are part of what is in dispute in the radical disagreement. Is this not, for example, why many Muslims – and Christians – are opposed to ecumenicism? Dialogue for mutual understanding *depoliticizes* the conflict.

Applying negotiation, problem-solving and dialogue approaches to identity/secession conflicts

By way of further illustration, we now apply the three main conflict resolution approaches in the communicative sphere to one class of intractable conflicts – identity/secession conflicts.

Principled negotiation and Khalistan

In *Beyond Machiavelli*, Roger Fisher and his colleagues offer a 'toolbox' for negotiators seeking agreed settlements to a range of intractable international conflicts:

> Every tool is intended to ask questions or to stimulate better questions. Better questions are not about who is right and who is wrong, or about one-shot solutions, but about the process for dealing with

conflicting views about right and wrong, and for dealing with the inevitable changes that lie ahead.[20]

Advice is given to negotiators from three perspectives: their own, that of the other, and that of a third party. From their own perspective, protagonists are advised to set aside 'What do I think is the best goal?' and substitute 'How shall you and I best proceed when each of us has different ideas about what ought to happen?' From the perspective of 'the other', the advice is to 'step into their shoes' and explore their perceptions, since: 'in each situation the key to the dispute is not objective truth but what is going on in the heads of the parties . . . the better we understand the way people see things, the better we will be able to change them.'[21]

From the perspective of third parties, the advice is to move from positions to interests:

> One way to contrast such differing priorities is to write out in parallel columns statements of positions that identify the dispute. These phrases record what each side is actually saying. Then, looking down first at their side and next at our own, we can write out phrases that suggest underlying reasons for our different positions.[22]

This is then applied to the Sikh secessionist conflict with the Indian government in the 1980s. The upshot of the advice given to the Sikhs was that they should set aside what they were 'actually saying' – 'The Sikhs require an independent state' – and substitute an articulation of their 'underlying interests', which Fisher saw as substantive, symbolic and domestic political:[23]

- a *substantive* interest in 'political representation, local control and prosperity for farms', protection from atrocities, and the 'ability to practice [the] Sikh religion in peace';
- a *symbolic* interest in the 'protection of minority Sikh rights' and a 'Hindu apology for past violence';
- a *domestic political* interest that 'Sikhs regain confidence in the Indian government'.

But now the Sikh demand for an independent state has disappeared. The radical disagreement (what both sides 'actually say'):

|(A) 'The Sikhs require an independent state'
 (B) 'India must remain united'|

has been transformed from the outset into a political compromise that falls short of full independence. The conflict is no longer intractable.

The *process* has determined the *outcome*. In this case, the Sikh bid for an independent state of Khalistan failed, and – to those for whom this outcome was wanted – the principled negotiation approach can be said to have been vindicated.

But compare this to a comparable radical disagreement about the independence of Pakistan in 1947. Here the first speaker is Mohammad Ali Jinnah addressing an ecstatic crowd of Muslim supporters. The second speaker is Jawaharlal Nehru articulating a response overwhelmingly endorsed by the Indian Congress:[24]

|(A) 'There are two nations on this sub-continent. This is the underlying fact that must shape the future creation of Pakistan. Only the truly Islamic platform of the Muslim League is acceptable to the Muslim nation.'

(B) 'Geography and mountains and the sea fashioned India as she is, and no human agency can change that shape or come in the way of her final destiny. Once present passions subside, the false doctrine of two nations will be discredited and discarded by all.'|

Here neither side is ready to make the move from incompatible 'positions' ('what the conflictants actually say') to a mutual rearticulation in terms of underlying and compatible 'interests' that mediators want them to substitute. Whereas the bid for Khalistan failed, the bid for Pakistan succeeded. The outcome led to unimaginable loss of lives and livelihoods. Whether the long-term outcome would have been better or worse if accommodation had been found within a united India is an unanswerable counterfactual. Either way, the reverberations echo to this day – for example, in Kashmir.

Problem-solving and Jerusalem

Continuing with the theme of identity conflicts, Jay Rothman (whose ARIA methodology in fact goes wider than problem-solving) has practised and written about engaging and transforming such conflicts with originality and insight. Taking the question of sovereignty over Jerusalem, he advocates '[m]oving from positional debating to real communication', which requires 'a lot of analysis of underlying motivations, hopes, fears of each other, especially in deeply rooted intercommunal conflicts'.[25] At the root of this is the distinction between negotiable interests and non-negotiable basic human needs for identity, security, autonomy and development. These are seen to lie at the bottom of intractable conflict. Needs cannot be divided. On the other hand, needs are non-zero sum – satisfying my need for

41

security and development can only be finally met by satisfying your need for security and development. In relation to Jerusalem, therefore, it is not territorial claims, or the land itself, that constitute the substance of what is at issue: it is by 'looking beneath the territory itself to the meanings that each side attaches to it' that the roots of the conflict can be discerned and 'common ground can be found'.[26] When conflict parties come to realize this, space is opened for engagement and transformation. Instead of remaining stuck in an endlessly repeated adversarial monologue of disbelief, mistrust and animosity, it is discovered that, at the deepest levels, 'each is alike in needs and motivations'. Only then will there be 'a new opening for peace, and therefore for true security'.

But during the present period of intractability, however possible all of this might become in future, at the moment historical experience has taught the conflict parties that their basic human needs can be guaranteed only by *sovereignty* – and the ability to defend it. This is what constitutes the radical disagreement.

Dialogue and the Sinhala–Tamil conflict

As a final example, Norbert Ropers invokes the Buddhist *tetralemma* in his analysis of the linguistic aspect of the Sinhala–Tamil conflict in Sri Lanka.[27]

Ropers uses the tetralemma to map out what he calls 'mental models' in the Sri Lankan conflict. The primary discourses of both Sinhala and Tamil mainstream parties are seen to be made up of potent religious-historical national narratives fired by claims to original settlement, inherited grievance and shared destiny:

> all parties have developed their own narratives or 'mental models' of the conflict, as well as options and possibilities of conflict resolution. These narratives and models have had tremendous impact on the way parties communicate and interact with each other. They often develop a life of their own and are deeply ingrained in the attitudes and behaviour of the respective collectives.[28]

Whereas a dilemma confronts two apparently incompatible alternatives, a tetralemma envisages four alternative stances on any controversial issue:

Position A	*Position B*
Neither Position A	*Both position A*
nor Position B	*and Position B*

42

Box 3.3 The tetralemma applied to the Sinhala–Tamil conflict

Position A	Position B
Unitary state or moderate devolution only	High-level autonomy or separate state
Neither A nor B	**Both A and B**
Power sharing is not the key issue: more important are genuine democracy, development, good local governance, etc.	Compromise – genuine power sharing, federalism, etc.

Position A	was that of the government and a majority of Sinhala mainstream parties.
Position B	was that of Tamil nationalist parties.
Neither A nor B	represented the position of a number of civil society groups, who argued that the 'real problems' were to do not with power sharing among political elites but with other unsatisfied needs.
Both A and B	represented the position of international peacemakers (e.g. Norway, the UN) – for example, a 'federal structure within a united Sri Lanka' (the formula agreed between the LTTE and the government of Sri Lanka in the negotiations in Oslo in December 2002).

Ropers uses the tetralemma to map out the interpretations and beliefs that make up the mental models driving the Sri Lankan conflict (see box 3.3). He hopes that the tetralemma can be used to transcend binary thinking: 'The tetralemma is a tool that has the potential of overcoming the binary logic of these two sets of attitudes and fears.'

It can now be seen that the radical disagreement at the heart of the conflict is not represented in the tetralemma. Radical disagreement is not a position but a relation – it is polylogical, not monological. Radical disagreement appears when the two antagonistic positions (A and B) are not treated separately, or transcended, but are presented together, as in the following example. The first speaker is the president of Sri Lanka at the time, Mahinda Rajapaksa. The second speaker was a prominent Tamil Tiger (LTTE) leader, V. Pirapaharan.

I(A) 'This blessed land will forever cherish, protect and value the fruits of the brave and courageous operation conducted by the Sri Lankan Security Forces to bring liberation to the people of the East, who for more than two decades were held hostage by the forces of vicious and violent terrorism.' (19 July 2007)

(B) 'We are at a crossroads in our freedom struggle. Our journey has been long and arduous, and crowded with difficult phases. We are facing challenges and unexpected turns that no other freedom movement had to face. The Sri Lankan government has split the Tamil homeland, set up military camps, bound it with barbed wire, and has converted it into a site of collective torture.' (27 November 2006)

This is what lay at the heart of linguistic intractability and constituted the main resistance against conflict resolution in the communicative sphere. The conflict parties were not yet ready to think and act in the way conflict transformation wanted. In the event, the Sri Lankan government succeeded in destroying the LTTE militarily in 2010 and brought that phase of the conflict to a close. This does not mean that approaches like that advocated by Ropers cannot succeed in future – they are certainly greatly needed in the aftermath of the Sri Lankan government's military victory if peace is to be consolidated, underlying needs are to be met, and the passions that may fuel renewed national struggle are to be assuaged. But, in the crucible of continuing and intractable intense political conflict such as that in Sri Lanka in the first decade of the twenty-first century, they proved in the end – after the false dawn of the 2002 interim peace agreement – to be premature.

Conclusion

This chapter has shown three things.

First, radical disagreement is not taken seriously in conflict resolution. Castigated as positional debate, or competitive debate, or adversarial debate, it is dismissed as an unproductive and all-too-familiar dead end which needs at the earliest opportunity to be set aside or transformed, not learnt from.

Second, this disregard rests on two main theoretical assumptions. One assumption is that radical disagreement is a superficial subjective feature of conflict and that, as such, it is merely functional for deeper causes (reflexivity). Another assumption is that radical disagreement is constituted by a coexistence of equivalent narratives, rationalizations, social constructions, psychological projections or historico-cultural posits (equivalence).

Third, in the light of this, when conflict resolution approaches are applied to examples of radical disagreement in intractable conflicts, it can be seen that the assumptions on which they rest are not yet appropriate, the contexts they presuppose do not yet exist, and the conflict parties they are dealing with are not yet ready to think or behave in the way they want. More work has to be done before these approaches become possible. The next chapter sets out what that work is.

4

PROMOTING STRATEGIC ENGAGEMENT

At this point it should be made clear that, in looking at cases where, so far, conflict resolution approaches do not work, I am in no way disparaging those approaches. On the contrary, dialogue for mutual understanding, interactive problem-solving and principled negotiation achieve remarkable results. These are, indeed, the communicative foundations upon which conceptual and cultural peacebuilding are constructed. What follows is an outline of another approach – conflict engagement rather than conflict resolution – that can work when conflict resolution is premature and can help to prepare the ground for its appearance or return. This should be seen, therefore, not as a replacement but as another string to the bow. In chapter 9 this will be termed *extended conflict resolution*.

It should also be made clear that what is proposed in this chapter is not the only suggestion for what can be done in intractable conflicts. As noted in chapter 3, the subjects of complex conflict, asymmetric conflict and intractable conflict have attracted a great deal of attention in recent years. In my book *Transforming Violent Conflict* (2010) I reviewed this literature and compared other approaches with my own (see box 3.2, p. 33). I will not repeat this here. But, to my knowledge, no other approach identifies radical disagreement as the chief impediment to conflict resolution in the communicative sphere or sees strategic engagement within and across conflict parties, including third parties, as the essential preliminary work to be done when so far conflict resolution does not gain traction.

Chapter 1 identified a capacity for second-order learning as essential in conflict resolution in the face of rapidly changing circumstances. Chapter 2 sketched the multifaceted and mutating lineaments of contemporary transnational conflict, which certainly demand that

46

capacity. Chapter 3 shifted to the communicative sphere – which both reflects and affects the other dimensions of transnational conflict – and identified linguistic intractability and radical disagreement as the chief impediments to conflict resolution. This chapter addresses the question what can be done about this.

The dictates of second-order learning suggest that, in order to answer this question, we should *acknowledge the impediment*, *try to understand it*, and *adapt practice accordingly*.

Acknowledging radical disagreement

We have noted how conflict resolution dismisses radical disagreement as 'adversarial debate', 'competitive debate' and 'positional debate'. It sees it as an all-too-familiar and unproductive dead end, a terminus to dialogue, that must from the outset be overcome, not learnt from.

Conflict engagement takes the opposite view. Radical disagreement is found to be not all too familiar but, perhaps, the least familiar aspect of intense political conflict. Nor is it a terminus to dialogue but, on the contrary, the chief form of dialogue in intractable conflict, namely what I call *agonistic dialogue*, or dialogue between enemies: 'agonistic dialogue is that part of radical disagreement in which conflict parties directly engage each other's utterances.'[1]

Agonistic dialogue is nothing other than the war of words itself at its deepest level. The word 'agonistic' comes from the Greek word for struggle: *agon*. It is not to be confused with 'antagonistic'. It has been made academically popular through Chantal Mouffe's 'agonistic' model of democracy (agonistic pluralism), although 'agonistic dialogue' means something somewhat different.[2]

When confronted by radical disagreement, Morton Deutsch advises conflict parties to eschew what he calls 'competitive debate':

> Place the disagreements in perspective by identifying common ground and common interests. When there is disagreement, address the issues and refrain from making personal attacks. When there is disagreement, seek to understand the other's views from his or her perspective; try to feel what it would be like if you were on the other side . . . Reasonable people understand that their own judgment as well as the judgment of others may be fallible.[3]

But what when reasonable people do not do this? What when conflict parties refuse to distinguish positions from interests and needs, resist reframing competition into shared problem-solving, will not convert adversarial debate into constructive controversy, do not change statements into questions or fuse horizons? What when they do not recognize the systemic nature of the conflict or when they have only a partial view of it, do not acknowledge the legitimacy of the other's narrative, are not prepared to transform the language and practice of power into a non-politicized 'ideal speech situation', and in general directly challenge the very bases on which third-party discourse analysis and third-party peace intervention are constructed? This is not a rare event. It is the norm in the intractable conflicts which are most resistant to conflict settlement and conflict transformation. Acknowledging this – and the key role that the phenomenon of radical disagreement plays in it – is the first step towards finding alternatives.

Understanding radical disagreement: heuristic engagement

The second step is to try to understand the phenomenon of radical disagreement itself. This means exploring the agonistic dialogue with the conflict parties. I call this *heuristic engagement* ('heuristic' comes from the ancient Greek word for 'find' or 'discover'). The initial stage of heuristic engagement is to listen to what conflict parties say individually in the context of radical disagreement. This will be illustrated in chapter 5 for Israelis and in chapter 6 for Palestinians. Conflict parties are found to be, not nearer, but much further apart than was realized. The further stages of heuristic engagement – exploring the resulting agonistic dialogue between the conflict parties and assessing third-party accounts – will be addressed in chapter 10. So we will return to this when the examples looked at in chapters 5 and 6 of the case study can provide the empirical evidence needed.

Adapting practice accordingly: strategic engagement

We have reached the central thesis in this book. The alternative to conflict resolution suggested by acknowledging and understanding radical disagreement is to move in the opposite direction – from conflict resolution to conflict engagement. In the practical field, this means a decisive shift to *strategic engagement*.

Strategic engagement begins, not between conflict parties, but within them, and not from where third parties would like them to be, but from where they are. It starts by promoting *collective strategic thinking* in which conflict parties address three main questions: Where are we? Where do we want to go? How do we get there? This is the first level of strategic engagement. In the case study this is exemplified in the work of the Palestine Strategy Group (PSG), the Israeli Strategic Forum (ISF) and the Palestinian Citizens of Israel Group (PCIG). The task of inclusive strategy groups is to promote sustained collective strategic thinking that is fed into the respective national debates at all levels. The aim is to fill the 'strategy gap' identified in each case as a major weakness. Particularly for 'challengers' (the Palestinians in the case study), the strategy gap is seen to be disastrous for the national project. So the long-term purpose is to build institutional capacity for collective strategic thinking and action at national level. This will be looked at in some detail in chapters 5 and 6.

Based on ongoing collective strategic thinking of this kind at conflict party level, the second level of strategic engagement is to promote strategic exchanges across and between conflict parties – not less radical disagreement but more. This is illustrated in chapter 7.

Finally, at the third level of strategic engagement, the role of third parties is clarified. Third parties – for example, would-be peacemakers – are seen also to be part of the conflict. They are not neutral or impartial or disinterested. They have their own preferred outcomes. They too, therefore, need to be able to think and act strategically – informed by the other two levels of strategic engagement. This is demonstrated in chapter 8.

Box 4.1 sets out the three stages of heuristic and strategic engagement – within conflict parties, across and between conflict parties, and by third parties.

Before considering how the three levels of strategic engagement can be 'placeholders' for a possible revival of conflict resolution even in the most severe conflict conditions, we need to address a prior question: What is implied by adopting a strategic thinking approach in the first place?

How to think strategically

What is strategic thinking? In this book, collective strategic thinking does not mean the same as private (or partisan) strategic planning behind closed doors and public manipulation. Much of the literature on strategic thinking is in effect about the latter – for example, in the areas of military strategy, commercial strategy, party political strategy and high-level national security strategy. Lawrence Freedman's

Box 4.1 Engaging radical disagreement

(A) Heuristic engagement

Level 1 Listening to what conflict parties say individually in the context of radical disagreement

Level 2 Exploring the resulting radical disagreement between the conflict parties

Level 3 Comparing third-party descriptions and explanations with examples of radical disagreements

Level 1 is illustrated in the case study in Part II and commented on further in chapter 10; levels 2 and 3 are discussed in chapter 10.

(B) Strategic engagement

Level 1 Promoting collective strategic thinking within conflict parties

Level 2 Promoting strategic exchange across and between conflict parties

Level 3 Promoting strategic involvement by third parties

Level 1 is set up in this chapter and illustrated in chapters 5 and 6. Level 2 is illustrated in chapter 7. Level 3 is illustrated in chapter 8.

monumental book *Strategy: A History* opens with these words: 'Everyone needs a strategy. Leaders of armies, major corporations, and political parties have long been expected to have strategies, but now no serious organization could imagine being without one.'[4] His book is divided into three main sections: 'strategies of force' (military strategy), 'strategy from below' (political and revolutionary strategy) and 'strategy from above' (commercial strategy). Strategy in this chapter refers more broadly to collective strategic thinking by identity groups engaged in conflict in order to determine where they are, where they want to be, and how they get there. In Freedman's words: 'strategy remains the best word we have for expressing attempts to think about actions in advance, in the light of our goals and capacities.'[5]

The difference between collective strategic thinking and private strategic planning/public manipulation is stark. The litmus test is how *alternatives* are presented. In the public presentation of partisan strategic planning, for example, all the advantages are listed on one side and all the disadvantages on the other. This may be clever politics, but it is poor – perhaps dangerous – strategy, because the complexity of most conflict environments means that this is to misrepresent the strategic choices. When it comes to the question of strategic futures for a whole society, the priority in collective strategic thinking, in contrast, is to weigh up strategic alternatives and to ensure that advantages and disadvantages are properly considered. Differences within the society also have to be acknowledged. Collective strategic thinking welcomes criticism. Strategic planning suppresses it. Under the pressure of decision, governments and leaderships may have to push through preferred policy. But it is the overall ability of a society to undertake collective strategic thinking and to translate this into effective strategic action that underpins its capacity for second-order social learning. A lack of this capacity is referred to as a 'strategy gap'.

In these respects, collective strategic thinking and action, as understood in this chapter, is perhaps akin more to what is sometimes called *theory of change* than to most forms of military, commercial, party political or national security strategy. Theory of change (roughly) promotes social change for the collective good by defining goals and mapping back to the requirements for getting there. In this way it defines 'outcome pathways' and the 'rationales' that connect them.[6] This shares important elements with the capacity for collective strategic thinking and action outlined below.

A brief idea of some of the main elements in collective strategic thinking can now be given (see box 4.2). This suggested outline has been developed through the work of the Palestine Strategy Group, the Israeli Strategic Forum and the Palestinian Citizens of Israel Group. It is offered as a guide to any groups and facilitators who would like to apply and adapt it. All these elements can be altered. No two applications are the same.

Let us briefly consider in turn the twelve elements of collective strategic thinking suggested in box 4.2. As an illustration we will refer to Palestinian and Israeli strategic thinking in preparation for the case study in Part II – and, in order not to overload this section, particularly the strategic thinking of Palestinians as the main 'challengers' to the status quo. Israelis, as possessors, have entirely different strategic tasks, as discussed in chapter 5.

1 *Strategic identity*
Collective strategic thinking begins with identity groups. Whose strategy is it? In complicated transnational conflicts there may be overlapping answers to this question. For example, the Palestine Strategy Group (PSG) is a group for all Palestinians – in Israel, in Gaza, in

Box 4.2   A guide to collective strategic thinking

WHO ARE WE?

1	*Strategic identity*	Managing overlapping constituencies – whose strategy?
2	*Strategic unity*	Attaining sufficient strategic unity to formulate strategy and sufficient strategic authority to implement it – a strategic prerequisite

WHERE ARE WE?

3	*Strategic context*	Analysing the status quo as a complex system
4	*Strategic balance of power*	Weighing the dialectic of strength and weakness

WHERE DO WE WANT TO GO?

5	*Strategic futures*	Evaluating scenarios to be promoted or blocked – desirability, attainability, likelihood
6	*Strategic goals*	Determining short-term, medium-term and long-term destinations

HOW DO WE GET THERE?

7	*Strategic paths*	Orchestrating complementary options
8	*Strategic alternatives*	Preparing for strategic either–or choices (Plan A, Plan B)
9	*Strategic means*	Assessing appropriate forms of power – how best to move down strategic paths

OPPONENTS, ALLIES AND COMMUNICATION

10	*Strategic opponents*	Looking at the chessboard from the perspective of the opponent
11	*Strategic allies*	Eliciting external support as a 'force multiplier'
12	*Strategic communication*	Winning the war of words

In the light of this: drawing up a task list and formulating tactics

Jerusalem, in the West Bank, and in the near and far diaspora. Each sub-group has distinct strategic needs and goals. Yet there is sufficient overall identity to make the PSG a natural forum for national strategic thinking. The Israeli Strategic Forum (ISF) is a strategy group for Jewish Israelis, because this is also a natural forum. Jewish Israelis want to work out their collective strategy across their own internal differences before they can engage with others – for example, non-Jewish Israelis. For the Palestinian Citizens of Israel Group (PCIG), on the other hand, the question of identity lies at the very heart of their predicament. They are a distinct identity group in terms of collective strategic thinking because their situation and needs are distinct from those of both non-Palestinian Israelis and non-Israeli Palestinians. And yet they could be members of a full Israeli Strategic Forum and are already members of the PSG. This gives them a key – and much neglected – strategic role in any outcomes that may or may not come out of the present struggle, as is made explicit in chapter 7. Other identity groups could also do useful work – for example, separate strategy groups for the Palestinian and Jewish diasporas. And a strategy group for all Israelis might emerge from the work of the ISF and the PCIG (a programme in 2014 entitled 'Strategic Thinking for Citizens' has pioneered this). In short, given the complexity of identity issues in transnational conflicts, it is only an interweaving of overlapping identity groups of this kind that can provide a sufficient basis for unlocking what is at issue. So the first strategic question here is 'Who are we?'

2 *Strategic unity*
With the question of 'strategic unity' we reach a *strategic prerequisite*. Identity groups always have internal differences. These may include different long-term goals (see point 6 below). There is no question here of plunging into the maelstrom of internal politics. But the strategic prerequisite is that, whatever internal differences there may be, there will be sufficient strategic unity to ensure that they do not make collective strategic thinking impossible. This is recognized as an absolute priority for the PSG – for example, managing differences between Hamas and Fatah. Without sufficient strategic unity there can be no national strategy. In addition to sufficient strategic unity to enable collective strategic thinking, there is a requirement for sufficient 'strategic authority' to implement it. This is usually a bigger problem in asymmetric conflicts for challengers than for possessors. For the PCIG, for example, this emerged as perhaps the prime first strategic goal, as shown in chapter 7.

3 Strategic context

Before determining where we want to go and how to get there, we need to know where we are. This is the strategic context or the status quo. The status quo plays different roles in strategic thinking in asymmetric conflicts depending on whether the strategist is challenger or possessor. For the challenger the status quo is what needs to be transformed. For both challenger and possessor the continuation of the status quo is likely to be one of the scenarios (possible futures) considered (see 5 below). And for possessors this may well be a desired strategic goal (see 6 below).

In transnational conflicts, the strategic context is a *complex system*. If challengers, like the Palestinians, want to transform the strategic context, then they must first understand this complexity. It is constituted across the different levels and sectors of transnational conflict discussed in chapter 2. As a system it is not enough to alter one or two aspects. The system as a whole will continually fall back into its default option sustained by all the other parts of the system. This is discouraging for challengers. On the other hand, the *strategic environment* within which the complex system itself is defined is constantly changing. The situation is *dynamic*. This means that the system may be 'hollowed out' from inside – sometimes in a way that is invisible on the outside – and can suddenly collapse or shift dramatically to a new equilibrium. This is the phenomenon studied in 'catastrophe theory', in which a small stimulus can trigger a disproportionate response. An example of this was the dramatic collapse of the complex governmental system across the Middle East triggered in December 2011 by the death of a Tunisian fruit seller. Another is the collapse of *apartheid* in South Africa.

The key strategic function of an analysis of the existing complex system, particularly from the perspective of the challenger, is to set out a template for the required coordination of complementary options orchestrated under 'strategic paths' (see 7 below). An example of this is the 'analytic matrix' produced by the PCIG as described in chapter 7.

4 Strategic balance of power

In intractable asymmetric conflicts, a strategic assessment of relative strengths and weaknesses plays a key role for those wanting to shape the future. The well-known SWOT analysis (strengths, weaknesses, opportunities, threats) is here split into two. Opportunities and threats are considered separately under 'strategic futures' (see 5 below). An important prior requirement for strategy is to weigh up the relative effectiveness of different *types of power* in different circumstances. These are likely to vary dramatically between possessors (top dogs) and challengers (bottom dogs), particularly where there is *qualitative* as well as *quantitative* asymmetry (e.g., one party is a state and the other party is not). But the relationship is also usually *dialectical*, meaning that strength and weakness can be ambivalent – in some situations a strength can also be a weakness and vice versa.

Kenneth Boulding defines power as an ability to get things done. He distinguishes between three 'faces' of power: threat power (do what I want or I will do what you do not want); exchange power (do what I want and I will do what you want); and integrative power (let us do this because we both want it).[7] In some cases threat power can be counter-productive. Over the long term Boulding argues that integrative power is the only kind of power that builds enduring community (nations, religions). Joseph Nye makes similar distinctions between 'hard power' and 'soft power'.[8]

In the Israeli–Palestinian conflict, for example, the Palestinian analysis stresses the great success of Palestinian strategy in eliciting international support for the legitimacy of the Palestinian cause, culminating in overwhelming endorsement through the UN General Assembly in November–December 2012. Conversely, Israel's total military superiority in Gaza in 2014 turned out also to be a weakness when the tiny proportion of Israeli civilians killed compared to the hundreds of Palestinian women and children killed triggered widespread international condemnation. The strategic task defined for Palestinians from this analysis is to convert their comparative ethical/legal strength into substantial change on the ground.

5 Strategic futures

In collective strategic thinking, identity groups look to the future. Here the essential strategic requirement before determining strategic goals is to identify and assess *scenarios* (possible futures). These may be good or bad from the perspective of the assessor. What may be good for one conflict party may be bad for another. The strategic aim in each case is to promote good scenarios and block bad ones. At the core of the analysis is not just *desirability* (whether particular scenarios are desirable or undesirable) but, above all, *attainability* (how easy or difficult it will be to bring the desired outcome about) and *likelihood* (how likely this will be). Extensive examples of this will be given in the case study. Analysing possible futures and assessing the desirability, attainability and likelihood of promoting or blocking preferred and unpreferred scenarios turned out to be the central task in the first PSG strategy report, *Regaining the Initiative* (2008). This underpinned the reorientation of Palestinian strategy that followed, as described in chapter 6.

6 *Strategic goals*

It is worth noting how far down the list of strategic elements the question of determining strategic goals appears. This is an important point. In order to discuss and agree strategic goals it is necessary first to use all the information acquired by thinking through the earlier stages. For example, in determining the sequence of strategic goals it is necessary to make a comparative determination between scenarios that may be more desirable but less attainable and scenarios that may be less desirable (although still desirable) but more attainable.

Two further points can be made.

Conflict parties often do not agree internally on long-term strategic goals. This is common in all complex societies. There may be fundamental disagreement about long-term vision – for example, for both Israelis and Palestinians, between a religious and a secular orientation. But this does not prevent a formulation of collective strategic goals any more than it prevents Scots, who disagree internally on independence, from sharing a common future.

The most significant aspect in the determination of collective strategic goals is the distinction between short-term, medium-term and long-term goals. This allows both cross-cutting alliances on shorter aims and flexibility in leaving an open future. Old vistas are likely to close down *en route*, and new vistas are likely to open in ways that cannot be anticipated. Sometimes the achievement of an interim goal may substantially alter the balance of possibilities looked at under point 5 and bring about a recalibration of future directions. All of this is essential to strategic flexibility.

7 *Strategic paths*

With strategic paths, we begin to look at the best ways of reaching our chosen destination(s). This is, in detail, evidently an elaborate and ongoing strategic task. Examples will be given in the case study. Three general main points can be made here.

First, for challengers such as the Palestinians, the range of options chosen must cover the range of elements that are seen to make up the existing complex system of the status quo, as analysed under 3 above (for example, at different levels and across different sectors). Otherwise the system as a whole will continue to resist change. It is like moving a sequence of dials on a complicated safe. Only when the right combinations are used will the door swing open.

Second, strategic paths here are best seen as *complementary*. The requirement is to go down several paths at the same time. This is what matches complexity and allows the conflict party to retain the initiative. If blocked down one path, progress can be made down another.

A third important point is that, even when cooperation may be impossible with another strategic player, it may still be possible to forge local partnerships on specific issues. This applies particularly to short-term strategic goals (see 6 above). On strategic journeys travellers may find themselves with 'strange bedfellows'.

The overall task under 'strategic paths', therefore, is to *orchestrate* options to optimal effect to match the different facets of the complex system being addressed (see 3 above). This will be an ongoing process.

8 Strategic alternatives

But sometimes we may meet a fork in the road or an impassible barrier. In that case it is no longer a case of orchestrating strategic paths but a case of choosing between strategic alternatives. This introduces the important issue of *Plan B*. Chapter 8 will end by stressing the fundamental significance of Plan B, not only for conflict parties but also for would-be third-party peacemakers. To an extraordinary extent the international community has no Plan B for the Israeli–Palestinian conflict. This is a fundamental weakness and a central task for what I call a 'strategic negotiation approach' (see chapter 8). It is a central 'strategy gap'. The same applies on a vaster scale, at the time of writing, to the lack of a capacity for coordinated collective strategic thinking about the future of the Middle East/ North Africa (MENA) region.

Where possible, if forks in the road ahead can be anticipated, it is important to prepare Plan B (or Plan C, etc.) carefully in advance. This can play two roles that both complement each other and are in tension. First, by planning assessment points where the viability of Plan A is recurrently reviewed, a conflict party will be ready to shift strategy quickly if need be. But, second, awareness of the imminent possibility of Plan B may be a powerful inducement to an opponent to comply with Plan A if the alternative is seen to be worse and the threat of deploying it credible. This lies at the heart of the current Palestinian 'two-track strategy' to be outlined in chapter 6 – and should lie at the heart of international mediation efforts.

9 Strategic means

'Strategic means' concerns *how* to travel down strategic paths. For the PCIG, for example, a major question for Palestinian Arabs in Israel is how far to cooperate with the existing Israeli system, and compete from within, and how far to boycott and challenge from outside. For Israelis the balance is between concession and repression. In most protracted conflicts the choice of violent means is a key consideration (whether to take it up or whether to drop it). The Palestine Strategy Group coined the term 'smart resistance' for ongoing assessment of the strategic effectiveness of violent and non-violent means. Peace processes often depend on persuading challengers to give up the violent 'armed struggle' (e.g., continue the struggle politically) and possessors to give up violent repression (e.g., share political power). The distinction between 'extremism of ends' and 'extremism of means' is key here.

10 Strategic opponents

This vital element in collective strategic thinking can be simply expressed. In answer to the question 'When playing strategic chess should you look at the board from the perspective of your opponent?', in my experience every strategy group answers 'yes'. Why? Not in order to 'understand' the other or to gain sympathy for the enemy, but in order to win. Chess players who do not do this are bad chess players. They will lose. This means identifying constituencies within the opponent's society which may be potential allies on particular issues, learning what messages are most likely to bring about desired results within the opposing community and leadership, and anticipating the opponent's strategic moves in order to counter them.

11 Strategic allies

The search for strategic allies is essential in transnational conflict for obvious reasons. Here a possessor state has advantages over a non-state challenger because of the greater resources a state player has at regional and global level. In most transnational conflicts – including Israeli–Palestinian and Israeli–Arab – it is if anything these levels of conflict which are the most important. This is somewhat played down in this chapter – and, indeed, in the case study except for chapter 8. Some attempt to remedy this will be made in chapter 9. In the most recent PSG plans for 2016–17, it is the regional dimension that has been identified as the most important focus for the group's analysis. The PCIG also emphasizes how Palestinian Arabs in Israel are no longer seen as merely an 'internal problem' for Israel but are increasingly gaining an international profile. This opens up another dimension for PCIG strategy.

12 *Strategic communication*

Finally, all the above is animated and enabled by the nature, energy and quality of strategic communication. Chapter 2 showed how, in transnational conflict, this is increasingly becoming a key strategic front. At the heart of the struggle – and for that reason at the heart of this book – is the 'war of words'. This is not just a matter of the content of the messages or the manner in which they are conveyed. Above all, it is a battle to determine the discursive ground on which the struggle is fought out. For example, one of the first acts of the PSG was to challenge not just Israeli and US discourse but also that of international peacemaking, with its misleading assumptions about equivalence, concessions and mutual recognition, when, given the gross imbalance in the situation, the language appropriate for Palestinian national liberation was seen to be above all one of *rights*. As the PSG report put it:

> A discourse is a framework of language within which verbal communication takes place. It is the discourse that determines what can and cannot be said within it and how this is to be understood. At the moment the Palestinian national struggle is nearly always discussed in terms of other peoples' discourses. This is like playing all football matches on other teams' pitches. It is always an away game – we begin one goal down. Palestinians must refuse to participate on those terms. We must explain and promote our own discourse and make this the primary language within which the Palestinian issue is discussed. Unfortunately the usual framework adopted by the international community is entirely inappropriate for the Palestinian case. This is a peacemaking discourse, which assumes that the problem is one of 'making peace' between two equal partners, both of whom have symmetric interests, needs, values and beliefs. This is the wrong discourse because there are not two equal conflict parties. There is an occupying power and a suppressed and physically scattered people not allowed even to have its own identity legally recognised.[9]

Summing up

In collective strategic thinking, identity groups look out over a huge and varied landscape. In learning how to read the terrain, choose their destinations and prepare for the journey, they may turn to the visionary. The visionary, with eyes fixed on the far horizon, can inspire them to set out. But the visionary does not understand political power and may fall over impediments along the way. So groups may turn to the politician. The politician does understand political power (particularly how to stay *in* power) and can help them to avoid the impediments. But the politician does not know how to use power to reach a distant goal. What the travellers need is the statesperson. The statesperson never loses sight of the long-term purpose of the voyage but understands the complexity of the route that must be taken. The statesperson is patient as well as determined, can move over, under or round impediments, can *reculez pour mieux sauter* (move back in order the better to leap forward), retains flexibility and can take advantage of sudden opportunities, keeps the initiative, constantly surprises opponents, and knows how to elicit assistance. The statesperson is the strategist.

Two main questions arise at this point. Why should conflict parties want to participate in such work at a time of intractability when conflict resolution gains no purchase? And how can this nevertheless help to maximize chances of a possible future revival of conflict resolution?

Why should conflict parties want to engage in strategic thinking when they are not ready for conflict resolution?

The best answer to this question is given by those involved in setting up and participating in the strategy networks mentioned above. More will be said about this in the case study. But here are responses by Palestinian and Israeli participants to give the main idea. On the Palestinian side one participant puts it like this:

> The overwhelming majority of the members of the project *Regaining the Initiative* are still in touch and extremely eager to further develop and continue the initial ideas they have agreed on and reached in their meetings and discussions. I have had the opportunity to speak with participants who are members of Fatah, Hamas, or women, student, academic, and human rights and democracy organizations. They all passionately agree about the desperate need to develop and sustain long-term Palestinian strategic thinking. Indeed, this approach has already had a real major impact. A few months ago I received a phone call from a senior member of the Negotiation Support Unit (NUS) of the Palestine Authority informing me that the Unit has discussed thoroughly the Palestinian strategy document and adopted several parts of it.[10]

On the Israeli side, a participant gives a comparable account:

> [As a result of internal divisions] the national conversation about the conflict has become a cacophony. To a large extent as time passes the discussion becomes increasingly polarised, filled with taboos and thus simplistic. This leaves Israeli Jews with no real capacity to agree on a common strategy . . . After so many decades of violence, and with Israel facing a truly complex rapidly changing reality, a mapping of alternative scenarios should be used to broaden the discursive space, alleviate some taboos, and legitimise a conversation on certain futures that are so far unspoken. This is a requirement if Israeli Jews are to take a well-informed decision about their future – one that takes seriously into account the domestic, regional and international constraints, costs and benefits.[11]

It can be seen that the main motive for conflict parties to engage in this work is not to do with attempts to understand the other or to solve a shared problem. It is to overcome internal divisions in order to attain national goals – in this sense it is to *win*. Both Israelis and Palestinians are deeply concerned about such internal divisions. In the case of Palestinians, these are multiplied by physical separation – in Israel, Gaza, Jerusalem, the West Bank, and the near and far diaspora. Without sufficient internal cohesion there can be no coherent and effective national strategy.

But is the aim of 'winning' not the antithesis of conflict resolution? Is it not just what principled negotiation, problem-solving and dialogue for mutual understanding want to transcend? In that case, how can it help to create conditions for their future revival?

How can strategic thinking be a placeholder for a revival of conflict resolution?

It is always possible that inclusive strategic thinking within conflict parties may deepen antagonisms and make things worse. Conflict parties may come to realize more clearly why they hate each other. But there are also a number of reasons why, nevertheless, such thinking may be able to act as a 'placeholder' when conflict resolution is not yet possible:

- Strategic thinking can 'mimic' conflict resolution.
- Overcoming internal divisions can often be a prerequisite for conflict resolution.

61

- The gap between elite decision-making and societal levels can be bridged.
- Channels of communication can be kept open that are otherwise closed.
- Issues can be raised that are otherwise not on the radar screen.
- The question of conflict asymmetry can be addressed.
- The role of third parties – especially would-be third-party peacemakers – can be clarified.

We briefly consider each of these in turn. The first three operate mainly *within conflict parties* at level 1. The next three operate mainly *across conflict parties* at level 2. The seventh relates to *third parties* at level 3.

How strategic thinking can mimic conflict resolution

Table 4.1 gives an idea of a number of ways in which, by its very nature, strategic thinking has characteristics that can help to give possible future conflict resolution initiatives more traction even in intense phases of conflict.

There is much that can be said about these ten features (see Ramsbotham 2010, pp. 177–80). Commenting briefly on them in pairs: numbers 1 and 2 can help to avoid the 'capture' of strategic thinking by

Table 4.1   Ten ways in which strategic thinking can mimic conflict resolution

1 Strategic thinking is inclusive.
2 Strategic thinking looks to the future.
3 Strategic thinking analyses the status quo as a complex system.
4 Strategic thinking evaluates scenarios (future possibilities) not just in terms of desirability but also in terms of attainability and likelihood.
5 Strategic thinking, on this basis, determines short-term, medium-term and long-term goals.
6 Strategic thinking prepares alternative routes (Plan A, Plan B, etc).
7 Strategic thinking distinguishes between different forms of power (threat, exchange, integrative).
8 Strategic thinking assesses strategic means in terms of relative effectiveness under different conditions.
9 Strategic thinking looks at the chessboard from the perspective of the opponent.
10 Strategic thinking takes care that strategic messages are expressed appropriately for different audiences.

any one faction and can temper preoccupation with past resentments; numbers 3 and 4 can go some way towards ensuring that analysis is sophisticated and realistic – not just wishful thinking; numbers 5 and 6 can add flexibility and an understanding that there are often many possible routes; numbers 7 and 8 can encourage evaluation of alternatives to violence; number 9 can open the way for consideration of enemy perspectives even though the aim is not to 'understand' but to 'win'; and number 10 can add greater critical awareness of what needs to be done to address and influence multiple audiences at the same time.

How overcoming internal divisions can be a prerequisite for conflict resolution

We have seen above how one of the main prerequisites for inclusive internal strategic thinking is 'strategic unity'. Strategic unity does not mean political unity between constituencies, parties or factions, but it does mean that internal differences must not make effective collective strategic thinking and strategic action impossible. Without strategic unity there can be no effective collective strategy.

But this can also contribute to increasing opportunities for future conflict resolution, because it is often internal divisions within conflict parties that are the main obstacles to peace processes between them. This is a well-known dynamic. Leaders who move towards political accommodation with opponents, for example, often thereby open dangerous space behind their backs that can be filled by more radical internal rivals. Innumerable peace processes have been derailed in this way.

How strategic engagement can help to bridge the gap between elite decision-making and societal levels

One of the most debilitating impediments to conflict resolution is the gap between decision-making elites and popular societal levels. Again and again, agreements made behind closed doors at elite level founder on 're-entry' into an unprepared public arena. Conversely, insights, possibilities and breakthroughs at societal or grass-roots level do not penetrate politicized party political hierarchies or official political and security institutions. This was one of the main reasons why the Oslo process began to lose momentum in the mid-1990s and why, even if there had been a breakthrough in the 2013–14 Kerry talks, most commentators doubted that either government could have carried this successfully through what would inevitably have been a prolonged implementation phase (see chapter 8).

Inclusive internal strategic thinking that is continually fed into the national debate at all levels can go some way towards remedying this. By its very structure, as many internal constituencies as possible participate in the strategic thinking. Strategic thinking is something that can be promoted in all parts of society. And the deliberate purpose of the enterprise is to operate at both societal and governmental levels and to bridge between the two. This is an essential strategic requirement without which it will be ineffective.

How strategic engagement can help to keep channels of communication open that are otherwise closed

Moving on to the opportunities opened up by collective strategic thinking within conflict parties for creating space for strategic exchange across and between them, figure 4.1 illustrates this process. In this model there are two conflict parties (A and B), each of which is internally composite (both contain extremists and moderates). This generates six *axes of radical disagreement*. Evidently this is a highly simplified model. There may be more than two conflict parties. There are many cross-cutting internal divisions. The terms 'extremist' and 'moderate' will vary across different issues and are themselves contested. Third parties have not yet been included. And so on. Nevertheless, the model is useful for illustrating the main dynamics involved. Above all, it clearly demonstrates one of the main reasons why it is best to begin not with radical disagreement *across* conflict parties (axes 1, 4, 5, 6), but with inclusive strategic engagement of discourses *within* them (axes 2, 3).

Radical disagreement is popularly identified with *Axis 1* – the disagreement between extremists (as normally defined). But this is, if anything, the least significant axis. As repeatedly demonstrated in the

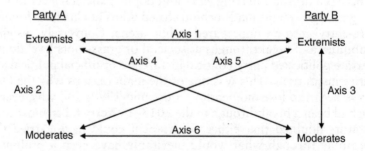

Figure 4.1   The hexagon of radical disagreement

exploration of agonistic dialogue, it is radical disagreement between moderates (as normally defined) that is much the most important element. Extremists often feed off each other and are mutually dependent.

Axes 2 and 3 are the key axes that constitute level 1 of the strategic engagement process. They form the basis for the possibility of maintaining inclusive strategic engagement between a majority on either side, even in times of maximum intractability. It is via axes 2 and 3 that the other axes remain operational.

Axes 4 and 5 are exchanges (often indirect) that are made possible only so long as axes 2 and 3 remain inclusive and Axis 6 remains active. Extremists (as normally defined) do not want to participate directly in, or to encourage, these axes of communication.

Axis 6 is the most crucial – and underrated – axis of radical disagreement. It is easy to assume that, since these are 'moderates' (for example, opposed to violence), there is bound to be agreement across this axis about most of the main issues. But that is not the case in intractable conflicts. On the contrary, this is where the central lines of radical disagreement lie and where agonistic dialogue that explores this is most urgently needed. An example is given at the beginning of the case study. In intractable conflicts, many if not most 'moderates of means' may be 'extremists of ends'. Anticipating chapters 8 and 9, in these cases it is more immediately important for peacemakers to maximize the number of extremists of ends who are moderates of means than to try to convert them into moderates of ends.

How strategic engagement can help to raise issues that are otherwise not on the public radar screen

This is a major outcome of promoting strategic engagement across and between conflict parties based on ongoing collective strategic thinking within them. Issues that do not otherwise emerge at all appear on the radar screen. And a shared language is available for addressing what were taboo subjects. It is these issues that often prove to be the crucial ones, as the case study demonstrates.

How strategic engagement can help to address conflict asymmetry

Similarly, a strategic engagement of discourses can reach deeply into the issue of asymmetry, which, as seen in earlier chapters, often lies at the heart of intractability. *Quantitative asymmetry* poses problems, but these are greatly compounded when there is also *qualitative asymmetry*. This means that conflict parties are seeking entirely different strategic goals. For example, as the first two chapters in the case study show, the primary strategic question for the possessor (Israelis) is 'Why should Israel give up anything at all?' Whereas the primary strategic question for the challenger (Palestinians) is 'How can Palestinians transform the status quo?' A central argument in this book is that the promotion of an institutional capacity for sustained collective strategic thinking is to the advantage of both possessors and challengers. But whereas for possessors the 'strategy gap' is dangerous, for challengers it can be fatal. Both the Palestine Strategy Group and the Palestinian Citizens of Israel Group recognize this. The promotion of a capacity for collective strategic thinking and strategic action is a powerful equalizer.

How strategic engagement can clarify the role of third parties

Level 3 of strategic engagement shows why, whatever they may themselves say – and believe – third parties are not neutral, impartial or disinterested in intractable conflicts. Even 'elicitive' or 'transformative' peacemakers – such as Norway or NGOs – know the outcome that they seek. They want to change the discourses of the conflict parties so that they become different to what they were before. They, too, want to 'win'. That is why third-party interveners, even if initially welcomed, so often end by quarrelling with all the conflict parties. Conflict parties expect third parties to support them. When they do not, conflict parties may turn against third-party peacemakers. They may then agree with each other that the third parties do not understand the situation at all.

And that is why, in the context of strategic engagement, third-party peacemakers also need a strategy in order to attain their strategic goals. As shown in chapter 8, these need to be factored in as scenarios in a strategic negotiation approach. In formulating their strategy, third parties would be wise to avail themselves of all the information provided by strategic engagement at the other two levels.

Conclusion

When faced with intractable situations that resist conflict resolution and with intransigent conflict parties who refuse to behave as conflict resolution wants, it is best to turn in another direction and to promote conflict engagement. Begin by taking the radical disagreement at the heart of linguistic intractability seriously. Conflict engagement entails listening to what conflict parties say (exploring agonistic dialogue – heuristic engagement) and promoting collective strategic thinking based on this (strategic engagement).

In the case study that follows, chapters 5 and 6 start at level 1 and look in turn at the Israelis and the Palestinians in these two ways. What do Israelis and Palestinians say? How do they think strategically?

Chapter 7 moves on to level 2 and discusses the promotion of strategic exchange across and between Israelis and Palestinians that is made possible as a result. It introduces the work of the Palestinian Citizens of Israel Group to show how new vistas – opportunities as well as challenges – are opened up when strategic engagement is widened and deepened in this way.

Chapter 8 proceeds to level 3 and considers the role of third parties. Why did the Kerry initiative fail in 2013–14? What lessons can be learnt by comparing principled negotiation with the strategic negotiation approach suggested in this book?

Part II begins with an example of why conflict resolution approaches do not yet work in the Israeli–Palestinian case.

Part II

Case Study: The Israel–Palestine Conflict

His Majesty's Government view with favour the establishment in Palestine of a national home for the Jewish people, and will use their best endeavours to facilitate the achievement of this object, it being clearly understood that nothing shall be done which may prejudice the civil and religious rights of existing non-Jewish communities in Palestine, or the rights and political status enjoyed by Jews in any other country.

> (UK Foreign Secretary Arthur Balfour, 2 November 1917,
> to the Zionist Federation via Baron Rothschild)

A century after the Balfour Declaration, the failure of attempts to reconcile the goal of 'a national home for the Jewish people' in Palestine with the 'civil and religious rights of existing non-Jewish communities' still constitutes what for many is the most intractable of all extant conflicts.

In this introduction to the case study we will begin with quite an extended illustration of the way in which conflict resolution approaches in the communicative sphere do not yet gain traction in intense political conflicts. This will illustrate the argument in chapter 3.

We will compare what the editor of a book on innovative attempts to overcome the radical disagreement at the core of the Israeli–Palestinian conflict says *about* the radical disagreement with an *example* of the radical disagreement itself taken from the same book. This suggests why conflict resolution approaches, based on such readings, so far fail. They do not engage with the chief verbal aspect of the conflict. In the rest of the case study we will try to remedy this by beginning with a heuristic and strategic engagement approach that forefronts radical disagreement from the outset.

What is the Israeli–Palestinian conflict about? Here is an account by the editor of an impressive and detailed survey called *Israeli and Palestinian Narratives of Conflict*. I will take this as characteristic of a whole swathe of interpretations:

> The Israeli–Palestinian conflict for primacy, power, and control encompasses two bitterly contested, competing narratives. Both need to be understood, reckoned with, and analysed side by side in order to help abate violence and possibly propel both protagonists toward peace. This is an immensely tall order. But the first step is to know the narratives, the second to reconcile them to the extent that they can be reconciled or bridged, and the third to help each side to accept, and conceivably to respect, the validity of the competing narrative . . .
>
> Juxtaposing the 'two justifying/rationalizing narratives' helps us to 'understand the roots of the conflict and the differentially distorted prisms that fuel it'. At the core of such narratives lie 'symbolic constructions of shared identity' or 'collective memories', which do not usually so much 'reflect truth' as 'portray a truth that is functional for a group's ongoing existence'. Each 'is "true" in terms of the requirements of collective memory'. Narratives are 'motivational tools'.
>
> What is required is a 'greater appreciation of the separate truths that drive Palestinians and Israelis', because this could 'plausibly contribute to conflict reduction'. The aim is 'to narrow, not eliminate, the chasm that separates one strongly affirmed reality from another. The lessons of this book are that the gulf between the narratives remains vast, that no simplified efforts at softening the edges of each narrative will work, and that the fundamental task of the present is to expose each side to the narratives of the other in order, gradually, to foster an understanding, if not an acceptance, of their deeply felt importance to each side.'[1]

Here the conflict resolution *prescription* (foster mutual acceptance of the validity of the other narrative) follows from prior *description* (these are coexistent truths) and *explanation* (their function is motivational). That is what dictates the adoption of a 'dialogue for mutual understanding' approach. So how adequate is this third-party description and explanation in the first place?

Let us begin with four main recommendations for action in the book that, it is suggested, might 'help abate violence and possibly propel both protagonists toward peace'. Then let us test these against an example of the radical disagreement in question.

1. Ilan Pappé advocates 'bridging the narrative concept' along the lines already initiated by the new 'post-Zionist' revisionist Israeli historians, among whom he is a prominent figure, in order to

narrow differences and, if possible, produce shared historiographical reconstructions.

2. Daniel Bar-Tal and Gavriel Salomon do not think that it is possible to overcome the way rival narratives oppose each other's fundamental truths, and, as psychologists, they hope to promote reconciliation by 'building legitimacy through narrative' – fostering mutual acknowledgement of sincerity and therefore validity by recognizing 'that there are two (legitimate) narratives of the conflict'.

3. Mordechai Bar-On recommends acceptance of the fact that the Zionist and Palestinian narratives 'negate the very existence of the foe as a collectivity' and suggests that the focus should rather be on a critical re-examination of the historical record by each side separately. He sees this as a particular task for the Palestinians.

4. Finally, Dan Bar-On and Sami Adwan aim to promote 'better dialogue between two separate but interdependent narratives' that 'are intertwined like a double helix' through their work on the production of parallel texts on the Balfour Declaration, the 1948 war, and the 1987 Intifada, including the idea of getting Israeli and Palestinian schoolchildren to fill in intermediate commentaries.

These are inspiring programmes. But what happens when they are applied to examples of the radical disagreements that they are attempting to mitigate?

We do not have to look far. We can take a contributor to the book itself as a spokesperson for the 'Palestinian narrative' and then provide an example of radical disagreement by combining this with the response of an Israeli contributor.

Nadim Rouhana is a highly regarded Palestinian conflict transformation specialist. How does his 'narrative' in the book relate to the editorial prescription and to the four suggested transformation approaches listed above? Let us look at each of the four recommendations in turn.

1. For Rouhana, 'bridging the narrative concept' cannot mean 'meeting the other half-way' when what is required is for Israelis to acknowledge the violence and injustice inherent in the Zionist project itself (as in fact Pappé does):

> From the moment Zionism was conceived, force has been a central component of its relationship with Palestinians. The seeds of protracted conflict are based in the relationship between colonizer and

colonized, and thus are inherent to the dynamics of the encounter between the Zionist movement and Palestinians. It has always been naïve or self-serving to think that a Jewish state could be established in a homeland inhabited by another people except through the use of force.[2]

2. In Rouhana's chapter, promoting reconciliation by 'building legitimacy through narrative' does not mean recognizing 'that there are two (legitimate) narratives of the conflict', because one of the narratives is fundamentally illegitimate:

> The encounter has been one between an indigenous people in a homeland defined by the political unit known as Palestine ever since the British mandate was established, and another group of people, the Zionists, who came from outside of Palestine, mainly from Europe, and developed a modern ideology based on three key principles: The Jews are a nation and should establish their own state . . .; A Jewish state should be established in Palestine . . .; Palestine [should] become the exclusive homeland of the Jewish people and not the land of both the Jewish people and the people of Palestine. Mainstream Zionists . . . did not seek partnership with the people who lived in Palestine to build a common homeland but rather [aimed] to transform the country into an exclusively Jewish homeland.[3]
>
> Genuine reconciliation requires facing historic truths, taking responsibility for past injustices, and framing future relations in terms of justice rather than power. Reconciliation would also require a major political restructuring to enable full equality between individuals and national groups in Palestine, a change that would be incompatible with a Zionist framework or with Zionism.[4]

3. For Rouhana, the idea that 'scholarly confrontations between conflicting narratives can be fruitful only if each side concentrates on self-criticism, not on condemning the other',[5] and particularly the notion that this is a task mainly for the Palestinians because Israel already has its revisionist 'new historians' and 'post-Zionists', does not cut ice. The 'Palestinian narrative' is an attempt to rescue a record of suppressed reality, whereas even 'left-leaning' liberal Israelis who promote the idea that 'both sides have equally legitimate narratives' are thereby covertly supporting the hegemonic Zionist cause and reinforcing the status quo:

> Left-leaning Israelis and Zionist groups seek official and unofficial diplomatic means to achieve the same result, while often paralleling the history of Zionism and the Palestinian national movement, arguing that both sides have equally legitimate narratives as well

as a history of violence, the need for recognition, and so on. This alternative approach seeks to achieve recognition of Zionism in return for a Palestinian state in the occupied territories.[6]

4. Finally, for Rouhana, it is not a question of 'promoting better dialogue between two separate but interdependent narratives' by producing parallel texts in both Hebrew and Arabic and inviting intermediate commentary so that 'hateful single narratives' are transformed into 'two mutually sensitive ones'. What are at issue, rather, are two other requirements.

First, the dominant narrative which supports and 'naturalizes' the unjust power asymmetry stands in need of deconstruction in order to expose its subconscious and repressed roots in guilt and fear: 'For obvious reasons, it is not easy [for Israelis] to face this fear, as it would mean challenging the national narrative and national and personal identity.'

Second, the marginalized narrative, which represents legitimate resistance to the injustice and a refusal to be suppressed or co-opted as 'one truth among many', needs to be reaffirmed:

For Palestinians, resisting the takeover of their homeland was a natural human reaction to injustice ... One of the most effective and least evident forms of resistance was the preservation of memories and the national narrative, at the core of which was a clinging to a right to the homeland – expressed now in the form of insisting on the principle of the right of return: Israel must be held responsible for the Palestinian exile, and the Jewish state in the Palestinian homeland must be denied legitimacy. This narrative is shared by all segments of Palestinian society, including Palestinians in Israel.[7]

In *Israeli and Palestinian Narratives of Conflict* the editor notes how some other authors 'take exception' to Rouhana's 'contribution'. What happens in these cases?

One of those to 'take exception' was Mordechai Bar-On, a 'veteran peace activist' (his own description) and an eminent research scholar at the Yad Ben-Zvi Institute in Jerusalem. Bar-On has great experience of Israeli–Palestinian dialogue and a sophisticated capacity to 'read-off' for his own partisanship: 'I have no doubt that my arguments have little chance of influencing Rouhana, as his oral arguments (at our meetings at Harvard University) not only failed to convince me but also made me angry.'[8]

So here is an example of radical disagreement at the heart of the linguistic intractability in the Israeli–Palestinian conflict. The speakers are co-contributors to the book, both are widely seen to be 'moderates',[9] and what they say would, I think, be generally endorsed by nearly all Palestinians in the first case and by nearly all Israelis in the second case. The first speaker is Rouhana, the second speaker is Bar-On.

|(A) 'Israel will have to face at least part of the truth that the country that they settled belonged to another people, that their project was the direct cause of the displacement and dismantling of Palestinian society, and that it could not have been achieved without this displacement. Israel will also have to confront the realities of the occupation and the atrocities it is committing, and will have to accept that Palestinian citizens in Israel are indigenous to the land and entitled to seek the democratic transformation of the state so that they have equal access to power, resources and decision making, and are entitled to rectification of past and present injustices.'[10]

(B) 'There are many historiographical faults in the way Rouhana tells the story. The main problem with Rouhana's thesis ... lies in his sweeping conclusion that "from the moment Zionism was conceived, force has been a central component of its relationship with the Palestinians" ... Is it not possible for a Palestinian such as Rouhana to understand that, in 1948, the Jews of Palestine, to their chagrin, could not but use force to defend themselves and impose a solution that was legitimated by a majority of nations? ... [T]here is no chance that I shall ever consider that my father and mother, who immigrated to Palestine as Zionists in 1924, were criminals. Nor do I consider my actions illegitimate when I gave the order "Fire!" and perhaps killed or wounded assailants in response to an ambush on the troop that I commanded on the way to Tel Aviv in December 1947. There is hardly any question that, in December 1947, the fire that later spread throughout the country was ignited at that time by the Palestinians.'[11]|

Evidently this example of radical disagreement is undeveloped. The second speaker does not yet directly address the central points made by the first speaker. And the first speaker does not yet answer back. More will be said about this in chapter 10. But already it can be seen why the editor's account of the radical disagreement at the heart of the Israeli–Palestinian conflict is not yet adequate. Neither of the speakers is saying that his utterance is a merely 'symbolic construction' or

74

a 'collective memory' that does not 'reflect truth' but only portrays a truth that is 'functional' for his group's 'ongoing existence'. They do not say that these are merely coexisting or equivalent 'narratives' at all. That they do *not* say these things is what makes this a radical disagreement. Not to acknowledge this is to miss the radical disagreement at the heart of the conflict.

That the editor realizes something of this is suggested by his comment:

> A next stage, too late for this book, would be for Jawad, Porat, Bar-On and others [he does not name Rouhana] to spend necessary hours together attempting to reconcile the discordant narratives, or at least delineating the precise contours of disagreement.[12]

This is, indeed, what needs to be done. It is what is surprisingly rarely done – as we have seen in chapter 3. What would happen if it was done? What would happen if the 'contours of disagreement' was first taken seriously and explored with the conflict parties? What would happen if conflict engagement (both heuristic and strategic) was not stifled but promoted? What would happen if this was done before attempts were made to resolve the conflict? In short, what would happen if, before trying to describe and explain narratives *of* conflict, prior efforts were made to understand and respond to narratives *in* conflict? The rest of the case study is an attempt to answer these questions.

5

STRATEGIC THINKING
FOR POSSESSORS: ISRAELIS

We now apply the two parts of the conflict engagement framework set out in chapter 4 to Israel. We want to learn what Israelis are saying (the first stage of heuristic engagement), and, in the light of this, we want to understand Israeli collective strategic thinking about the future (the first stage of strategic engagement). The former shows what blocks conflict resolution. The latter clarifies what can – or cannot – be done about it. And the overarching strategic question for Israelis as possessors is: Why should Israel give up anything at all?

Heuristic engagement:
why conflict resolution fails – what Israelis say

The first thing to get away from is the prevailing third-party assumption noted in chapter 3 that what is in question is a merely subjective 'Israeli narrative'. As if 'subjective' perceptions, thoughts, feelings, ideologies – and arguments – can be explained away in terms of political rationalization of interest, social construction, psychological projection, and so on, and can thereby be divorced from the 'real' core issues that make up the 'objective' conflict over 'scarce goods' such as land, wealth and power. Any time spent listening to what Israelis say dispels this assumption. Israelis are not referring to what is merely subjective. Israeli arguments and claims cannot be divorced from the harsh 'objective' realities and bitter lessons of history that have generated them.

Despite all the internal differences – which we will look at in chapter 7 – what has been most striking about Israeli discourses over the years has been the impassioned consensus that binds the nation together at times of crisis. And this has been most of the time since the foundation of the state in 1948 – not to mention the experience of the *yishuv* (pre-state community) before that. This underlying national consensus on key political issues has, if anything, intensified rather than decreased in the opening years of the twenty-first century, affected by changing internal composition and dramatic external events.

At the risk of some misunderstanding – to be clarified in chapter 10 – I will try to give a flavour of this by commenting on three 'realities' that powerfully influence internal Israeli discourse and can be uncovered only by heuristic engagement.

The reality of lived experience

Born in a period of nationalism, colonialism, socialism and imperial rivalries in the late nineteenth century, what had for centuries been preserved as religious Zionism became political Zionism – the longing for an independent national home in the land of Israel (*Eretz Yisrael*). It was very much a minority movement to begin with. Ninety per cent of Jews in the world lived in Europe (50 per cent in tsarist Russian lands). The more wealthy among them saw themselves not as a separate nation but as citizens of the countries they lived in – and had lived in for centuries. In Europe these were mainly *Ashkenazim* ('German' Jews), who in large part both embraced and contributed mightily to the development of 'Western' Enlightenment values in general. They spoke the languages of the countries they lived in. Poorer Jews, living in the *shtetls* (small towns) particularly of Eastern Europe, tended to speak *Yiddish* (a Germanic language written in Hebrew characters).

What changed this and persuaded millions to leave mainland Europe for Britain, America – and Palestine – over the next decades? It was the reality of persecution and anti-Semitism on a massive scale. Theodore Herzl – widely seen as the founder of modern Zionism – wanted to be an ordinary German and while at university joined patriotic German societies. He was rejected. And his response was then shaped by the reality of the deep anti-Semitism revealed in the Dreyfus affair in France. This was an ancient pattern going back nearly 2000 years to the destruction of the previous Jewish state by the Romans in 70 CE.[1] Since then Jews had been scattered and lived in non-Jewish countries subject to recurrent massacre and expulsion – for example, perhaps a quarter of European Jews were killed at the time of the first crusade (roughly 1000 CE). After that, massacres and expulsions continued throughout the Middle Ages in Europe – including in 1492, when Jews were forcibly converted or driven out of newly united Spain (these were the *Sephardim* or Spanish Jews). During the time when modern political Zionism was forming, ferocious persecutions (*pogroms*) were perpetrated in the Russia of Tsar Alexander III. All of these made up the reality of lived experience. These were not just 'subjective' constructs or narratives.

After the First World War, the text of the promise made in the 'Balfour Declaration' was reproduced in the wording of Britain's League of Nations mandate for 'Palestine'. Map 5.1 shows the 'carve-up' by the colonial powers (chiefly Britain and France) of the lands of the defeated Ottoman Empire in which mandatory Palestine made up the land to the west of the river Jordan. The land to the east – widely also seen as part of Palestine – formed the bulk of the new kingdom

Map 5.1   The carve-up of the Middle East after the First World
War (including mandatory Palestine)

79

of Transjordan. At the time of the 1922 census, the Jewish population made up about 10 per cent of the population of mandatory
Palestine (it is estimated that before the advent of Zionism – in the
early 1880s – at the time of the 'old *yishuv*', this figure had been 3 to
4 per cent). In the 1920s and 1930s tensions rose as Jewish immigration continued (by the early 1930s the Jewish population made up
some 17 per cent of the whole). But the lived reality that did most
to shape opinion in the *yishuv* was the advent of the Nazi regime in
Germany in 1933 and the great Arab revolt in Palestine that broke
out in 1936. Kristallnacht in Germany in November 1938 convinced
many European Jews that ideas of integration in Central Europe were
illusory. And in Palestine in 1936: 'The Jewish community was militarily weak and vulnerable. It would have been easily defeated had
Britain not intervened to restore law and order.'[2]

This experience demonstrated the implacable hostility of Arab
leaders, notably Haj Amin al-Husseini, Grand Mufti of Jerusalem,
and their determination to 'drive the Jews into the sea' if they had
the power to do so. And it persuaded most of those who had hitherto
resisted the insistence of 'hard-line' revisionists, inspired by Ze'ev
Jabotinsky, that the Jewish community must arm itself and create an
'iron wall' of military power as the only sure defence against annihilation, that this was indeed necessary. As it was, the brutal crushing of
the Arab uprising by the British major-general Bernard Montgomery
'broke the back of the Arab national movement' for the next decade,
while, conversely, part of the irregular Jewish *Haganah* ('defence') was
effectively professionally armed and trained by the British in 1941–2
to help defend Palestine from advancing German forces under Rommel
(for example, the Palmach regiment; British funding stopped after the
battle of El-Alamein). This helps explain Jewish military success – in
contrast to 1936–9 – in the first part of the War of Independence
between December 1947 and May 1948.

In 1937 the Peel Commission had advised a partition of mandatory
Palestine. The Jewish state would have occupied only 5000 square
kilometres, punctuated by a 'mandated area' enclave from Jerusalem
to Jaffa (see map 5.2). The remaining area would have been united
with Transjordan to form a much bigger Arab–Palestinian state. The
Jewish Agency accepted the proposal. The Grand Mufti refused. Had
Arabs accepted the plan, and had there been no ensuing violence, the
Israeli–Palestinian conflict would already have been over.

This experience was replicated on a grander scale ten years later,
but not before Britain had once again reneged on a promise by
issuing a White Paper in 1939 which effectively abandoned the

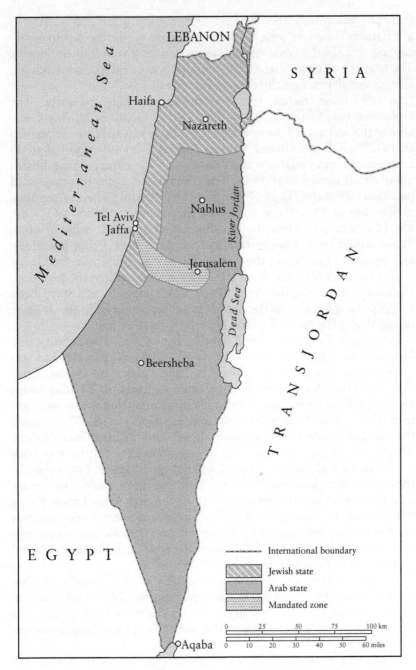

Map 5.2   The 1937 Peel Commission proposal

Balfour Declaration and the Peel Commission offer and advocated a binational state in which Jewish numbers would be permanently capped at a third – once again Jews would be a vulnerable minority. The lesson was clear. The *yishuv* could rely only on its own strength. It must not depend on third-party promises.

In 1947 these lessons were repeated and strongly reinforced. The Holocaust was finally ended by the defeat of Germany in May 1945. One of the first acts of the new United Nations was to set up a commission (UNSCOP, the United Nations Special Committee on Palestine) to make recommendations for Palestine on the expiry of the British mandate set for 14 May 1948. The commission again recommended partition (see map 5.3). In November 1947 the UN General Assembly, in Resolution 181, voted to accept the recommendation (33 votes for, 12 against, 10 abstentions including, characteristically, Britain). There would be a Jewish state and an Arab state living peacefully side by side. Once again the Jewish Agency accepted and the Grand Mufti, together with the Arab states in the UN, rejected the proposal. Had they accepted, the Arab (Palestinian) state would have been roughly the same size as the Jewish state. Once again, in the absence of hostilities, the conflict would effectively have ended.

Instead, in December 1947 fighting broke out. The action came in two phases. Between December 1947 and May 1948 the war was between the forces of the *yishuv* and the Palestinian Arabs. After that, the announcement of the new State of Israel on 14 May 1948, together with the invasion of Palestine by armies from the seven countries of the Arab League, inaugurated a period (1948–67) in which the conflict became one between Israel and its Arab neighbours. These events have been the focus of huge historical controversy both within Israel and outside, which I will not go into here. But, as one of the leading 'new historians', Avi Schlaim, puts it, this is 'not to suggest that the conventional Zionist version of the first Arab–Israeli war is based on myth rather than on reality', since 'it is precisely because this version corresponds so closely to the personal experience and perceptions of the Israelis who lived through the 1948 war that it has proved so resistant to revision and change.'[3]

The outcome of the fighting was victory for the Israelis, so that by the time of the armistice at the beginning of 1949 Israel made up 78 per cent of mandatory Palestine, with the remaining 22 per cent (Gaza and the West Bank) under the rule of Egypt and Jordan respectively (see map 5.4).

Three lessons were learnt. The historic significance for the Jewish people of the Zionist achievement was overwhelmingly confirmed.

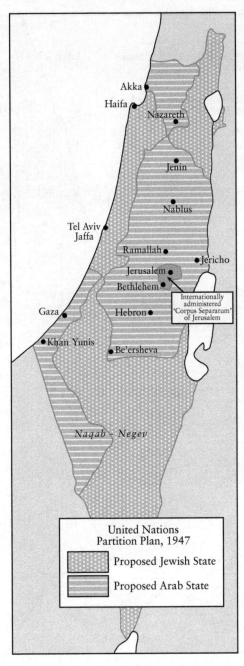

Map 5.3   The 1947 United Nations partition plan

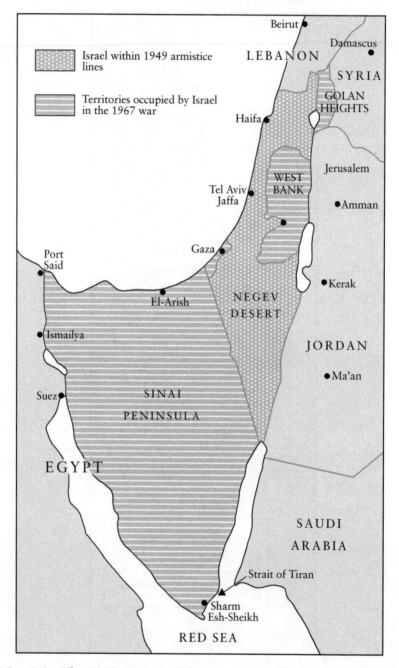

Map 5.4   The 1949 armistice lines and Israeli gains in the 1967 war

The responsibility of the Arabs for not creating their own state in Palestine and the danger that their implacable hostility posed against the very existence of Israel was reinforced. And the essential necessity for Israel to build an 'iron wall' to protect itself instead of relying on outside support was underlined. For example, in the early weeks of 1948, before the Israeli declaration of independence, the American administration had changed its mind and tried at the last minute to dissuade the Jewish leadership from announcing a Jewish state. Outsiders, who did not live in the region or understand it, could not be trusted.

Here are two indications that these lessons had been well learnt:

> The State of Israel! My eyes filled with tears, and my hands shook. We had done it. We had brought the Jewish state into existence ... From this day on we would no longer live on sufferance in the land of our forefathers. Now we were a nation like other nations, master – for the first time in twenty centuries – of our own destiny. The dream had come true – too late to save those who had perished in the Holocaust, but not too late for the generations to come. (Golda Meir)[4]
>
> [The 1948 victory] seemed to show the advantages of direct action over negotiation and diplomacy ... The victory offered such a glorious contrast to the centuries of persecution and humiliation, of adaptation and compromise, that it seemed to indicate the only direction that could possibly be taken from then on. To brook nothing, tolerate no attack, cut through the Gordian knots, and create history by creating facts seemed so simple, so compelling, so satisfying that it became Israel's policy in its conflict with the Arab world. (Nahum Goldmann)[5]

But this achievement remained precarious. Barely twenty years later, in the early 1960s, Israel faced if anything an even graver danger. Knowing with hindsight the outcome of the June 1967 'Six-Day War' can obscure the searing experience of living through it. Inspired by the fierce pan-Arab nationalism of President Nasser in Egypt, bolstered by his apparent success in the 1956 Suez war, Israel was confronted with the prospect of a concerted attack by Egypt, Syria and Iraq. This threat was so great that it led to a collapse in the confidence of Prime Minister Ben-Gurion in the early 1960s and his resignation. In a letter to US President Kennedy dated 26 April 1963, he wrote that what had happened to the Jews in Europe during the Second World War might now be repeated in the Middle East if the Arabs continued their hostility: 'It may not happen today or tomorrow, but I am not sure whether the state will continue to exist after my life has come to an end.'[6] The future Israeli premier Yitzhak Rabin also had a temporary breakdown (on 23–4 May 1967).[7]

85

Once more historical controversy surrounds these events. But again there is no doubting the sense of intense national anxiety in Israel – for example, during the two-week 'period of waiting' that followed Nasser's actions in mobilizing Egyptian forces, removing UN peace-keepers from Sinai, and closing of the Straits of Tiran to Israeli shipping. Invasion by Lebanon, Syria, Iraq, Jordan and Egypt was imminent. On 26 May 1967 Nasser declared that, now that Arab forces were strong enough, 'if we were to enter a battle with Israel, with God's help we could triumph . . . The battle will be a general one and our basic objective will be to destroy Israel.'[8]

> To Israelis it was a war for survival, fought against a steady drumbeat of threats to Israel's very existence. Israelis never forget the fear of annihilation that prevailed on the eve of the war, or the digging of mass graves in anticipation of vast civilian casualties.[9]

The astonishing – in some eyes miraculous – outcome of the 1967 war left Israel in control of the whole of mandatory Palestine and more (see map 5.4). Again the three lessons from 1948 were reinforced – in this case with the added warning never to trust security assurances by the UN.

At an Israeli cabinet meeting on 19 June 1967 it was agreed to offer peace with Egypt on the pre-1967 borders, and with Syria so long as the Golan heights were demilitarized and water access was guaranteed. A decision on Jordan was deferred. This proposal was communicated to the USA. Famously, General Dayan said that he was 'waiting for the phone to ring' with offers of peace terms from the defeated powers. None came. Instead, in their meeting between 28 August and 2 September 1967 at Khartoum, the eight leading countries of the Arab League agreed the 'three noes': no peace with Israel, no recognition of Israel, no negotiations with Israel.

So it was that the reality of the lived experience of the creation and defence of Israel shaped the discourse of Israelis. This lived reality is still what is referred to in that discourse. Israelis today live very close to those events and in some cases personally remember them. The reason Israel controls the whole of mandatory Palestine is because otherwise it would have been annihilated. It was an existential war of defence, not a conquest by choice.

Between 1967 and 2000 the national struggle once again changed character. Peace was eventually made with Egypt and Jordan (but not Lebanon or Syria). The contest then reverted to being mainly an Israeli–Palestinian conflict with the emergence of the Palestine Liberation Organization (PLO) under Yassir Arafat as the widely recognized legitimate representative of the Palestinian people. The unexpected and spontaneous 'First Intifada' (1987–1993) further changed perceptions in Israel (prompting calls for immediate harsh repression, but suggesting that over the longer term the status quo was unsustainable). The 1988 PLO declaration of independence for a Palestinian state in Gaza and the West Bank, with its implied recognition of the State of Israel, and Arafat's renunciation of violence in December of that year opened the way for what came to be called the 'Oslo process'. The idea of a 'two-state solution' was revived. This reached its climax during the US presidency of Bill Clinton. In 1993 Israeli Prime Minister Rabin and PLO Chairman Arafat shook hands on the White House lawn (with the US president visibly cajoling a reluctant Rabin to do so). In 1995 came the 'Oslo II' agreement. The assassination of Rabin and Palestinian counter-violence brought Likud under Binyamin Netanyahu to power. But by the turn of the millennium Labor again formed a government under Ehud Barak, and in 2000, in the last year of his presidency, Clinton tried to bring about a lasting and final settlement at Camp David. What happened next forms the latest chapter in the lived experience of Israelis and will be described below.

The reality of deep history

But first there is another dimension of reality to be recognized. It is again fashionable for conflict resolution analysis – and sophisticated Western social and political science analysis in general – to treat history as 'imagined' or 'constructed' in relation to 'national and religious myths'. These are consequently seen as precipitations of knowledge/power in which hegemonic discourses generate 'regimes of truth' by determining the rules by which 'true' and 'false' are recognized and accepted as such. This – largely invisible – production of knowledge is effected through control of the education system, the media, and all the other manifestations of the 'ideological apparatuses' that shape the society in question – always in the interest of the powerful.

But, as will be discussed further in chapter 10, generalized attacks on the very notion of fact, reality and truth of this kind – however profound the insights they may give in their own terms – apply indiscriminately across the board and thereby miss the particularity of the fierce clash of claims and refutations that constitutes agonistic dialogue. For that reason, I will argue, they drop out of the equation (or are themselves involved in the dispute) in the radical disagreements that lie at the heart of linguistic intractability. What they assume is not what is said by the conflict parties in question – whether challengers or possessors. The conflict parties – including Christians and Muslims, as indicated at the end of this section, as well as 'seculars' within Israel and elsewhere who reject biblical authority entirely – are already profoundly embroiled, on one side or another, in these contestations. There is no 'impartial ground' from which the struggle can be loftily surveyed.

In this case the deep history that underlies prevailing patterns of Israeli discourse is the very foundation that forms Jewish identity in the first place – and has preserved it for millennia. Why have the Israelites or Hebrews survived, whereas the Jebusites, Amalakites, Midianites, Philistines, etc., have not? The main answer to this question given by historians such as Simon Schama in the monumental first volume of his *The Story of the Jews* is that the Jews were the 'people of the book'.[10] It was the deep history recorded in the Hebrew Bible (*Tanakh*) and law (*Talmud*) – attached to living rituals handed down in Jewish marriage arrangements and family life – that enabled them to persist. The subtitle of Schama's book is *Finding the Words*. If you are an ultra-religious (*haredi*) boy today, you recite and discuss these texts for hours a day in pairs in *yeshivas* (religious schools). If you are not religious, this still forms the basis of family life in the celebration of festivals, weekly family gatherings for the *Shabbat* (Sabbath), and rites of passage.

That is why reductionist accounts that 'explain away' this inherited history or expose 'the invention of the Jewish people'[11] do not affect the reality of the power of deep history. They wash over it. The same applies to internal critiques, such as those of the Israeli 'new historians' or 'post-Zionists' since the 1990s, as will be noted below.

And the history that is told is one of exile and return, physical and spiritual. Abraham's journey to the promised land. Exile in idolatrous Egypt and return (*aliyah*, ascent) to the high land of Israel under Moses – where later David and Solomon built the first temple in Jerusalem. It is in the hills of Jerusalem and Judaea (now the West Bank), not the coastal plain, that the encounter with YHWH (God) took place.[12] Exile for the second time in Babylonia, where 'by the waters of Babylon we sat down and wept when we remembered Zion' (Psalm 137:1), followed by a second miraculous return and the building of the second temple. Exile, for the third time, after the destruction of the Jewish state in 70 CE, and a third miraculous return in 1948. In 1967 Jerusalem and the site of the temples were once again Jewish. The wheel had come full circle.

But the reality of this deep history is felt not only in relation to the 14 million Jews worldwide today but also in relation to nearly 4 billion Christians and Muslims – half of humanity.

Three-quarters of the Christian Bible (the Old Testament) is made up of the Hebrew scriptures. The first words of the New Testament are: 'The book of the generation of Jesus Christ, the son of David, the son of Abraham'. And the last words – from the end of the Book of Revelation – are: 'I Jesus . . . am the root and offspring of King David . . . Surely I come quickly. Amen', to which St John the Divine (author of the Book of Revelation) says: 'Even so, come, Lord Jesus.' As a result, the heated debate about the Balfour Declaration in the British cabinet in November 1917 was clinched by 'gentile Zionists' such as Prime Minister Lloyd George, who recognized the Holy Land as the land of the forefathers of the Jewish people. And the promise of salvation 'at the end of times' in the Book of Revelation inspires the mass of evangelical 'Christian Zionists' in the USA to see the events of 1967 as a demonstration of the working out of God's plan in history. This exerts a much bigger influence on the US Congress than the relatively small 'Jewish lobby'. Jewish Americans constitute barely 2 per cent of the US population, they are internally divided (critical voices from supporters of J Street challenge the orthodoxy of AIPAC (the American Israel Public Affairs Committee)), and most Jewish Americans traditionally vote Democrat.

The Qur'an was dictated verbatim in Arabic by the archangel Gabriel. The *qibla* (direction of prayer) for the first Muslim *umma* (community of believers) in Medina was towards Jerusalem, because at that time Mecca was still idolatrous. The Prophet went on his 'night journey' to Jerusalem guided by Gabriel (Sura 17, *Al-Isra*, Qur'an) and from there was taken into heaven, where he met Joseph, Moses and Abraham (*hadith*, supplementary teachings). And in the *Hajj* (pilgrimage to Mecca) more than 2 million Muslims a year today process seven times around the Kaaba, the house of God, the holiest site in Islam – built by Abraham and his son Ishmael. All the prophets before Muhammad recognized in the Qur'an – including Jesus – were Jewish.

The reality of the security imperative

Now we return to the period between 2000 and the present day. Here two events above all have shaped prevailing patterns of contemporary Israeli discourse.

The first is what happened in 2000. The Camp David talks between Israeli Prime Minister Barak and Palestinian leader Arafat, brokered by US President Clinton, failed. This is the reason given by Clinton's chief negotiator and Middle East envoy, Dennis Ross:

> To this day, Arafat has never honestly admitted what was offered to the Palestinians . . . [W]ith 97 percent of the territory in Palestinian hands, there would have been no cantons, Palestinian areas would not have been isolated and surrounded. There would have been territorial integrity and contiguity in both the West Bank and Gaza, and there would have been independent borders with Egypt and Jordan. Had Nelson Mandela been the Palestinian leader and not Yasser Arafat, I would be writing now how, notwithstanding the limitations of the Oslo process, Israelis and Palestinians had succeeded in reaching an 'end of conflict' agreement . . . Arafat either let the Intifada begin or, as some argue, actually gave orders for it . . . Arafat was not up to peacemaking.[13]

The full story of what was on offer in July 2000, the 'Clinton parameters' presented later in the year, and the final negotiations at Taba in January 2001 (when Clinton and Barak were effectively no longer in power) is highly contested.[14] For most Israelis, however, Palestinians had yet again refused a chance of a Palestinian state. But it was what happened next that was the seismic shock. No doubt provoked by a visit by Ariel Sharon to the Temple Mount in Jerusalem, the Second (Al-Aqsa) Intifada erupted in September 2000. This was very different to the First Intifada and included suicide attacks inside Israel itself. In the single month of March 2002, for example, 127 Israelis were killed – given the relatively small size of the Jewish Israeli population this was equivalent to twice the number that had been killed in the attack on the 'twin towers' in the United States in September 2001.

> The Palestinians may have been provoked beyond endurance by the brutality of Israeli power. Nevertheless, resorting to firearms was a mistake of historic proportions. The key to success of the first intifada lay in its non-violent nature. By resorting to violence in 2000, the Palestinian leadership reneged on its principal pledge under the Oslo accord. Palestinian violence destroyed the Israeli peace camp; it persuaded Israelis from all points along the political spectrum that there is no Palestinian partner for peace . . .[15]

The entire Israeli discourse was transformed. For example, this was a death knell to any further influence from Israeli 'post-Zionist' new history after its brief flourishing in the 1990s:

> [A]lmost immediately after the outbreak of the Second Intifada a reinvigorated Zionist consensus, which had somewhat eroded at the height of the Oslo days, reasserted itself with force. Public discourse in Israel was reshaped along strictly consensual lines.[16]

And all of this was further compounded by the events of 2007. Many if not most of the suicide attacks had been claimed by Hamas and Islamic Jihad. In 2005 Israeli Prime Minister Sharon evacuated Gaza – despite passionate opposition from some 8000 Jewish settlers living there. In the 2006 elections to the Palestinian Legislative Council (the legislature of the Palestinian National Authority or PA) Hamas, to the surprise of many, won 74 of the 132 seats, and a National Unity Government was formed. In June 2007 Hamas fighters seized control of Gaza in a bloody coup and expelled Fatah and other Palestinian Authority (PA) officials. The firing of indiscriminate mortar shells and Qassam rockets from Gaza into Israel immediately increased – 2807 altogether in 2007, including for the first time Katyusha rockets – an average of four or five a day. Fatalities reached a peak in 2008, leading to Israel's punitive response in December–January 2008–9. What government could possibly act otherwise?

The Hamas takeover of Gaza convinced most Israelis that this is also what would happen if Israel similarly evacuated the West Bank and handed over to a weak Palestinian government. The collapse of Syria in 2012 and the advent of Islamic State to within a few miles of the Israeli border demonstrated to most Israelis the inescapability of this view. Standing with the Mediterranean at one's back and looking east, a few miles away lies the Jordan valley; further east are more than 2 million Palestinian Arabs in Jordan; beyond them is Iraq; beyond Iraq is a rabidly anti-Israeli Iran on the verge of acquiring nuclear weapons; beyond Iran are the 'Stans' (Uzbekistan, etc.) – a vast ocean in which Israelis are outnumbered 50 to 1 by Arabs and 250 to 1 globally by Muslims. There is only one Jewish state. There are twenty-two Arab states.

Iran sends weapons to Hamas in Gaza to be used indiscriminately against Israeli civilians and thereby shares the stated intentions still enshrined in Articles 22 and 23 of the 1988 Hamas Charter:

[Pro-Zionist forces] were behind the French revolution, the Communist revolution, and most of the revolutions throughout the world ... Concerning local and international wars ... they were behind the First World War in which they destroyed the Islamic Caliphate, picked the material profit, monopolized the raw wealth, and got the Balfour Declaration. They created the League of Nations through which they could rule the world. They were behind the Second World War, in which they became fabulously wealthy through the arms trade. They prepared for the establishment of their state; they ordered that the United Nations be formed, along with the Security Council, so that they could rule the world through them. There was no war that broke out

91

anywhere without their hands behind it ... Today it is Palestine and tomorrow it may be other countries, because the Zionist scheme has no bounds; after Palestine they want to expand from the Nile River to the Euphrates. When they have occupied the area completely, they look toward another. Such is their plan in the *Protocols of the Elders of Zion.* That is the best proof of what is said.[17]

A reading of the Hamas Charter is all it takes to silence most Israeli internal criticism of current strategy. That is why Palestinian attempts at national reconciliation between Hamas and Fatah – seen as a fundamental prerequisite for Palestinian strategy, as shown in chapter 6 – is viewed in Israel as an existential threat by terrorists committed to the destruction of Israel.

Conclusion – why conflict resolution fails

It can be seen that the preceding section – 'What Israelis say' – deliberately does not qualify the account by calling it 'an Israeli perspective'. The realities of lived experience, deep history, and the security imperative cannot be dismissed as a 'subjective' penumbra surrounding the 'real' conflict. To suppose that they can is to misread the nature of the linguistic intractability that bars the way to the three conflict resolution approaches discussed in chapter 3: dialogue for mutual understanding, interactive problem-solving, and principled negotiation.

There are many imaginative ongoing attempts to foster *dialogue for mutual understanding* and *interactive problem-solving* in the Israeli–Palestinian conflict.[18] They often achieve remarkable results. But, up to the time of writing, they have not so far affected the core of the conflict. Using examples discussed in chapter 3, we can see why, for most Israelis, it is not yet time to foster 'inquiry, co-creation, and listening, the uncovering of one's own assumptions and those of others, a suspension of judgment and a collective search for truth' (*dialogue*) or to promote 'an effective cooperative problem-solving process in which the conflict is the mutual problem to be resolved cooperatively' (*problem-solving*). Nor, in the language of *principled negotiation*, to be discussed further in chapter 8, is there yet sufficient trust 'to understand the interests of the other so that both can jointly generate options that are mutually advantageous and seek agreement on objective standards for resolving opposed interests'.

So it is that the crushing of the Second Intifada by 2005 meant that most Israelis lost interest in the Palestinian question. Except as a 'scare tactic', it hardly featured in the March 2015 Israeli election, for example, as discussed further in chapter 7. Instead, the conflict moved into a fourth phase. For the second time (the first being 1948–67) the focus shifted away from the Israeli–Palestinian conflict and towards wider regional – and global – horizons. Israeli preoccupations were once again international: the dangers (but also opportunities) from the post-2011 turmoil in the Arab world; the threat from armed *jihadism* on Israel's doorstep with the possibility that sub-state groups might acquire 'dirty bombs' and the means to deliver them; the development of 'iron dome' and other defences against such threats; and the mortal danger posed by a nuclear-armed Iran.

In conditions of linguistic intractability it is heuristic engagement that shows why conflict resolution does not yet work. But is there an alternative? In order to find out, we need to look in the opposite direction. We need to turn away from conflict resolution and towards strategic engagement.

Strategic engagement – what can be done? Promoting collective internal strategic thinking

In the rest of this chapter we will take an admittedly small-scale example to illustrate the potential of a large-scale enterprise. The logic of conflict engagement in intense political conflicts is that, when conditions are not yet ready for conflict resolution *between conflict parties*, it is best to begin by promoting collective strategic thinking *within them*. On this basis it is then possible to open new space by promoting strategic engagement *across conflict parties* and by encouraging appropriate strategic thinking and action *by third parties*. That will be the theme of chapters 7 and 8.

What follows is illustrated by the experience of the Israeli Strategic Forum (ISF) between 2007 and 2015. Here is a participant's description of the original make-up and continuing purpose of the ISF (a shortened version was given in chapter 4):

> The main criteria for selecting the participants was that together they represent the major currents of thought in Jewish-Israeli society ... The group thus included several members of the Knesset with diverse political views, former heads of the security services (GSS, IDF), leading business people, key religious and spiritual leaders (ultra-orthodox, national-religious, [secular] Jewish renewal), prominent social activists, well-respected journalists, senior academics and various celebrities and publicly known figures ... To a large extent the group's thinking was led by the assumption that internal cohesion is the key to resolving

the problems of Israel's Jewish population ... This is as a result both of social cleavages (religious–secular, socio-economic, left–right, Ashkenaz–Sepharad, immigrants–natives) and of the pressures caused by the Israeli–Palestinian conflict ... As a result the national conversation about the conflict has become a cacophony. To a large extent as time passes the discussion becomes increasingly polarised, filled with taboos and thus simplistic. This leaves Israeli Jews with no real capacity to agree on a common strategy ... After so many decades of violence, and with Israel facing a truly complex rapidly changing reality, a mapping of alternative scenarios should be used to broaden the discursive space, alleviate some taboos, and legitimise a conversation on certain futures that are so far unspoken. This is a requirement if Israeli Jews are to take a well-informed decision about their future – one that takes seriously into account the domestic, regional and international constraints, costs and benefits.[19]

Up until now this chapter has given an impression of Israeli consensus on the great existential issues. As can be seen from this quotation, the opposite is also the case: there is a complex 'cacophony' of voices in Israel, reflecting the extraordinary diversity of the population, made up as it is of innumerable acts of *aliyah* (immigration to Israel) from all over the world. Over a very short period, speakers of many languages and from many countries have come together, learnt Hebrew, and forged a new nation. In the 1990s, for example, nearly 1 million Russian Jews arrived in Israel, profoundly changing the demographic – and political – landscape. An increasing proportion of the population – particularly in Jerusalem – is *Haredi* (ultra-orthodox), following *halakha* (religious law) and cut off from the modern secular world. This will be re-emphasized in chapter 7. Israelis speak forthrightly and with passion, and it is hard to think of a topic that is not debated and contested vigorously. Such, certainly, has been the experience in the Israeli Strategic Forum.

At the time of writing the work of the ISF has gone through three phases: 2007–9, 2010–12 and 2013–15. We end this chapter by commenting on two of these: how to think strategically (methodology) and the collective evaluation of possible futures that is made possible as a result (substance). We will look at the third phase in chapter 7.

Methodology:
how to think strategically in a complex environment

First, Israeli participants in the Israeli Strategic Forum have emphasized the importance for Israel of basing collective analysis on ongoing awareness of the rapidly changing context within which future policy needs to be determined. Why is it in the interest of Israelis to promote a methodology for thinking strategically in a complex environment? Because the alternative is short-term crisis response in which poor strategic decisions are often made. If collective internal strategic discussion is suppressed, what is left is partisan strategic planning behind closed doors and public manipulation. Policy reverts automatically to the default option. Alternatives are presented as if all the strategic advantages lie on one side and all the disadvantages on the other. As we have seen, this will suit some constituencies – those in power may have an incentive to shut down strategic debate. But the counter-argument in the ISF is that this is against the long-term interest of Israel. It may be clever politics, but it is poor strategic thinking. Strategic reality is not like that. In a rapidly changing political environment, 'linear' strategic analysis that does not factor in complexity is bad strategy.

A flavour of 'complexity thinking' as presented, discussed and applied in ISF sessions is given in box 5.1.

Box 5.1   Non-linear strategic thinking in a complex environment

A complex adaptive system is defined as a group of interrelated elements that exhibit non-linear relations. The more elements and interrelations, the higher the level of complexity in the system. In particular, six features are seen to drive change within a complex system:

- connectivity and interdependence of elements;
- emergence and self-organization – the system comes out of the accumulated choices of all the individuals operating within it;
- chaos – in the technical sense that simple known changes can produce very different and therefore uncertain results;
- systemic memory and path dependency – today's dynamics are channelled by yesterday's constructions;
- feedback effects – negative feedback dampens or stabilizes the system, while positive feedback amplifies the system;
- evolution and adaptation – the system as a whole responds to a continually changing environment.

Rather than solving a problem in linear style, as in traditional strategic thinking, therefore, the aim is to understand a complex ecology and learn how to operate successfully within it.

Source: Moty Cristal and Orit Gal, ISF workshop presentation, Haifa, 2010.

An example of poor decision-making in the absence of such capacity that was analysed in detail by the ISF was the Israeli response on 31 May 2010 to the attempt by MV *Mavi Marmara* and other ships in the 'Gaza Freedom flotilla' to break the Israeli blockade of Gaza.[20] This was an instance of instinctive (over)reliance on the default option of military action, with what were at the time unforeseen consequences. Another more recent example of strategic complexity would be the highly ambivalent outcome of Operation Protective Edge in Gaza (8 July–26 August 2014), to be noted further in chapter 7.

One of the main conclusions from this phase of the ISF's work was the recommendation – supported across the group – that a strategic thinking unit should be set up by the Israeli government, formally protected from party political interference, and tasked to provide the kind of ongoing complexity analysis that hard-pressed policy-makers do not have the time or political freedom to provide.

Substance: filling the public strategic thinking gap

So what happens when collective strategic thinking of the kind espoused by the Israeli Strategy Group is consistently applied? What is the outcome in terms of ongoing strategic evaluation of possible futures that the methodology makes possible? Rather than emphasize the many creative ideas that also emerged, this section will focus, somewhat negatively, on the main strategic reasons why the internationally preferred outcome of an independent State of Palestine, 'living peacefully side by side with the State of Israel', so far gains such little political traction in Israel.

The main upshot of extensive ISF analysis and discussion is to illuminate, as only strategic engagement can, why what we will call Scenario (A) – an independent and sovereign Palestinian state as specified in successive UN General Assembly and Security Council resolutions – is at the time of writing not yet a serious strategic option for Israel. For example, it was not on the radar screen in the 2015 election – although since then, as discussed in chapter 7, the Labor Party has at last produced a short strategy paper called a *Comprehensive Diplomatic-Security Plan* (7 February 2016).

In addition to the deep inhibitions uncovered through heuristic engagement looked at earlier, what strategic engagement chiefly adds here is an understanding of how *strategic alternatives* play out. As seen in chapter 4, unlike private strategic planning and public manipulation, serious strategic thinking is, through and through, *comparative*. Options are not considered in isolation but are continually

Box 5.2   Possible futures

Scenario (A)   An independent Palestinian state as internationally agreed

Scenario (B)   Permanent effective Israeli control over the whole of mandatory Palestine

Scenario (C)   Indefinite continuation of the status quo – incremental Israeli settlement in the West Bank and international life support for an otherwise unviable Palestinian Authority

Scenario (D)   Final accommodation between Jewish Israelis and Palestinians in mandatory Palestine without a Palestinian state

evaluated against each other. This is the hallmark of strategic thinking and is what partisan strategic planning most tries to suppress. Strategic thinking, in contrast, welcomes critiques of current policies in order to guard against complacency and keep the widest range of options open to optimize standards of decision-making and maximize flexibility. Strategic thinking continually looks for the *best* options (or *least bad* options) in the circumstances.

We will illustrate this with what is admittedly a much simplified set of scenarios (possible futures) (see box 5.2) as recurrently discussed in the ISF. More detailed analysis would show how these are not mutually exclusive, but can – and do – overlap.

If Scenario (A) (a Palestinian state) is compared with Scenario (B) (permanent Israeli control of the whole of mandatory Palestine), then the main argument *in favour* of Scenario (A) is twofold.

First, that the long-term dangers of Scenario (B) are greater. This is a strong (albeit as yet muted) argument inside Israel and an increasingly unanimous argument outside Israel. The main dangers of Scenario (B) are seen to involve *demography* (the existing overall Palestinian majority in mandatory Palestine as a whole), *legitimacy* (if it does not give Palestinians equal rights, Israel becomes an apartheid state and forfeits international legitimacy) and *security* (never-ending unrest and increasing local and regional radicalization not permanently containable by purely military means). Current right-wing Israeli refusal to countenance a Palestinian state is seen to lead inexorably to some form of bi-national state shared with Palestinians in which there will no longer be a Jewish majority.

Second, in comparison, Scenario (A) is seen to offer an end of conflict, regional normalization, and acceptance of Israel within the

97

Box 5.3   The Arab Peace Initiative, 2002

Emanating from the conviction of the Arab countries that a military solution to the conflict will not achieve peace or provide security for the parties, the Council of Arab States:

1. Requests Israel to reconsider its policies and declare that a just peace is its strategic option as well.
2. Further calls upon Israel to affirm:
   (i) Full Israeli withdrawal from all the territories occupied since 1967 . . .
   (ii) Achievement of a just solution to the Palestinian refugee problem to be agreed upon in accordance with UN General Assembly Resolution 194.
   (iii) The acceptance of a sovereign independent Palestinian state on the Palestinian territories occupied since June 4 1967 in the West Bank and Gaza Strip with East Jerusalem as its capital.
3. Consequently, the Arab countries affirm the following:
   (i) Consider the Arab–Israeli conflict ended, and enter into a peace agreement with Israel, and provide security for all the states of the region.
   (ii) Establish normal relations with Israel in the context of this comprehensive peace. . . .
4. Calls upon the government of Israel and all Israelis to accept this initiative in order to safeguard the prospects for peace and stop the further shedding of blood, enabling the Arab countries and Israel to live in peace and good neighbourliness and provide future generations with security, stability and prosperity.
5. Invites the international community and all countries and organizations to support this initiative.[22]

Arab world (see the main provisions of the Arab Peace Initiative, box 5.3, offered in 2002 by the Arab League and subsequently reaffirmed), together with untold opportunities for Israeli high-tech know-how to flourish within a region desperately in need of it. The future of Israel, as the nation-state of the Jewish people, would be secured. This would also allow for a rediscovery of – and international recognition for – the deep spiritual values on which the State of Israel was founded, which are seen from this perspective to have been distorted, if not all but lost, under the relentless pressures of ongoing conflict and occupation.[21]

So why do these powerful arguments – widely regarded as self-evident outside Israel – cut so little ice at the time of writing in central Israeli politics? In addition to deeper reasons uncovered through heuristic engagement considered earlier in this chapter, the answer given by strategic engagement of the kind developed in the ISF is that, however things might appear to 'well-wishers' from the outside who do not live in Israel, that is not the strategic reality for most of those who do.

In the comparison between Scenario (A) and Scenario (B), for example, however great the supposed long-term dangers of Scenario (B) may be (accompanied as they often are by 'assurances' from those who remain implacably hostile to Israel's existence),[23] they are still distant and therefore uncertain. In contrast, withdrawal from the West Bank under Scenario (A) is immediate and far more dangerous. It would leave a security vacuum likely to be filled, as in Gaza after 2005, by forces bent on Israel's destruction. These forces are already rampant a few kilometres away – in normal times you can comfortably drive from Jerusalem to Damascus for an evening meal and then back again. An unstable Palestinian state would not be able to resist further future demands, such as a 'right of return' for millions of perhaps radicalized Palestinian refugees registered through UNRWA (the UN Relief and Works Agency). And Israeli experience over the past century has shown how delusory it is to rely on outside 'guarantees' from powers whose prime concern is their own national interest, not the survival of Israel. In addition, any attempt to evacuate settlers from Judea and Samaria would lead to the collapse of the government that attempted it.

But that is not the key strategic consideration. As strategic engagement makes clear, the most immediate strategic choice facing Israel is not between Scenario (A) and Scenario (B). It is between Scenario (A) and Scenario (C) – the status quo. This is the decisive consideration. Israel always has a better strategic option than Scenario (A), namely a continuation of the situation as it has evolved since 1988 – a state of affairs that is, for Israel, neither an occupation nor absorption of Judea/Samaria into Israel.

The three main component elements of Scenario (C) are:

- the division of the West Bank into Areas A and B (40 per cent of the land), which contain most of the urban and rural Palestinian population, and Area C (60 per cent of the land), which remains under full Israeli control (see map 6.2);
- the setting up of the Palestinian Authority (PA) in Areas A and B, funded by the international community but with continuing

Israeli/US control, committed to suppressing security threats to Israel;

- continuing sporadic bilateral negotiations brokered by the USA as the sole legitimate peace process.

These three components of 'Oslo' are seen largely to neutralize the dangers inherent in a manifest embracing of Scenario (B). They also 'cover' and leave open the progressive accumulation of 'facts on the ground' that are seen in some quarters to prepare the way for other future planned scenarios – such as unilateral partition of the West Bank, with Egypt and Jordan assuming responsibility for residual Palestinian populations.

Two further elements make up the status quo. First, the Hamas–Fatah split, which allows Israel to do a separate deal on Gaza and perpetuates Palestinian division. Second, the complex regional conflict that enables Israel, for example, to operate in alliance with Egypt and Saudi Arabia in opposing Iranian support for Hizbollah in Lebanon and Hamas in Gaza and to provide Israeli 'iron dome' technology, funded by the USA, to regional defences against this threat. Israelis are happier with this existent, familiar and controllable reality than with the unknown uncertainties and dangers associated with withdrawal from the West Bank.

In this way strategic engagement clarifies why Scenario (A) – the preferred international 'solution' – is not yet taken seriously at the time of writing in mainstream Israeli politics. And, looking ahead to chapter 8, it helps to specify what would need to happen – for example, what third parties would need to do – in order to change this.

Beyond this, it may be noticed that, so far, there has been no mention of the possibility of a 'one-state solution', whether in the form of a unitary democratic state, a bi-national state, or some other variant on this theme. The reason is that, despite the continuing popularity of the 'two-state solution'/'one-state solution' mantra, particularly in third-party discourse, the latter is as yet empty of strategic content – even among Palestinians, although many now rhetorically embrace it. There is no serious 'one-state solution'. Although there are plenty of Israelis who support such ideas – or variants of them, as will be seen in chapter 7 – these options are not yet on the main strategic horizon. In chapter 8 I will argue that it is important that Scenario (D) – final accommodation without a Palestinian state – *does* appear on the strategic radar screen, not just of Israel and of the Palestinians, but above all of the international community. The argument there will be that its absence as a serious strategic option has been a significant – even fatal – flaw in third-party attempts to mediate a final settlement.

It is by continually arguing through possible futures that cross-cutting scenarios, otherwise not considered, may then emerge: for example, negatively, how 'one state' may eventually break up – albeit by more bloody means – into two (or more) states; or, positively, how 'two states' might prove to be the best way eventually to approximate to 'one state' – such as through future forms of voluntary confederation between an Israeli and a Palestinian state (perhaps including Jordan).

Opinion polls repeatedly suggest that a majority of Israelis still support a 'two-state solution'. But what these polls miss out is, first, that 'a Palestinian state' means different things to different people and, second, that there is a bigger majority who in the same breath say that Palestinians are 'not yet ready' for it (mightily intensified at the time of writing – for example, between October and December 2015, when twenty-two Israelis were killed and 200 wounded by Palestinians, and more than ninety Palestinians were killed).[24]

If that is the case, what are the alternatives? And how can these be evaluated and compared? This – the experience of the ISF suggests – is where the main strategy gap in the public debate in Israel now lies.

Conclusion

The first stage of heuristic engagement – listening to what Israelis say – uncovers the deep reason why so far conflict resolution does not work in Israel.

The first stage of strategic engagement – promoting collective strategic thinking in Israel – shows why, since 2000, there has been so little serious public discussion about future strategic options in Israel.

To sum up, here are some of the key strategic questions identified by the Israeli Strategic Forum:

- What would need to change for Scenario (A) (a Palestinian state) to become viable for Israelis, or is it definitively rejected?
- If the latter, is Scenario (C) (the status quo) sustainable and, if so, how?
- If it is not sustainable, how viable will a more exposed Scenario (B) (permanent Israeli control) be over the longer term, and what forms might it take?

- What would Scenario (D) – a realistic and acceptable final accommodation without a Palestinian state – look like? Would it be desirable? Would it be attainable? Would it be likely?

The main conclusion of the ISF is that the interplay between and around these questions constitutes the missing public security debate in Israel. The further conclusion is that this is damaging for Israel, because to suppress rather than encourage strategic debate reduces the quality of decision-making and dangerously decreases the capacity for 'second-order social learning', as discussed in chapter 1.

6

STRATEGIC THINKING FOR CHALLENGERS: PALESTINIANS

This chapter begins with an illustration of collective strategic thinking by Palestinians. It is taken from the most recent summary paper produced by the Palestine Strategy Group (PSG) at the time of writing and sums up work done by the PSG since the collapse of the Kerry talks in April 2014 (to be discussed further in chapter 8). While the details of the paper will be out of date by the time this book is published, part of it is reproduced here as an example of 'filling the strategy gap' – building capacity for sustained collective strategic thinking and action across hitherto politically divided and geographically scattered constituencies.

From the beginning of its work in 2007, the PSG was unanimous that internal disunity and the lack of a capacity for sustained collective strategic thinking had been a disastrous weakness for the national cause. Filling the strategy gap was seen as a prerequisite for the national liberation struggle:

> Palestinians have been historically outmanoeuvred, politically neutralized, and made totally dependent on international handouts. Or have they? A newly released Palestinian strategy document which outlines strategic political options gives witness to a renewed breath of fresh air in the Palestinians' struggle for freedom and independence.
>
> Over the past several months, I participated together with a group of 45 Palestinians from all walks of life, men and women, on the political right and left, secular and religious, politicians, academics, civil society, business actors, from occupied Palestine, inside Israel, and in the Diaspora. We were a group that is a microcosm that reflects the dynamics of Palestinian society. We could not all meet in one room anywhere in the world because of the travel restrictions that Israel has created. Nevertheless we continue to plan and to act. Our mission is to open a

discussion on where we go from here: What are the Palestinians' strategic options, if any?

After several workshops in Palestine and abroad and a continuous online debate, we have produced the first iteration of *Regaining the Initiative: Palestinian Strategic Options to End Israeli Occupation*, published in Arabic and English. The document reflects an alternative to an official but impotent Palestinian discourse that will very shortly, in the judgement of most Palestinians, run head-on into a brick (cement) wall.[1]

The 2008 Palestine Strategy Group report proved influential as a catalyst, as noted by another participant:

The overwhelming majority of the members of the project *Regaining the Initiative* are still in touch and extremely eager to further develop and continue the initial ideas they have agreed on and reached in their meetings and discussions. I have had the opportunity to speak with participants who are members of Fatah, Hamas, or women, student, academic, religious, and human rights and democracy organizations. They all passionately agree about the desperate need to develop and sustain long-term Palestinian strategic thinking. Indeed, this approach has already had a real major impact. A few months ago I received a phone call from a senior member of the Negotiation Support Unit (NUS) of the Palestine Authority informing me that the Unit has discussed thoroughly the Palestinian strategy document and adopted several parts of it.[2]

Two further PSG reports followed in 2011 and 2014.

An account of the situation in January 2015 after the failure of the Kerry talks, based on contributions by PLO executive committee member Hanan Ashrawi and Palestinian President Mahmoud Abbas, concludes:

The Palestinian narrative points to a broader problem underlying the peace talks: the Palestinian leadership has all but lost faith in the American-led peace process – causing them instead to pursue a strategy that's dramatically different than anything they've attempted in the past 20 years.

The Palestinians have been considering such a move since at least 2008. That year a group of senior Palestinian political and civil society leaders met to write a report (*Regaining the Initiative*) on the peace process under the auspices of the Palestine Strategy Group . . . Within roughly a year, the Palestine Liberation Organization's executive committee began exploring an idea in line with the PSG approach, asking the UN to formally recognize Palestine as a state . . . This gave rise to Palestine 194: the Palestinian Authority's campaign to become the 194th internationally recognized state in the United Nations. . . . By November 2012, Palestine had been granted non-member observer status by the UN General Assembly.[3]

A Post Oslo Strategy (June 2015) summarizes previous PSG reports and contributory papers and sets out clearly the admitted complexity of the new 'two-track' strategy that the current situation now demands. Box 6.1 gives the opening pages of the report (this is an English translation of the Arabic original).

Box 6.1 *A Post Oslo Strategy*: opening section

It is hoped that the suggested framework for strategic action presented in outline here will encourage participation by as many Palestinians as possible in helping to formulate the next decisive phase of our struggle for national self-determination, independence and the achieving of our historic rights. It is built on work done by the Palestine Strategy Group since 2007, and derived from expert workshops and focus groups since October 2014.

For 21 years the Oslo process has constrained our national liberation strategy. While purporting to be a peace process that would lead to the creation of a Palestinian state as set out in successive UN resolutions (Scenario A), it has in reality been a mask behind which Israeli governments have pushed ahead with the 'Greater Israel' project of deepening effective control over and judaizing most of mandatory Palestine (Scenario B). The collapse of the Kerry initiative in April 2014 has exposed the flaws in the US sponsored bilateral negotiations and the delusion that it could lead to a just solution. Given the contradiction between almost universal international endorsement for a Palestinian state on 22% of the land, and progressive illegal Israeli settlement on the same land intended to make this impossible, we have to dismantle the component parts of the Oslo system by moving down both tracks simultaneously – working towards Scenario (A) (a future Palestinian State) and opposing Scenario (B) (further consolidation of Greater Israel).

The right of the Palestinian people to self-determination is a right enshrined in international law. By correlation so is the right of the Palestinian people to independence in the State of Palestine. However, it is clear that ending Israel's military occupation of Palestine can only be achieved through a political deal with Israel. Therefore, the objective of any strategy must be to change the existing power dynamics that have made a negotiated settlement that results in an independent Palestinian state impossible. This involves exerting pressure on Israel by using a number of tools. The purpose of exercising this leverage is to make a final status deal the least bad option for Israel.

So this report calls for a post-Oslo strategy that adopts dual parallel tracks. The first track continues to work towards achieving liberation and statehood on the 1967 borders, albeit now via an internationalized route, not a bilateral negotiation route. The second simultaneous track is to demand and fulfill Palestinian individual and collective rights in the absence of a state and in accordance with international law. This means abandoning the uni-track approach: **either** resistance **or** political settlement. It must be **both** at the same time within a comprehensive strategic plan. The experience of the last 20 years of peacemaking confirms that searching for a political solution without resistance is ineffective. By the same token, resistance without a clear and agreed upon political track lacks strategic purpose.

Elements of the post Oslo strategy

The first element (Track 1) is to redouble efforts to build international support for our independent, contiguous, and sovereign Palestinian State on the borders of 1967 and the fulfillment of Palestinian historic rights including the right of return. Unlike the 'Palestinian state' that several Israeli politicians expressed a willingness to accept, which is largely emptied of the central features of a modern nation-state such as sovereignty, the majority of Palestinians view a sovereign and independent Palestinian state on the borders of 1967 as a minimal frame within which they put an end to the Israeli military occupation and colonisation and materialise and enjoy national self-determination, besides realising other individual and collective rights and achieving justice for the refugees. Realising these claims and rights is the glue that binds together our national struggle for self-determination. It is what commands overwhelming international support and it is what Israel seeks to undermine through policies of separation, blockade and fragmentation of the Palestinian geography and demography. The unity of the Palestinian cause must not be jeopardized.

But this can no longer be done via bilateral negotiations with Israel brokered by the United States as under the Oslo process. It can only be done via a new strategy that aims at changing the balance of power, including an internationalized route in which any future negotiations play the role of implementing what has already been internationally endorsed. It is Israel – protected by the United States – that has closed the bilateral negotiation route by continuing to carve up, expropriate, annex and colonize the territory being negotiated over. The UN has explicitly acknowledged that the PLO has developed successfully the capacity to run a democratic and peaceful state, founded on the rule of law and living in peace and security with its neighbors. Palestine largely fulfills the legal and technical criteria for UN membership, including statehood, in as far as the Occupation allows. Only Israel blocks Scenario (A). Here an international conference based on international law and successive UN resolutions is a preferred route.

The second element (Track 2) is to oppose and resist the existing 'one state reality' imposed by Israel that deprives Palestinians of basic human, civil and political rights enshrined in international law. We must resist in every detail the tightening web of illegal expropriation and colonization of Palestinian territory, and the discrimination and apartheid practiced against Palestinian people. The emphasis needs to be on linking popular resistance in the occupied territory and by all Palestinians with a synchronized local, regional and international campaign that utilizes all kinds of legitimate resistance in coordinated strategy in the West Bank, Gaza and the Diaspora. Track 2 means insisting on full and equal national rights throughout Mandatory Palestine and for all Palestinians, which entails dismantling the divisive colonial system. This track is gaining increasing support among Palestinians, but we do not yet call this a 'one state solution' for reasons given below.

The key to this strategy is to end the long held confusion between strategies for national liberation and rights-based strategies. It is not either-or. It could and must be both. We are aware of the difficulties of following these two tracks at the same time. It is likely to be misrepresented as a switch from a 'two-state solution' to a 'one-state solution'. It is not. As explained in the conclusion, the alternative at the moment is not yet between a 'two-state solution' and a conceivable eventual 'one-state solution' – although both of these nevertheless remain possible future scenarios. The immediate choice is between self-determination for Palestinians (Scenario A) and the existing one-state reality – Greater Israel (Scenario B) which we aim to block. The aim is to dismantle the delusory option of a permanent continuation of the *status quo* in order to expose this fundamental choice in Israel and within the international community. The post-Oslo two-track strategy is not a threat to future solutions, but on the contrary the only way to save the prospects for such a meaningful resolution.

The two tracks are inseparably intertwined. Scenario (A) will only come about when Israel and the international community understand that the alternative – Scenario (B) – is worse, because it will entail endless conflict, endless instability, increasing costs, and an unpredictable outcome. In addition, since the internationalized route to Palestinian self-determination is now likely to be a long one because Israel will oppose it and the US will veto UN Security Council resolutions, we can no longer be expected as in the past to hold back indefinitely from opposing Scenario (B) by all means at our disposal. We have been asked to wait long enough. The time for waiting is now over. We must act. The two tracks do not contradict one another. They complement one another.

One concrete proposal for action that follows from this analysis would be to remove the ambiguity under Oslo by persuading the international community to confront Israel with an existential choice. Is its presence in the West Bank including East Jerusalem and effective control of Gaza a military occupation or not? If it is an occupation, as the international community has repeatedly decreed, then its – supposedly provisional – custodianship should be brought to a swift end after what is now nearly fifty years. If, on the other hand, Israel insists on not recognizing its

107

military rule as an occupation, then there is no justification for denying equal rights to everyone who is subject to Israeli control and rule, which is the entire area of historic Palestine. This includes the right to vote for whatever government exercises that control. Israel can no longer go on avoiding this choice under the cover of the ambiguities of the Oslo status quo. Independently of any Israeli response, or lack of response, the international community can then act accordingly in line with its own commitments. We can go on aiming to influence this, while reserving our own position (going down both tracks at the same time) and continuing to increase the cost to Israel of Scenario (B).[4]

Our post Oslo strategy is guided by the following principles:

- The long term goal of our strategy is national independence and national self-determination and achieving individual and collective rights including the right of return to refugees and equality to the 1948 Palestinians.
- It is a national strategy that includes all Palestinians wherever they may live. The aim is to regain the unity of the nation and transform their lives.
- Our strategy does not close down any options or paths that may lead to the strategic goal – it will adapt to a situation where there is a Palestinian state and to a situation where this is not yet possible. It is 'both and' not 'either or'. For 21 years the possibility of there not being a Palestinian state was not part of the national strategy, confining our strategy to act only in the context of an emerging state. In light of the current geo-political reality in Israel, this must end.
- Our strategy is based on the clear understanding that it is only when the power imbalance is redressed that we will achieve our goals. The limits of Israel's preponderance in military power were demonstrated in the outcome of the third war on Gaza. Our power is the steadfastness of our people, the justice of our cause, and resistance in all its forms including the growing global movement for boycott, divestment and sanctions (BDS). Our strategic aim is to convert legitimacy power into real transformation on the ground.
- The justice of our cause rests on the dramatic contrast between the unethical basis of the Greater Israel project and the ethical basis of our strategy. The Greater Israel strategy is based on claims of rights for Jews that are thereby denied to Palestinians. The Palestinian strategy demands rights for the Palestinian people that are equal and reciprocal with those of any other people. Peoples are equal in dignity and rights.
- A central requirement of our strategy is to inspire and galvanize the mass of the Palestinian people – civil society in its widest sense – and not just elites in both the formulation and implementation of the national liberation strategy.

- It is a central principle of our strategy that the initiative and drive for national liberation and self-determination must come from and be guided by Palestinians. We cannot—and must not—rely on others to do it for us.

The ultimate aim of our post-Oslo two-track strategy is to unleash the full potential for collective action by our people. A far greater range of action is envisaged than has been available before. We can retain the initiative, move simultaneously in different directions, constantly surprise our opponents, and never rest until we have dismantled the web of control, dispossession, discrimination and oppression that has shackled us. This is in every sense a strategy for national *liberation*.

Source: Palestine Strategy Group, August 2015

The rest of *A Post Oslo Strategy* is made up of an analysis of the changing *parameters* (conditioning factors), *policy implications* and *action points* that need to be coordinated in the new national strategy. Five main 'arenas for action' were identified.

Arena (1) Internal national reconciliation, institutional renewal, and popular resistance

How can the Palestinian people be unified and collectively inspired to seize the historic opportunity to achieve national liberation?

This was made up of *national reconciliation* (for example, between Fatah and Hamas), *institutional rebuilding* (for example, of the Palestine Liberation Organization (PLO) as the overarching frame for national aspirations, and also recalibration of the role of the Palestinian Authority (PA) away from *de facto* collaboration in occupation and towards leadership in resistance, including the vital question of the succession to Mahmoud Abbas), and *national resistance* (the PSG coined the term 'smart resistance').

Arena (2) Eliciting support from the region

How can the universal regional sympathy for our cause be harnessed into effective support?

This section was chosen as one of the two main topics for further analysis by the PSG in 2016. In line with the principle behind the idea of 'strategic negotiation' to be set out in chapter 8, the focus is on linking internal strategic thinking *among* Palestinians to the international strategic *context* which is likely largely to determine the outcome:

> Overwhelming popular sympathy for the Palestinian cause throughout the region should be a great source of strength for our strategy. The upheavals that continue to convulse the region, however, make this difficult to harness ... In these circumstances the policy implication is to try to avoid entangling alliances with particular factions, which can backfire and bring adverse and often unanticipated reactions from other parts of the system. Instead, we should identify what specific roles relevant to our strategy different countries can play and then work systematically to activate these.

Arena (3) Eliciting support from the international community

How can the overwhelming international legitimacy of our cause be translated into tangible transformation on the ground?

This section was informed by a separate prior 44-page PSG paper on recourses via international law: *A Diplomatic Strategy for National Liberation* (June 2015). Possible strategic recourses were identified and evaluated along Track 1 (actions to promote a Palestinian state) and along Track 2 (actions in case there is no Palestinian state). They included:

- a continuing drive to attain further international recognition (particularly in Europe);
- further moves through the UN Security Council and General Assembly;
- greater use of international courts and tribunals:

  > we need to have a plan for the day after the advisory opinion, which must include a coherent and effective media strategy to overcome the failure to take advantage of the advisory opinion issued by the International Court of Justice on 9 July 2004 [which ruled that the Israeli security barrier was illegal];

- an escalation of the Boycott, Divestment, Sanctions (BDS) campaign;
- a revival of the idea of UN protection in the wake of the Gaza attack along the lines of the international protectorate for Kosovo that resulted in the EU giving Serbia ninety days for direct negotiations to produce an agreement followed by swift recognition for Kosovo by most EU states: 'This should have happened in 1998 in the case of Palestine when the Oslo interim phase ended with no agreement.'

Arena (4) Influencing the public debate in Israel and the cost–benefit calculations of the Israeli leadership

How can Israel be confronted by the reality of the existential choice between ending its occupation, colonization and control of Palestine and accepting equal rights for all Palestinians, or international isolation?

This was identified as another major focus for attention in 2016. As noted in box 6.1, it was clearly understood that the strategic purpose was to change the cost–benefit calculations of different scenarios within Israeli society and by the Israeli government. A major positive feature of the strategic engagement approach, as argued in Part I, is its central emphasis on the importance of influencing the internal dynamics of the other party:

> In the end, as the possessor, it is Israel that has to come to understand – or be made to understand – that in cost–benefit terms persistence with Greater Israel policies under scenario (B) is self-defeating, and will lead to mounting confrontations, financial burdens, security risks, and international isolation. On the other hand, fair resolution of the conflict – in whichever form – will bring lasting security, international endorsement, and big financial and other benefits.
>
> The policy implication here is that stripping away the 'peace process' system is the only way to confront Israel with this stark alternative. Up to now, there has been no strategic debate in Israel because the illusion of the no-risk Oslo process [the status quo] has always seemed better than the risks of Scenario (A) while at the same time removing most of the risks associated with open acknowledgement of Scenario (B) (this is the ambiguity that the suggested proposal for action on page two of this report [the paragraph that begins at the bottom of page 107 in this chapter] seeks to remove).

Arena (5) Communications

How can our superior ethical and legal case be made manifest? How can we win the war of words?

The fifth arena was seen to permeate all the others:

> The new strategic parameter is that in the cyber-age winning the war of words can be as important as winning the war of weapons – sometimes more so (it is possible to win a war and lose the peace). As noted under strategic principles at the beginning of this paper, the ethical superiority and manifest justice of our cause in comparison with the Israeli attempt to claim rights that are thereby denied to Palestinians is a major strength

111

of our strategy. This is an arena where Palestinians have made big gains over the past years. In November 2012 UNGA 67/19 overwhelmingly accorded Palestine non-member observer status with 138 votes for, 9 against, 41 abstentions, and 5 absentees. At the time of writing, 137 out of 193 UN member states have recognized Palestine.

This is the conclusion of *A Post Oslo Strategy*:

> The suggestions for action set out here are not systematic or exhaustive. It is up to elected leaderships to formulate official policy. They are offered as stimuli for participation by as wide a range of fellow Palestinians as possible . . .
>
> Earlier in this paper it is suggested that the 'two-state solution'/'one-state solution' alternative does not correspond with reality. The immediate alternative is between Palestinian self-determination as embodied in full independence on the one hand, and apartheid as manifested in the Greater Israel project on the other. Alternatives to partition (as we know it) that do not necessarily encompass a Palestinian state lie over the horizon. These include malign possibilities, as well as benign forms of possible future federation, confederation, or bi-national, consociational and other types of political arrangement between the two sides. It is helpful that these are discussed in terms of possible future scenarios. But the passage from the current one-state *de facto* reality to any of these outcomes in the absence of a sovereign Palestinian state that fully embodies the Palestinian right to national self-determination is likely to be turbulent. In the meantime, what is strategically damaging about the 'two-state solution/one-state solution' language is that it draws attention away from the existing one state reality. Opponents of Palestinian statehood can then attack the former (the indeterminateness of the idea of a possible future one-state *solution*) and thereby ignore the latter (the unsustainability of the existing one-state *reality*). That is why we would do well to nuance it in our strategic lexicon.
>
> For 21 years, the Oslo process has furthered the Greater Israel project. Now that the Oslo process has come to an end, our strategy must be to continue the struggle for national self-determination through our own state albeit via the international rather than the purely bilateral route. At the same time, being gradually freed from the shackles of Oslo, we must also in parallel challenge the Greater Israel project in its entirety. We must expose and resist Israeli policies of expropriation, colonization, annexation, separation and apartheid. We must act across the board with a full range of integrated strategic actions that unite our people and link local to international campaigns. Our aim is to transform the lives of all Palestinians so that our national rights – equal to and consonant with the rights of other nations – are fully protected and realized.

112

Heuristic engagement:
why conflict resolution fails – what Palestinians say

Based on the work of the Palestine Strategy Group (PSG), we can now briefly illustrate the deep national discourse that underlies Palestinian strategic thinking of the kind illustrated in *A Post Oslo Strategy*, and why, in the face of this, conflict resolution so far fails.

In the introduction to Part II we noted Nadim Rouhana's summary, which he claims 'is shared by all segments of Palestinian society, including Palestinians in Israel':

> Israel will have to face at least part of the truth that the country that they settled belonged to another people, that their project was the direct cause of the displacement and dismantling of Palestinian society, and that it could not have been achieved without this displacement. Israel will also have to confront the realities of the occupation and the atrocities it is committing, and will have to accept that Palestinian citizens in Israel are indigenous to the land and entitled to seek the democratic transformation of the state so that they have equal access to power, resources and decision making, and are entitled to rectification of past and present injustices.[5]

Here we can unpack this further with reference to the first Palestine Strategy Group Report *Regaining the Initiative: Palestinian Strategic Options to End Israeli Occupation* (2008). We will do this in the form of snapshots at twenty-year intervals taken from PSG reports.

1948

In the cataclysmic shock of the *Nakba* (disaster), a Jewish State of Israel was suddenly imposed on the indigenous population by immigrants from another continent. Half the original population was driven out within a few months. Many of their descendants still carry the keys of their lost ancestral homes.

The outrageous injustice of the *Nakba* is the foundation of Palestinian discourse. In the words of *Regaining the Initiative*:

> Above all it is important to combat a central idea in the peacemaking discourse that what is at issue is two equivalent 'Israeli' and 'Palestinian' 'narratives'. No doubt there are Israeli and Palestinian narratives. But what is centrally at issue is not a mere Palestinian narrative, but a series of incontrovertible facts – facts of expulsion, exclusion, dominance and

113

occupation bitterly lived out by Palestinians day by day over the past 60 years and still being endured at the present time. This is not a narrative. It is a lived reality. Finding the best strategy for ending this lived reality is the main purpose of this Report. Transforming the discourse within which it is discussed is a major part of that effort.[6]

The discursive battle is to make the Palestinian discourse the primary language within which the Palestinian issue is discussed, not because it is a narrative, but because it is *true*. This is not just an abstract discussion but essential to Palestinian strategy:

> Palestinians are of course ready to enter serious negotiations. They are more ready to do this than Israelis. But such peacemaking has to be defined within a context that genuinely aims to deliver Palestinian national aspirations and rights. Anything less is simply not peacemaking, but a confirmation of continuing – and deepening – occupation and repression.[7]

That is why, as *A Post Oslo Strategy* puts it, 'strategies for national liberation and rights-based strategies' are two sides of the same coin. From the outset Palestinian discourse has placed central emphasis on *international law* in framing the successive stages of the national struggle:

- UN Security Council Resolution (UNSC) 194 (1949) on the right of return for Palestinian refugees – compliance with which was a condition for Israel's admission to the UN;[8]
- UNSC 242 (1967) (confirmed in UNSC 338 (1973)) requiring Israel to withdraw from occupied territories;
- UNSC 1515 (2003) (reaffirming UNSC 1397 (2002)), unanimously adopted by the Security Council, enjoining an end to 'the occupation that began in 1967', advocating the 'emergence of an independent, democratic and viable Palestinian state living side by side in peace and security with Israel', and recognizing the 2002 Arab Peace Initiative as a 'basis' for proceeding.[9]

The appeal is to *elementary justice* and *basic international values* as explicitly recognized by all 'civilized nations'.

1967

After the Six-Day War in June 1967, Israel imposed military rule on the remaining 22 per cent of mandatory Palestine (Gaza and the West Bank). The Palestinians in those territories now became – and remain – stateless. On 22 November 1967, UN Security Council Resolution 242 clearly stipulated a 'withdrawal of Israel armed forces from territories occupied in the recent conflict'. Yet, from the outset, illegal Israeli settlement of the occupied territories was deliberately and systematically planned and exercised. This has continued – for fifty years – up to the present day (the current number of Israeli settlers on Palestinian land is – according to some criteria – nearly 600,000). With this second blatant ongoing violation of internationally endorsed principles, the '67 Palestinians now joined the '48 Palestinians as victims of injustice.

Here again the 2008 PSG report (from which the paragraph above is taken) further stresses how this is absolutely not a question of 'alternative equivalent discourses'. The report emphasizes the dramatic discrepancy between the universal ethical/legal basis of Palestinian national strategy, based as it is on the principle of equality of rights for all individuals and peoples, and Israeli national strategy, which is based on the opposite: a denial of Palestinian rights and the promotion of Jewish rights at the Palestinians' expense. These are 'ethnic', not 'universal' rights. The report points to the ways in which successive Israeli governments have shown no interest in recognizing Palestinian rights of any kind – neither equal *individual citizens' rights* for Palestinians in Israel, nor *collective rights* for Palestinians as a national minority in Israel, nor *indigenous rights* for Palestinians anywhere in mandatory Palestine, let alone *national self-determination rights* for Palestinians, even on 22 per cent of their ancient homeland. This is in marked contrast to Israeli government insistence on full *individual citizenship rights* for all Jewish Israelis; the *collective privileges* of the Jewish 'majority' in Israel to determine the nature not only of Israel but of the whole of Palestine; the *indigenous 'law of return'* by which any Jew worldwide has an automatic right to Israeli citizenship, including, in practice, settlement in the 22 per cent of mandatory Palestine beyond the 1949 'green line'; and *self-determination rights* only for the Jewish people in their own, increasingly 'Jewish', state.

This is the deep underlying discursive basis of the strategic thinking in *A Post Oslo Strategy*, and it can be seen as central to the comparison of relative strategic strengths and weaknesses in it.

1988

In 1988, against the background of the First Intifada, the PLO leadership in exile in Tunisia made the crucial offer to Israel, which should have led directly to an end-of-conflict agreement. This is how the point is put in *Regaining the Initiative*:

> In November 1988 the Palestine Liberation Organisation, recognised by Palestinians as their sole representative, made the extraordinary sacrifice of accepting the existence of the State of Israel and determining to establish an independent Palestinian state on the remaining 22% of historic Palestine in accordance with UN Security Council Resolutions 242 and 338 (Palestinian National Council Political Communique, Algiers, 15 November, 1988).[10] Has a national movement ever made a concession on a similar scale? To this day this remains the basis for official Palestinian strategic objectives. Yet for twenty years these objectives have not been realised. Why? In negotiations Israelis repeatedly say 'we do all the giving and the Palestinians do all the taking'. This is the opposite of the truth. Palestinians continue to demand no more than 22% of their historic land. It is Israel that has done all the taking through continuous government-backed settler encroachment on this remaining 22%. The aim has been to create 'facts on the ground', now reinforced by the 'security wall', in order to reduce the land left for a future Palestinian state below even 22%. Indeed the longer-term aim has been to make a Palestinian state impossible. This is not just a Palestinian 'perspective'. These are facts. At the time of writing Israeli government-backed settler encroachment is still continuing relentlessly despite the negotiations. Palestinians know that Israel is not yet a serious negotiating partner. It is on the basis of these facts and on this understanding that the strategic objectives for Palestinians are set out in the next section.[11]

2008

By 2008 this was the situation described in *Regaining the Initiative*:

> On the sixtieth anniversary of the Nakba, Palestinians find themselves as far away from realising their strategic national objectives as ever. Expectations from the current phase of negotiations, launched in the final year of the Bush administration in the USA, are very low. The 'Annapolis' initiative is seen to promise, not more, but less than previous attempts, such as those made in the final year of the previous Clinton administration. The 'Road Map' includes deeply ambivalent conditioning factors unacceptable to Palestinians, such as talk of 'provisional borders' and the open-ended acknowledgement of changing 'facts on the ground' contained in the American 'Letter of Guarantees' of 2004. With the passing away of the first generation of Israeli leaders and deep shifts in the demographic make-up of Israeli society through changing patterns of immigration and ideological commitment, Israel lacks the unity and strong leadership necessary to deliver the genuine negotiated two-state

agreement that is the only acceptable outcome for Palestinians. Above all, as outlined in the Executive Summary, Israel sees no need to do this, given its widespread assumption that a two-state solution is always available and belief that there are in any case more attractive alternatives to a negotiated agreement that perpetually remain open.[12]

In the event, although, according to Israeli Prime Minister Ehud Olmert, he and Palestinian President Mahmoud Abbas nearly achieved a breakthrough in 2008 ('We were very close, more than ever in the past, to completing an agreement in principle that would have led to an end of the conflict between us and the Palestinians'),[13] the situation changed dramatically with the return to power of the Likud leader Binyamin Netanyahu in 2009. As in his earlier period in power (1996–9), the three subsequent Netanyahu terms of office (2009–13, 2013–15 and 2015–) soon dissipated any such prospects. The 2011 and 2014 PSG reports noted how the leaders of major government coalition partners in Israel openly advocated policies such as removing Palestinians in the 'little triangle' from Israel (Avigdor Lieberman) and permanently carving up the West Bank in solidarity with the settlers (Naftali Bennett). Many members of Netanyahu's own Likud party also opposed a Palestinian state. And Netanyahu himself, on the eve of the March 2015 election, explicitly appealed for electoral support by a public assurance that there would never be a Palestinian state on his watch. The three Gaza wars (2008–9, 2012, 2014) in each case preceded Israeli elections.

During this period, *A Post Oslo Strategy* refers to 'the tightening web of illegal expropriation and colonization of Palestinian territory, and the discrimination and apartheid practiced against Palestinian people' that continued inexorably. Attention is drawn to the continuity in Israeli long-term planning for the permanent absorption of the West Bank into 'Greater Israel' – as shown in a comparison between the original post-1967 'Allon Plan' (map 6.1), the 1995 Oslo II arrangements (map 6.2), the current post-separation barrier situation (map 6.3), and Naftali Bennett's future plans for permanent partition and annexation (map 6.4). As Israeli cabinet discussions since June 1967 repeatedly show, the main inhibition on Israeli annexation of the West Bank has been reluctance to take in the Palestinian population living there. Maps 6.1 to 6.4 show the various Israeli attempts over the subsequent fifty-year period to square this circle – still the main strategic preoccupation of the Israeli right. That is why all the maps share the same basic contours.

Faced with all this, it becomes clear why, for Palestinians, conflict

Map 6.1   The 1967 Allon Plan

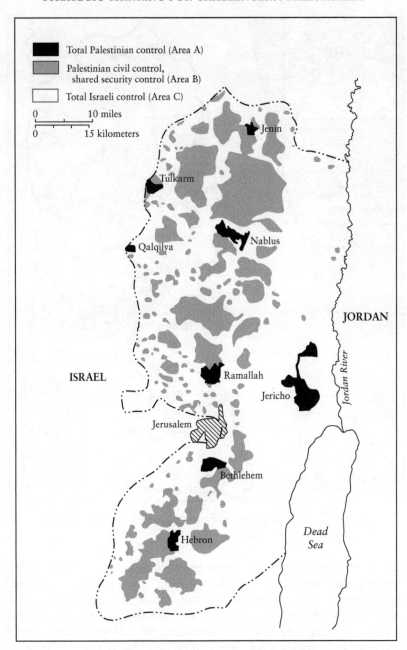

Map 6.2   The Israeli–Palestinian Interim Agreement on the West
Bank and the Gaza Strip (Oslo II), 1995

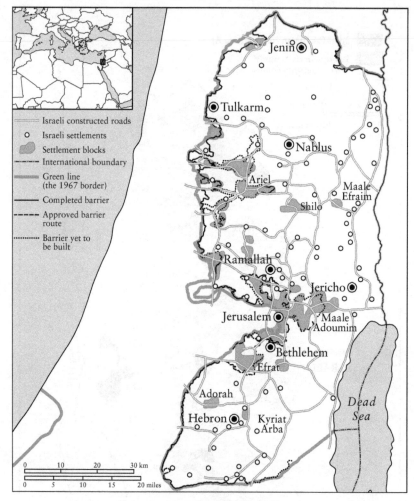

Map 6.3   The separation barrier and Israeli settlements
on the West Bank

resolution initiatives that promote 'dialogue for mutual understanding' or 'interactive problem-solving' or 'principled bilateral
negotiation' – but at the same time ignore the pre-existing and
continuing reality of exclusion, occupation and repression – do not
work. They are rejected as 'normalization'. Normalization tries
prematurely to pacify what needs to be challenged and, by drawing
a false veil of equivalence over an unequal situation, perpetuates
inequality. This is the main (negative) insight that the first level of

Map 6.4   The Bennett Plan

121

hermeneutic engagement – listening to what conflict parties individually say in radical disagreement – reveals in the case of Palestinian discourse.

This can easily lead to despair. In her book *Return: A Palestinian Memoir* (2015), for example, Ghada Karmi gives an anguished account of her horror and dismay when she returned to Palestine after nearly sixty years in Britain, intending to stay and play her part in the national struggle. Her family had left Jerusalem in 1948. She was shocked by the brutality and injustice of the Israeli occupation and the way the Palestinian Authority, instead of leading the Palestinian struggle, had been co-opted into serving the occupation. She felt paralysed by the 'spectrum of despair' in Gaza and disheartened by the ubiquity of Israeli control in the West Bank, where the locals had forgotten the national effort and were taken up with the daily struggle to survive. Most young Palestinians wanted to study in America, 'the very country which perpetuates Palestinian misery by giving Israel the arms it uses against the Palestinians'. As she eventually flew back to London and saw the lights of Tel Aviv twinkling beneath her, Karmi thought: 'Flotsam and jetsam, that's what we have become, scattered and divided. There's no room for us or our memories here. And it won't ever be reversed.'

But that is not the only response.

Strategic engagement – what can be done? Promoting collective internal strategic thinking

We return, briefly, to *A Post Oslo Strategy*. Instead of looking backwards in despair – the incubator of violence – it can be seen that strategic thinking looks forwards with hope. Recent opinion polls since the end of the Kerry initiative (for example, in September 2015) suggest that a majority of Palestinians – particularly young Palestinians – now favour a 'one-state solution' and support a 'resumption of violence'. But, as *A Post Oslo Strategy* clearly shows, on their own, such yes/no responses to pollsters' questions mean little unless properly thought through and discussed within the context of wider strategic implications and strategic alternatives.

Many of the main features of strategic thinking noted in chapter 4 can be seen in *A Post Oslo Strategy*. The main focus is on balance of power – the capacity of Palestinians to shape their own destiny. The prerequisite of strategic unity is clearly recognized and set out. The challenge to overcome the greatest Palestinian weakness

– fragmentation – by building 'internal national reconciliation', 'institutional renewal' and regenerated leadership is seen to be daunting, but to be within the power of Palestinians.

The interlocking elements that make up the complex system of the 'Oslo' status quo are also analysed. There are no illusions about the difficulties and dangers in reversing the fragmentation of the West Bank into areas A, B and C, undoing the complicity of the PA in the occupation, and ending 'bilateral' negotiation as practised in the past. The instability that looms in the search for a successor to Abbas is recognized. It is seen to be essential to retain international support – and not jeopardize the large number of Palestinian livelihoods dependent on it (30 per cent of GDP on some estimates, including about 140,000 Palestinian Authority employees). But the judgement is that the status quo persists only with Palestinian compliance and can therefore be ended without it.

Changing the balance of power means neutralizing Israeli military preponderance with the overwhelming international legitimacy of the Palestinian cause – and the concomitant illegitimacy of Scenario (B) (Greater Israel) once the mask of Scenario (C) (the status quo) has been stripped away. The new Palestinian strategy is seen to have made great strides here in the years since 2008 – for example, the overwhelming international endorsement of Palestine as a non-member observer state by the vote in the UN General Assembly in December 2012. The central strategic task is to convert international legitimacy into reality on the ground.

The reordering of short-term, medium-term and long-term strategic goals around the parallel two-track strategy – of simultaneous pursuit of Scenario (A) (a Palestinian state) and blocking of Scenario (B) (Greater Israel) by resistance and a demand for equal rights throughout Palestine in the absence of a Palestinian state – is understood to be difficult to balance and open to danger – for example, of Israeli partition of the West Bank and unilateral withdrawal. But the flexibility provided is seen to reflect the existing situation accurately and to allow Palestinians to retain the initiative whatever the likely turn of events.

In attaining these ends, *A Post Oslo Strategy* advocates 'smart' resistance – a term coined in *Regaining the Initiative* in 2008 – and the central importance of competing with Israel at regional and global levels, where again Palestinians are seen to have many advantages and therefore opportunities to 'balance power'. It is understood that it is in Israel's interest for Palestinian resistance to become violent (plain-clothes Israeli military *provocateurs* already foment this) – providing international credibility for fierce Israeli response. This might include the military reoccupation of Areas A and B on the West Bank, which would increase the burden of occupation for Israel, but might fatally jeopardize the Palestinian gains already made. In such volatile conditions it is hard to control mass resistance.

It is also clearly understood that the chessboard must be seen from the perspective of the opponent. The aim is to alter Israeli perceptions – at both government and societal levels – of the relative costs and benefits of different scenarios. This opens up a whole new strategic agenda, as will be emphasized in chapter 7.

The central importance of the regional and international context as a critical arena in the struggle between Israeli *realpolitik* and the Palestinian potential to orchestrate a potent 'force-multiplier' in order to balance power is fully realized.

Fundamental to all this is the importance of 'winning the war of words' so that the national struggle is fought on the ground of Palestinian discourse (legitimate equal rights for all individuals and peoples), not on the ground of a premature international 'peace' discourse that assumes an already existing equivalence and equality.

Conclusion

The first level of heuristic engagement – understanding Palestinian discourse – reveals the depth of suffering endured by the Palestinian people over the past seventy years, demonstrates why, so far, conflict resolution does not work, and highlights the current levels of despair that, at the time of writing, are stoking the danger of an explosion into an even more violent third intifada.

The first level of strategic engagement – Palestinian collective strategic thinking – on the other hand, shows how strategic thinking can be an antidote to despair, how it can channel anger into determination, and how it can convert frustration into the creation of new paths ahead and new means for getting there.

Strategic thinking cannot give back the past. But, by transforming despair into hope, it can give back the future.

7

STRATEGIC ENGAGEMENT WITHIN, ACROSS AND BETWEEN CONFLICT PARTIES

The last two chapters were about the first level of heuristic engagement (understanding what conflict parties individually say) and the first level of strategic engagement (collective strategic thinking within conflict parties). In this chapter and the next we look at the strategic engagement across and between conflict parties that can result from this and at the role of third parties.

Strategic engagement between the Israeli Strategic Forum (ISF) and the Palestine Strategy Group (PSG)

Chapter 5 attempted to convey something of the current overall Jewish Israeli response to the Israeli–Palestinian and Israeli–Arab conflict. Heuristic engagement showed how the realities of lived experience, deep history and the security imperative have shaped Israeli strategic thinking in general. A study of collective strategic thinking then explained why, particularly since 2000, the option of a Palestinian state in Gaza and Judea/Samaria has so far not been seriously debated in successive Israeli elections (up to and including that in 2015).

Chapter 6 presented a summary of collective Palestinian thinking at the time of writing (*A Post Oslo Strategy*), followed by an account of the Palestinian discourse that underlies it.

Both chapters, taken together, show how prevailing Israeli and Palestinian discourses miss each other almost entirely. Conflict resolution does not gain a foothold. Conflict parties are not nearer, but much further apart than was supposed. This theme is developed further in chapter 10.

125

In this chapter, in adapting practice accordingly, we want to correct any misleading impression that may have been given earlier that Israeli and Palestinian discourses are monolithic. On the contrary, we seek to show how new opportunities are opened up for strategic engagement across and between complex internal and external divides by the work of the Israeli Strategic Forum (ISF) and the Palestine Strategy Group (PSG) (as well as by a third group, the Palestinian Citizens of Israel Group (PCIG)) and to demonstrate how this can create spaces of possibility that are otherwise not available. In addition, since internal division is one of the main impediments to external resolution, the attempt to overcome the former in collective internal strategic thinking also helps to alleviate the latter. This does not guarantee success, of course. But chapter 4 suggested reasons why chances are likely to be enhanced. The alternative is a breakdown in communication and a frozen situation where strategic exchange does not take place at all and conflict resolution – peaceful management, settlement, transformation – is permanently blocked.

We can illustrate this in relation to the national election in Israel in March 2015. Here, according to opinion polls, although the 'right' in the security debate has been in the ascendancy since 2000 for reasons seen in chapter 5, there are still many more on the 'left' than might be supposed.[1]

Yet this potentially critical debate does not translate into central political discussion during national elections in Israel. It is a remarkable fact that, even though the three military offensives in Gaza (2008–9, 2012 and 2014) immediately (some say deliberately) preceded elections, the Palestinian question itself hardly appeared on the party political radar screen in the elections themselves. In each case, intense international criticism strengthened the internal perception that Israel was misunderstood, misrepresented and on its own. Voting in the end came down not so much to socio-economic or other issues, but to the question of 'territorial compromise'. And the political right succeeded in framing this as a stark choice between the two alternatives: *either* peace *or* security. As Hilik Bar, secretary-general of the Labor Party and deputy speaker in the Knesset, put it, this was at the root of the marked absence of serious public strategic debate in Israel in the 2012 and 2015 elections, as noted in chapter 5: 'The right has convinced the Israeli public – and us [in the Labour Party] – that the possibility of peace is ruled out because there is no Palestinian partner.'[2]

That this was not because of a lack of differentiation in the policies formally espoused by the political parties can be seen from box 7.1. Nor is it even true that voters in general 'moved to the right' in 2015.

Box 7.1   The spectrum of political opinion on a Palestinian state in the March 2015 Israeli election

There are 120 Knesset (parliament) seats. So to form a government a coalition leader must command at least 61 seats – as Binyamin Netanyahu, leader of the Likud party, does at the time of writing.[4]

In the 2015 election, right-wing parties variously favoured annexation of Area C and cantonization of the West Bank (Jewish Home: 8 Knesset seats), differing forms of Greater Israel or a much circumscribed Palestinian entity (Likud: 30 seats), and an emphasis on strengthening Jewish identity through annexation of Jewish settlements and removal from Israel of border Arab towns (Yisrael Beiteinu: 6 seats). Ultra-orthodox parties were focused on other issues and have traditionally been divided on the Palestinian question, with membership more hawkish than leaders, but unanimous in opposition to the division of Jerusalem (Shas: 7 seats; Torah Judaism: 6 seats). The two newer centrist parties, Yesh Atid (11 seats) and Kulanu (10 seats), concentrated more on economic issues but, although in favour of a Palestinian state in principle, did not see the Palestinian leadership as capable of delivering this in practice. The left-wing and centre-left parties Meretz (5 seats) and the Zionist Union (Labour and Hatnuah: 24 seats) formally supported a 'two-state solution' but, particularly in the case of the Zionist Union, were decidedly muted about this in the run-up to the elections. The new Joint Arab List (a grouping of three Arab parties and a communist Arab/Jewish party: 13 seats), reflecting diverse communist, nationalist and Islamist stances, uniformly demanded an end to occupation but differed on whether to support two states (Hadash) or to favour one democratic state (Balad).[5]

Binyamin Netanyahu's Likud party took seats mainly from other right-wing parties. But, symptomatic of right-wing success in making the security issue central and in defining it in either/or terms was Netanyahu's crucial intervention shortly before the vote, when he declared 'if I am elected there will be no Palestinian state'.[3]

Behind the four scenarios discussed in chapter 5 lie further variations and options that have not yet publicly engaged each other (see box 7.2).

Faced with this situation, Hilik Bar himself, who heads the Knesset Caucus to Resolve the Arab–Israeli Conflict, produced a strategy paper (a 'diplomatic framework') in October 2015, in order to challenge the rightist formulation *either* peace *or* security and to substitute the alternative formulation *no* future security *without* peace. Bar hoped that this might tap into a new and potentially large centre-left coalition in Israeli politics that would gain hugely electorally if wider

Box 7.2   Scenarios revisited: further variations

Scenario (A): a Palestinian state	Includes various left-wing options: Israeli settlers remain in Palestine; two states, one homeland; confederation between Israel, Palestine (and perhaps Jordan); parallel sovereignty
Scenario (B): Greater Israel	Includes various right-wing options: unilateral partition, with possible Egyptian and Jordanian participation; dependent 'pseudo'-states in Gaza and perhaps residual West Bank areas
Scenario (C): status quo	Continuing ambiguity about occupation – permanent 'management', not 'resolution': indefinite hold on area C and settlements; promotion of 'economic peace'; costs met by international community; security controlled via Palestinian Authority; bilateral negotiations as only peace process; separation of Gaza under Hamas; regional deals with Egypt, Saudi Arabia, etc.
Scenario (D): final accom- modation without a Palestinian state	As yet strategically undefined: some form of unitary democratic or bi-national state (as scenario (A) recedes, increasingly favoured by many Palestinians)

economic, social and other issues could at last be freed from the shackles of the right's negative security stranglehold. It would then be possible to break the dominant frozen default option, favoured by the prime minister, of 'managing' the status quo and condemning internal critiques as a betrayal of Israel. Perhaps at last a full public strategy debate about options for settling the Palestinian question might again move centre stage in Israeli politics. In Bar's words:

> Over my dead body will we not have a peace plan in time for the next election. It is unacceptable that the party of Yitzhak Rabin, who was murdered trying to bring peace, hid the flag of peace for the last two elections. I will not allow this to happen.
> Saying there is no partner for peace is an excuse for diplomatic stale-mate. My outline protects Israel's vital interests, keeps Jerusalem united,

solves the Palestinian refugee problem outside Israel's borders, leaves the majority of settlers in their homes, strengthens Israel's position in the world and gives Israel a boost in its unflinching war on terrorism. The current leadership's approach is to 'manage' the conflict in a way that will inevitably lead to a one-state reality that endangers Israel's Jewish majority and thus would spell the end of the Zionist enterprise. Let us not kid ourselves. Today we are told that PA President Mahmoud Abbas is 'not a partner for peace', but in the bi-national state to which the right is leading us, Abbas will be a partner – in the cabinet. And Khaled Mashaal is head of Hamas's political wing today, but in the bi-national state to which the right wing is leading us, he will head a political party that will compete in democratic elections.[6]

Bar proposed Israeli recognition of a demilitarized Palestinian state subject to satisfactory negotiations based on 1967 lines, widening consultation to include 'moderate' Arab governments and the EU, an Israeli response to the Arab Peace Initiative, an undivided Jerusalem as capital of the two states, a resolution of the Palestinian refugee problem outside the borders of Israel, and – most boldly – the idea that some Jewish settlers might remain in the new Palestinian state. The leaders of the Zionist Union party, Isaac Herzog and Tzipi Livni (who had been Israeli negotiator during the Kerry talks) welcomed, but did not yet fully endorse, the Bar proposal.

Since then, in February 2016, a new Labor Party plan has been adopted at a party conference called a *Comprehensive Diplomatic-Security Plan.*[7] Only two pages long, it retains a commitment to an eventual 'two-state solution'. But in the meantime it seeks to meet the mounting wave of 'Palestinian terror' and to avoid a slide into 'the reality of one Arab-Jewish state' through proposing interim measures that 'ensure national security' by accelerating 'physical and geographical separation between the two peoples' – such as completing the construction of the 'separation barrier' and dividing Jerusalem along ethnic lines. Israel must 'avoid construction outside of the settlement blocs' and 'transfer more civil powers to the Palestinian authority'. The importance of 'regional dialogue' is emphasized by including 'moderate states' such as Egypt and Jordan in the process – and officially responding to the 2002 Arab Peace Initiative. The paper endorses the 'broad outline' of previous initiatives going back to 'the Clinton parameters of December 2000' and including the recent Hilik Bar proposal.

However unsatisfactory many of these provisions may be from their perspective, such formulations open a major opportunity for Palestinian strategy along the lines identified in *A Post Oslo Strategy*. Here, as seen in chapter 6 (p. 111), the ultimate aim is to exert enough leverage on Israeli opinion and on Israeli decision-makers so that 'a final status deal' comes to be seen as 'the least bad option' for Israel:

> In the end, as the possessor, it is Israel that has to come to understand – or be made to understand – that in cost–benefit terms persistence with Greater Israel policies under scenario (B) is self-defeating, and will lead to mounting confrontations, financial burdens, security risks, and international isolation. On the other hand, fair resolution of the conflict – in whichever form – will bring lasting security, international endorsement, and big financial and other benefits.

In a public discussion at Harvard University in September 2015 between Hilik Bar (a participant in the original phase of the ISF) and Husam Zomlot (director of the PSG), some of these issues began to be properly argued out.[8] The main point in the strategic engagement was not that there was general agreement. There was not. On the contrary, it started to become clear exactly where and why the proposal that Bar hoped would form a nucleus for a revived centre-left alternative in Israeli politics was in that form not yet compatible with many aspects of the strategic formulation so far reached by the PSG (for example, in *A Post Oslo Strategy*). The point was that here, at last, was the beginning of a serious *strategic engagement of discourses* across and between conflict parties – an exploration and arguing out of *differences* – the essential (and hitherto missing) prerequisite for opening up the whole complex that makes up the current impasse.

But, before pursuing this further, we will first look in the rest of this chapter at the significance of an entirely new front in strategic engagement. We turn to a third initiative, the work of the Palestinian Citizens of Israel Group (PCIG) between 2012 and 2015 in relation both to the ISF and to the PSG. Palestinian Arabs in Israel, uniquely, could be participants in both a possible future Israeli Strategic Forum, as Israeli citizens, and also in the Palestine Strategy Group, as Palestinians. As noted in chapter 4, this conflicted identity lies at the heart of their predicament. Moreover, Palestinian citizens are those most likely to be affected whether there is a Palestinian state (for example, by being involved in land swaps) or no Palestinian state (for example, by subsequent (re)definition of Israel as a national home for the Jewish people). Palestinians in Israel could be either spoilers who challenge a settlement based on '67, not '48, or enablers who offer a bridge for transformed understanding. Yet they did not feature in the 2013–14 Kerry talks. So it is of critical significance to determine, through the process of collective internal strategic thinking, what Palestinians Arabs in Israel say. What follows is taken from the first (as yet unpublished) draft of the PCIG strategy report, produced in 2015: 'Strategic Thinking for Palestinian Arabs in the State of Israel'.

The Palestinian Citizens of Israel Group (PCIG): 'Strategic Thinking for Palestinian Arabs in the State of Israel' (2015)

The 1.7 million Palestinian Arabs in Israel, or Palestinian Citizens of Israel, make up more than 20 per cent of the Israeli population. This is a very large percentage. For example, Scottish citizens of the UK constitute only about 8 per cent of the total UK population. These are mainly descendants of the original pre-1948 Arab inhabitants who stayed behind after the 1948 exodus (so they are sometimes referred to as the '48 Palestinians).[9]

For a long time after the shocks of 1948 and 1967, the Arab population in Israel was an 'invisible, identity-less and potentially de-Palestinianized group'.[10] This began to change in 1976, when, in protest against the persistent and cumulative 'Judaization' of territory in Galilee in Israel and elsewhere, including confiscation of Arab land, the 'Day of the Land' demonstrations erupted, in which six Palestinians were killed. It was at that time that the High Follow-Up Committee was established (1982), made up of the Arab heads of local authorities[11] and other major Arab organizations and political parties in Israel. The Follow-Up Committee is now given *de facto* (but not *de jure*) recognition by the State of Israel. The situation was compounded at the time of the Second Intifada after October 2000, when Palestinian Arabs were caught up in the violent confrontations of the Al-Aqsa Intifada, subsequently investigated by the Orr Commission.

The Future Vision documents

But the real breakthrough came in 2006–7 with the publication of the four Future Vision documents.[12] These were produced in response to the Jewish Israeli Kinneret Charter (*Amant Kinneret*), with its focus on the 'Israelization' of the Arabs in Israel. In the Palestinian Citizens of Israel Group analysis ('Strategic Thinking for Palestinian Arabs in the State of Israel', hereafter referred to as PCIG (2015)), this watershed in national self-awareness was seen to be driven by 'a rise of the middle classes as social groups with a degree of power and influence on local

131

governance'. The Future Vision documents 'aimed to break through a stagnated reality' and expressed 'the aspirations of the Palestinian Arabs in Israel as a national minority with civil rights'. Nevertheless, in the PCIG analysis, the Future Vision documents did not yet constitute strategic thinking. For example, they presented a list of demands that were not integrated with each other or related to a clear analysis of the complex system that so far blocked them. The documents outlined 'a desired finish line, but did not discuss how to get there'. And there was little further consultation, marketing or development. The reaction from the Jewish majority was fiercely negative.[13]

The Palestinian Citizens of Israel Group

The Palestinian Citizens of Israel Group (PCIG) was formed in 2012 to fill this 'strategy gap'. Participants came from across the Arab Palestinian community spectrum. Three-day meetings of the full PCIG took place in Oxford, Jerusalem, Haifa and Istanbul, preliminary consultations with community leaders and activists were held, and further input from twenty-five other prominent members of the community were incorporated. Strategic thinking was seen as a prerequisite without which Palestinian Arabs in Israel would never be able collectively to formulate, let alone achieve, their aims – 'strategic thinking is a necessary prerequisite that precedes strategic planning and implementation':

> Strategic thinking represents a new experience in our society. It seeks to analyze the system, monitor what scenarios may develop, and examine the possible options for changing reality through a study of obstacles, opportunities and preferred strategies in determining short-, medium- and long-term goals.[14]

At exactly the time that the first draft report was completed in 2015, one of the main recommendations of the group had already been realized through the formation of the new united Joint Arab List in the March 2015 Knesset elections, as noted above – at the time of writing still precarious. The leader of the Joint List, Ayman Odeh, strongly supported the PCIG initiative.

Strategic identity

Palestinians in Israel are 'an indigenous national minority and part of the Arab Palestinian people and Arab culture and civilization in general'.[15] This conflicted identity defines the particularities of the

132

strategic enterprise, distinct as it is from both that of Jewish citizens of Israel and from that of non-Israeli Palestinians.

The existing situation

Given this ambivalence, Palestinians in Israel are faced with a particularly complex strategic terrain that is full of apparent contradictions.

In relation to Israeli society and the Israeli state, for example, some impulses in Israel have been to try to equalize economic, educational and other opportunities for Palestinians as individual citizens: 'there have been attempts by some in Jewish and Zionist circles in Israel to view us as a part of the state with policies adopted to pull us away from the Arab and Palestinian cultural and political space.' On the other hand, the more powerful currents in recent years in Israel have been in the opposite direction. The shift to the right in Israeli politics is seen to have intensified policies of discrimination, exclusion and oppression that are overtly ethnic and colonial: 'rightist tendencies have dominated the economy and permeated society accompanied by a belief in the ability to manage the conflict with the Palestinians rather than solve it': 'Several influential members of the elite have persisted in viewing us as a "fifth column" and agents of the "enemies" of the state.'[16] But there are also complications in relation to the wider Arab world. There are unclear relations 'between us and the Arab nation, which has descended into a state of disarray and has become exhausted with religious conflict and disintegration.'

In order to map out this complex terrain, the PCIG report offers a sophisticated *analytic matrix* of the status quo that sets out different *levels* along one axis (local, national, Palestinian, regional, international) and different *sectors* along the other axis (political, legal, socio-economic, cultural, demographic/geographic). This is the complex that Palestinians in Israel want to transform. The matrix is subsequently carried through to the analysis of scenarios that follows, and then on to the structuring of future paths or options that arise as a result.

Strategic unity

From the beginning a common theme among those consulted by the PCIG was the prior need for Palestinians in Israel to build sufficient internal unity to formulate and carry out collective strategic thinking and action. There is a complicated ethnic and religious make-up of the Palestinian presence in Israel – for example, it is difficult to include in collective strategic thinking the radical northern branch of the Islamic Movement in Israel, led by Raed Salah (the southern branch is more moderate). But it is essential that such differences in perspectives and doctrines: 'should not prevent the Palestinian Arabs in Israel from coordination, cooperation and creating partnerships for action and struggles in regard to collective procedures and steps that can be taken collectively.'[17] The key question of 'strategic authority' – a capacity to implement strategic thinking – was also identified as critical in the report, as noted further below.

Internal democracy

Equally fundamental – and recurrent – in discussions and consultations by the PCIG was the insistence that the strategy must not be imposed top-down, but must reflect genuine, wide-ranging and continuous attempts to elicit the concrete needs and aspirations of the mass of the Palestinian people in all parts of Israel – from the Palestinian towns and villages in Galilee in the north to the Bedouin towns and villages in the Negev in the south:

> The report, along with the working team, views this as being done through rebuilding the map of requirements and interests via a dialogue among all active forces with people in their towns, institutions and frameworks. This is a condition that prevents circumvention of the masses or bypassing their true needs or interests.[18]

It is acknowledged that authoritarianism and lack of internal democracy is a weakness in Palestinian society in Israel, as noted below.

Strengths and weaknesses

Imbalance of power is seen to be the defining factor. How can it be rectified? This requires an analysis of comparative strengths and weaknesses. Palestinian strengths are summarized under the following headings:

- the justice of our cause
- the historic and cultural depth of our society within its wider Arab surroundings
- our longstanding experience of living with the Jewish community and state – creating a bilingual society in which each community possesses broad knowledge about the other community

- historic acceptance of partnership with the Jews in Palestine
- ability to grant or retract legitimacy for Israeli democracy
- preparedness to live with any solution and settlement – flexibility in adjusting
- an advanced network of civil society institutions and an expansion of the middle classes able to activate these
- a youthful society – most of its members are under forty
- struggles thus far have been distinctively peaceful and non-violent
- relations with regional and global forces including international bodies
- support for our cause in international conventions and treaties relating to rights of minorities.

Palestinian weaknesses include:

- geographic distribution that hinders transformation into a bloc (population centers on the outskirts)
- weak economic structure (economy subordinate to the Jewish city, high rates of poverty and prevalence of violence)
- social structure that is sectarian or familial – severe divisions among the elite
- widening gap between the leaders and elite on the one hand and the masses on the other
- educational system that is inadequate, not independent, weak and does not make a student qualified for life and its challenges
- absence of an all-inclusive political framework for collective decision-making (e.g., decline in effectiveness of the Follow-Up Committee)
- undemocratic political culture that lacks coordination and cooperation and suffers from factionalism and division
- political culture that suffers from reactivity and absence of initiative and that is always searching for foreign patronage for protection
- regional variables are reflected upon us causing further division and internal tensions.[19]

At the heart of Palestinian strengths in Israel is 'the moral superiority of our cause'. This gives 'enormous energy to work and influence reality' – for example, to lobby international forums. Palestinians in Israel are supported by 'international law and conventions and treaties relating to human rights, national, linguistic, cultural and religious minorities and similar documents relating to indigenous peoples including ideas of equal citizenship, justice and equitable distribution of resources and power':

> Above all, our participation in legislative elections in Israel since 1949 has given us the power to grant – or withhold – legitimacy from the indigenous society in the country to the immigrant society ... This means that we can connect our desire to correct the imbalance of power between the state and ourselves in Israel to its desire to obtain the regional and international legitimacy outside Israel that it seeks.[20]

Strategic scenarios

The PCIG analysis of scenarios – possible futures – differs from those considered in chapters 5 and 6 because of the different situation in which Palestinians in Israel find themselves. Under each of the three futures – a Palestinian state, a continuation of the status quo, and a one-state outcome – good and bad possibilities are foreseen for Arab Palestinians in Israel, with 'historic reconciliation' at one end of the spectrum and 'escalation' or even 'expulsion' at the other. In addition, there is a fourth scenario under which Islamic extremism in the region directly threatens Israel's borders. In each case, scenarios are considered in relation to the matrix of levels and sectors mentioned under the status quo above, and emphasis is placed on the 'fluidity' of scenarios and on the 'intersections' between them.

We will not try to reproduce the carefully compared scenarios in turn here. But, in brief:

(A) Within the *separate Palestinian state scenario*, two contradictory developments may result for Palestinians in Israel. There may be 'a relaxation in the relation and things may stabilize to complete normalization on the basis of joint living founded on justice and equality', or:

> There is a tendency in Jewish Israeli society to demand 'compensation' for a strategic geographic 'compromise' in the space through economic-demographic pressure on Palestinian Arabs in Israel by affirming the Jewishness of the state and resettling the settlers in residential areas of Palestinians at the expense of their development and expansion of their towns. There have been statements and proposals to this effect by Jewish Israeli leaders ... This escalation might bring back the idea of population exchange or the coercive annexation of the Palestinian Arab population in Israel to the neighboring Palestinian state with unilateral border modifications, or the initiation of a new phase where the state presents the Palestinian citizens with a choice either to waive their collective and civil rights in Israel or cross over to the Palestinian state.[21]

(B) The *continuation of the status quo scenario* may also result in contradictory developments:

> Such a development of the status quo may lead to some type of opening or relaxation in the relation between the state and its Palestinian citizens, especially since such a track will increase the size of the middle class and improve its condition and deepen the network of mutual interests between such middle class groups and the state and Jewish society.
>
> As for the escalation track, however, oppression may be extended to the subjugation of protest and solidarity activities, as happened during the most recent two assaults on Gaza when the state crushed Palestinian (and Arab-Jewish) protest with an iron fist. This was combined with an escalation in the rhetoric of hate and incitement against Palestinians, coupled with legislation directly prejudiced against Palestinian Arabs in Israel restricting their rights both as a group and individuals, while granting further privileges and resources to Jewish citizens collectively and individually.[22]

(C) A *one-state scenario* might evolve towards reconciliation and greater equality on the one hand – in the direction of a possible future approximation to some sort of bi-national state – or towards more oppressive Jewish superiority on the other, which would be:

> a stone's throw away from an open apartheid regime where the entire country between the river and the sea is governed by racial segregation laws, spatial isolation and a legal and constitutional structure that absolutely favors the Jewish people in Israel over the Palestinian Arabs in everything.[23]

(D) Finally, there is a fourth *external threat scenario* in which regional insecurity will directly threaten Israel in the form of the arrival of radical Islam on its borders. An existential choice will then be demanded of its Palestinian citizens. The demand will be for complete loyalty to Israel in its struggle against its Islamist enemies:

> Palestinian society would then be torn on the issue of recruitment into the political and war effort of the state that is defending itself and its citizens – including the Arabs. Some are likely to cooperate with the state at all levels, culminating in the recruitment of more Palestinian Arabs into the army.[24] This would entirely change the relationship and discourse. More than at any other time in the past, however, the Palestinian Arabs will stand before the strict choice imposed by Jewish society and the state, which says 'you are either with us or against us!' In such a situation, it is meaningless to delve into the minute details, distinctions and differences in determining the general policy towards

the Palestinian Arabs, and it might not even be possible to assume a position of neutrality. Escalation here is existential as far as Israel is concerned and it might propel it to radical solutions such as expulsion of Palestinian Arab groups outside its borders.[25]

Strategic goals

Long-term (twenty to forty years), medium-term (ten to twenty years) and short-term (five to ten years) goals are envisaged. It can be seen that this is a very long perspective. Shorter-term 'preliminary strategies' over the next five years follow on from this below.

In brief, over the question of long-term vision, 'it is difficult to ascertain whether or not there is consensus among the Palestinians in Israel, especially as regards ideologies and beliefs.' For example, there are Palestinian Arabs in Israel who 'dream of an Islamic state where there is no separation between the religion and the state', whereas others believe in the attainment of a secular state 'where there is complete separation between state and religion'. Nevertheless, such differences in long-term vision are common in other countries, and 'it must not be changed into an obstacle in the face of agreement on public issues and common objectives in the medium and short terms.'[26]

Over the medium term, 'there are goals at two levels: the internal level and the level of the relation with the state.' At the internal level the goal is 'to achieve an effective democratic collective will and capacity to deliver it', as detailed below. At the level of relations with the state:

> the goal is to achieve equality constitutionally, legally and practically both individually and in terms of recognition of us as a national group that is entitled to its rights as stipulated by international conventions relating to the rights of minorities and indigenous populations. It is necessary to connect the struggle for rights in these areas with the struggle undertaken by other [Jewish] groups in the state to be fair to them. It is important to join forces in the struggle with others in Israeli society, so here we are referring to a partnership strategy with the Jewish community.[27]

Over the short term, the goal is to combat current Israeli government plans to pass legislation 'opposing our society based on ethnicity' and to support 'current projects and plans that envisage limited financial transfers for urban development and advancing economic facilities particularly in the employment sector', while not letting this be seen as a substitute for full equality.

Strategic options: complementary and alternative

The strategic options (paths) identified as leading to these goals match the matrix developed under the 'existing situation' (status quo) above. We cannot list the intricate web of interlocking strategic options here. But one central issue arises when there is a fork in the road and a choice may have to be made between two different broad directions. The main thrust of the report stresses cooperation with the Israeli political process (e.g., through representation in the Knesset, as has been the case since 1949) and reform from within. But at a certain point, if the current rightward trend in Israeli politics continues with further ethnically based and oppressive legislation, it may be necessary to move in a different direction and boycott what will by then have become an intolerable straitjacket:

> We may find that strategic – and not only tactical – Arab–Jewish partnership is a necessity, because every scenario drawn up later short of overt expulsion includes coexistence of Palestinians and Jews in the same space. Yet we might also discover the strength of using boycott as an action strategy in some cases, especially if the rightist forces in Israel enhance the nationalistic categorization process within the borders of the state.[28]

Both paths are seen to be legitimate and may need to be fine-tuned and combined if occasion demands.

Strategic means

The PCIG report is clear that strategic means must be consonant with strategic ends. The strategic goals of Palestinians in Israel are morally and legally compelling. This is identified as a central – in the end decisive – strategic strength. So this entails that the means must also be entirely consonant with international standards:

> Among the weaknesses of Arab Palestinian politics in Israel in the past has been the fact that it has been associated from time to time with external Arab centers and patronage, and in some instances has taken the form of association with a dictator or a totalitarian project that is rejected by Palestinian Arabs as citizens in Israel. Since our struggle rests on its moral and international legal strength, the means used to promote it must not contradict those principles – violent methods used could lead to our losing the fairness of our narrative and the war of narratives in its entirety. This relationship between means and ends, therefore, remains a key component in any strategic plan.[29]

139

The report ends by specifying the immediate priorities of *building internal capacity and empowering the community* (strategic legitimacy and authority); *engaging and influencing the Jewish-Israeli public* (including engagement with the Israeli Strategic Forum (ISF)); *clarifying relations with the Palestinian national movement* (for example, through engagement 'across the green line' with the broader Palestine Strategy Group (PSG)); and *invoking the support of regional and international allies and winning the war of words.* On the key issue of relations with the Jewish majority:

> we realize that any change in the status quo that leans towards improving our circumstances may be interpreted in the mentality of the Jewish society – in Israel and among the elites – as being an existential threat. This is due to the complex of fear of destruction resulting from the experience of the Jewish people in Europe prior to arrival in Palestine. We think that our community has instinctively understood this and so has worked tirelessly on non-violent political action as a historic choice to induce change.[30]

Emphasis is laid on exploring the potential for alliances with progressive Jewish constituencies in Israel that are also struggling for equality and justice:

> In our struggle we will benefit from possible partnerships with sectors in Jewish society that share our goal and vision regarding the idea of equality or democratic values or fair distribution of resources. Of course, this matter requires careful scrutiny of the map of allies, supporters and potential partners in each field of work and in following up on the outlined goals.

Although it is well understood that this may involve complicated trade-offs:

> As for other vulnerable segments in the Jewish community, which we may look to for advocating for the Palestinian Arab society here, they may be busy competing for the status of victimhood and attracting governmental aid/subsidies. Therefore, they may actually stand against the track of improvement and incite against the Arabs rather than advocate for them.[31]

Nevertheless, the overall thrust of the report is that, if there is ever to be proper Arab–Jewish partnership in Israel, the precondition has to be that Israel becomes a state in which Arab Palestinians *want* to be citizens:

> In light of what we view as a future that clearly consists of coexistence in most scenarios, we need to think seriously about adopting partnership

as a final strategy, as this emphasizes the potential of coexistence, joint action, joint production and a joint future. Doing so is part of shouldering responsibility for the desired future.[32]

Strategic engagement between the Palestinian Citizens of Israel Group (PCIG) and the Palestine Strategy Group (PSG)

Strategic engagement between the PCIG and PSG is innovatory and of great importance but will not be dwelt on here. This is now identified as a major project for the 2016–18 phase – Palestinian strategic thinking 'across the Green Line'. Here some PSG members are wary of separate PCIG strategic thinking because it may divide the Palestinian cause. The PSG sees itself as the 'mother' of the whole enterprise – and Palestinian Arabs in Israel as already represented in the PSG. But PCIG members, while acknowledging this, also want to emerge from under the shadow of both Israeli and Palestinian elites in order to define their own needs and aspirations. Here the PCIG sees itself as a possible 'bridge' because of its insight into, and understanding of, Israeli society.

Strategic engagement between the Palestinian Citizens of Israel Group (PCIG) and the Israeli Strategic Forum (ISF)

But what of engagement between Palestinian citizens of Israel (the minority) and Jewish citizens of Israel (the majority)? Here is the key new strategic terrain that is opened up by prior and ongoing collective strategic thinking within these identity groups. For all those wanting to transform the situation, this is the critical 'strategic gap' – the almost total absence of strategic engagement on this issue in Israel – that first needs to be filled before other alternatives become visible, let alone politically possible.

We saw in chapter 5 that, in 2012–15, in parallel with the creation of the Palestinian Citizens of Israel Group, the Israeli Strategic Forum was at the same time undertaking its third project – this time focused more within Israel than outside. This phase has been organized and run by the Van Leer Institute, Jerusalem. The title chosen for the project was 'Paths to a More Equal Israel', and a preliminary report was produced in September 2015 (as yet unpublished) called 'Is There a Path to a More Equal Israel?', hereafter referred to as ISF (2015).

141

Given space constraint – and confidentiality – the detailed discussions will not be commented on here. But one recurrent theme will be indicated because of its central bearing on the issue of Palestinians in Israel:

> Membership [of the Israeli Strategic Forum in this phase] is drawn from many sectors of Israeli Jewish society: ultraorthodox, secular, settler movements, Mizrahim [Jews of Middle Eastern and North African descent], Ashkenazim [Jews of European descent], people from different social classes, men and women, from left and right of the political centre, and from opposite ends of the Israeli spectrum . . . Due to this unusual mix, the participants were able to understand and reflect the dynamics and heterogeneity of Israeli-Jewish society, in a way that many research groups cannot.[33]

The need for collective strategic thinking is generated by the group's overarching commitment to overcoming internal (seemingly intractable) disputes to the point where collective strategic thinking and action becomes possible. Despite deep internal differences and 'fault-lines', ISF members share common ground and commitment to the best possible shared future for Israel. This includes common concern to create a 'more equal Israel', seen as integral to the enterprise. A central premise in our collective strategic thinking is that clear recognition of the depth and complexity of internal differences is essential for developing a strategic capacity to manage them. To gloss over or ignore internal differences for the sake of agreement is not in the overall strategic interest of the collectivity – in this case Israel.[34]

In relation to the Palestinian issue, the ISF was sharply divided:

> Even the definition of the Israeli–Palestinian conflict was under negotiation, with some group members seeing the problem as one of an *occupation*, which means that Israel has responsibility for the equality and inequality of all people living between the River [Jordan] and the Sea [Mediterranean]; while others framed it as a *security threat*, which positions the Palestinians in the West Bank exclusively as an external threat, which does not need to be considered in debates about equality and inequality in Israel.[35]

Nevertheless, because of the inclusive nature of the ISF, even those who did not want to engage with Palestinians outside Israel found that this could not be separated from the question of struggles for greater levels of equality within Israel.

At the very heart of all the discussions about equality in Israel was the recurrent theme of relations between Mizrahi (Middle Eastern) and Ashkenazi (European) Jewish Israelis – on some measures (such as the Central Bureau of Statistics, which uses father's place of birth as an index), some 30 to 35 per cent of Israeli Jews have Mizrahi (Asian and African) ancestry.[36] Most Mizrahim came to Israel in the 1950s and afterwards from surrounding predominantly Arab countries:

> The question of relations between Mizrahim and Ashkenazim – including relations between centre and periphery, class and economic differences, the tension between the European Zionist ethos and Mizrahi identity, the import of this tension for understanding inequality in Israel and the processes needed to change it – was the connecting thread among all the topics discussed – bringing together national political, regional, religious and socio-economic issues, as well as the core values of the society – narrative, history, association and vision.[37]

The epicentre of this highly charged strategic interchange was the question of the core symbolic talismans of European Zionism itself:

> The most turbulent discussions had to do with the key Zionist symbols: the *halutz* (pioneer) and the *kibbutznik* (resident on an agricultural collective, the original settlements in Israel); the status of the Holocaust as a unique and central historical event as well as its impact on the relations among Jews in Israel; and the perception of the Israeli Defense Forces (IDF) as a melting pot and as a site of morality and equality in regard to the internal relations among sectors in Israel . . .

In other words, many Mizrahim challenged key aspects of the prevailing Eurocentric narrative presented in chapter 5.

It was at once recognized that this raised profound issues in relation to the question of Palestinian citizens of Israel:

> It is worth noting that this is extremely similar to the way many Palestinian citizens analyze Israeli and Zionist hegemony. This is one of the conclusions we believe makes the group's work different to others – to understand these things as part of an Ashkenazi shaping of Zionism and Israel, as opposed to something all groups consent to and follow . . .[38] Some of the participants argued that the hierarchy of European (superiority) and Arab (inferiority) that accompanied Zionism and the Israeli regime can explain the situation in the Occupied Territories as well.[39]

On the other hand, as anticipated in the PCIG report described above, this does not mean that it is possible for Palestinian and Mizrahi Israelis to work together. On the contrary:

> Many times, and in different contexts, group members involved in the struggle for equality in Israel, for example that of the Mizrahi Jews in Israel, stressed that they find it hard to support the struggle for Palestinian rights. According to them, this is because every time

143

underprivileged Jewish groups demand equality, the response they receive from members of more privileged groups in Israel (e.g. the Ashkenazi, left of centre, elite) is that, while their struggle might be important, it can wait as Palestinians 'suffer more'. Some participants even called it the 'Ashkenazi-Palestinian alliance'.[40]

We have reached a critical point in the analysis. The role of Mizrahi Jewish citizens in relation to Palestinian citizens in Israel lies at the epicentre of the current impasse and has highly ambivalent or ironic features that emerge only through internal collective strategic thinking and subsequent strategic engagement of the kind set out in this book.

The connection to internal Israeli electoral politics

The 'Mizrahi vote' has played a key role in Israeli electoral politics ever since the 1977 'revolution' in which the 'right-wing' Likud party effectively replaced the 'left-wing' Labor Party as the 'natural party of government'. Since then Likud has been supported by a preponderance of Mizrahi votes. This remains the case even though Mizrahim predominate in the less privileged social strata and on the 'periphery' of elite Israeli society, so that on socio-economic issues they might be expected to support parties on the 'left'. But that is not the case. In the 2015 election, for example, in Jerusalem, with its Mizrahi majority, Likud received 24 per cent of the vote and Zionist Union (mainly Labor) only 10 per cent. In Tel Aviv, on the other hand, with its Ashkenazi majority, Meretz received 13 per cent of the vote and Zionist Union 34 per cent. Zionist Union won in twenty-eight of the thirty-three wealthiest cities; Likud won in sixty-four of seventy-seven Israeli cities lower down the socio-economic scale.[41]

Here, then, is a crucial challenge for Arab Palestinians in Israel, one that needs to be explored in strategic engagement between the PCIG and the ISF if the declared PCIG strategic goal of 'partnership as a final strategy' is ever to become possible. This in turn links to the electoral 'revolution' called for by Hilik Bar, as noted at the beginning of this chapter.[42] As the PCIG report concludes, under almost all scenarios (short of expulsion), Jewish and Palestinian Arab citizens will continue to live together in Israel. According to several opinion polls, most Palestinians in Israel would rather live in Israel than in a Palestinian state. A pilot study of workshops, in which ISF and PCIG members (and others) pioneered the possibility for a strategic exchange of this kind ('Strategic Thinking for Citizens'), made it clear that on almost no major issue (for example, whether there should be a Palestinian state, or whether it would be good for Israelis if President Bashar al-Assad in Syria were toppled) did all Palestinian Israelis think one way and all Jewish Israelis think another way.[43]

Conclusion

This chapter has shown how new possibilities for strategic exchange can be opened up across and between identity groups, based on ongoing collective strategic thinking within them. In the first part of the chapter, this was seen to apply to strategic engagement between Israelis and Palestinians in general. In the second part, it was seen to apply also to Palestinians citizens of Israel, in relation both to non-Palestinian Israelis and to non-Israeli Palestinians. The strategic terrain is found to be more complex than was realized. Strategic options are seen to be more varied. This brings new challenges but also new possibilities for change, and can thus inform the efforts of third parties to play a more substantial role at the third level of strategic engagement. Prospects for success in negotiation depend on a comparison between *alternatives*. This theme is taken up in the next chapter.

8

THE KERRY INITIATIVE AND THE ROLE OF THIRD PARTIES

In this chapter we look at the remarkable attempt between July 2013 and April 2014 by US Secretary of State John Kerry to broker a final settlement to the Israel–Palestine conflict. This will cast light on the role of third parties in mediating intractable conflicts. The central argument compares the principled negotiation approach (PN) in conflict resolution looked at in Part I with what Amira Schiff and I call the strategic negotiation approach (SN) that forms the third level of strategic engagement. This chapter is based on our joint article.[1]

The argument is that, in intractable asymmetric conflicts, principled negotiation (PN) needs to be guided by a prior strategic negotiation approach (SN), which focuses on the prerequisites that make principled negotiation possible. SN is not pre-negotiation, nor is it pre-pre-negotiation. It has a broader remit that connects internal strategic thinking within conflict parties to the wider conditioning context at different levels (local, national, regional, international) within which the negotiations are set.

The chapter begins with the ten 'elements' described by chief Palestinian negotiator, Dr Saeb Erekat, as constituting the 'Western' approach to negotiation.[2] He sees these as characteristic of the negotiation process in the Israel–Palestine conflict with which he has been engaged since the time of the 1993 Oslo Accords. Erekat has been involved in Palestinian negotiations at the highest level throughout this period and has been head of the PLO's Negotiations Affairs Department since it was set up in 2003. In this capacity, he attributes what we will still call the 'principled negotiation' approach to Roger Fisher of the Harvard Negotiations Project[3] and, in particular, cites the advice and training given to Palestinians through the internationally backed Negotiations Support Unit for the Palestinian Authority in Ramallah.[4] In an interesting recent study he argues that these principles were anticipated by the fourth Muslim Caliph, Ali Bin Abi Taleb.[5]

In relation to the third level of strategic engagement that is the topic in this chapter, a strategic negotiation (SN) approach sees would-be third-party peacemakers not as neutral, impartial or dis-interested, but as immersed in the conflict and therefore themselves in need of an effective strategy to bring about the outcomes they desire. In this enterprise they would be wise, therefore, to inform themselves as much as they can about what is revealed at the other two levels – collective strategic thinking within conflict parties and strategic engagement across and between them – as discussed in earlier chapters.

Conflict resolution: the elements of principled negotiation

The elements of principled negotiation as understood by the chief Palestinian negotiator include the four 'basic points' listed in Roger Fisher's and William Ury's original definition in *Getting to Yes* (1981) that we looked at in chapter 3 (pp. 30–1). These were to separate the people from the problem; to focus on interests, not positions; to invent multiple options for mutual gain; and to ensure that the result is based on objectively verifiable standards. These four elements appear in Erekat's list as elements (iii), (iv), (v) and (vi) respectively. Guided by John Murray's and Terry Barnett's 'Negotiation training workshop' paper (2007), Erekat also includes *alternatives* ('best alternatives to a negotiated agreement') (ii), *com-munication* (vii), and *commitment* (viii). In addition, we will add three further elements that Erekat refers to but does not number: the nature of the negotiation process itself (i), the requirement that 'moderates' rather than 'extremists' prevail (ix), and the role of third parties (x).

Box 8.1 gives the full set of ten elements that are seen to define a conflict resolution ('principled') approach to negotiation. The focus from the outset is on negotiation communication *between* the conflict parties. And the aim is to set aside the radical disagreement at the core of the conflict in order to search for mutual accommodation, if not consensus.

Box 8.1   The elements of principled negotiation

(i)   The starting point in principled negotiation is the negotiation process itself. It begins with the hypothetical proposition: *if* negotiation is to be successful, *then* these are the elements that must constitute it. Everything else follows from this.

(ii) 'Conflict parties are not obliged to accept an agreement that is worse than available options in the event that no agreement is reached.'[6] This refers to the 'best alternative to a negotiated agreement' (BATNA). The process must be voluntary and unconstrained.

(iii) Separate the people from the problem. Any animosity in relations between the individuals and institutions involved should be suspended so that all parties can 'deal with disagreements in a creative way' and thus 'improve the possibility for all parties to work jointly'.[7]

(iv) Focus on interests, not positions. Conflict parties should set aside 'positional debate' or radical disagreement (what they say they want) and focus instead on their 'basic interests' (why they want what they say they want). These are often non-zero sum and therefore more amenable to mutual accommodation. Positions are superficial. Interests (or needs) are the 'underlying reasons for those positions'.[8] Conflict parties may not at first realize this.

(v)   Invent multiple options looking for mutual gains before deciding what to do. 'Options comprise the possible space of possibilities available to the parties for reaching an agreement. An option can be put forward on the table of negotiations, and the agreement will be ideal if it takes place as a result of what is best for the set of options, especially if all the possibilities of common gains for the parties have been used well.'[9]

(vi) Insist that the result is based on some objective standard. 'Results should be based on objective or fair standards' if the agreement is to be legitimate. 'Legitimacy points to the fairness of the agreement and all parties express satisfaction with an agreement that is based on external landmarks, principles and standards outside the will of the parties.'[10]

(vii) Communication should be kept open throughout, so that 'each party understands the other party even if both parties are in disagreement.' Conflict parties should listen carefully to each other and, above all, avoid the 'blame game': one party 'should not blame others'; there should be 'no blame' and 'no accusations'.[11]

(viii) Premature commitment should be avoided, because otherwise 'each party will present the positions they think will help them in strengthening their negotiation ground, and this will lead to neglecting the search for common ground on which to reach an agreement that takes into consideration the interests of both parties.'[12] The aim is to reach final agreement, so commitment should be left to the end.

(ix) It is important that moderates prevail, not extremists who refuse to compromise, because 'the overall aim is to find common ground, with the objective of reaching an agreement on the basis of a win–win formula.'[13]

(x) Third-party mediators should gain the trust of all parties by being neutral, impartial and disinterested.

Why did the Kerry initiative fail between July 2013 and April 2014?

We are now in a position to gain insight into why the Kerry initiative failed during this period. The following background section is taken from the work of Amira Schiff.[14]

Background

In late March 2013, John Kerry, Secretary of State in the Obama administration, initiated diplomatic efforts, following a three-year hiatus, to renew direct negotiations between Prime Minister Binyamin Netanyahu and Chairman Mahmoud Abbas. Kerry set a very ambitious initial target for the talks, which were renewed in July 2013: a comprehensive peace treaty for a two-state solution within about nine months. The Palestinians committed to enter the talks and not to walk away from the negotiating table, and they promised to freeze all unilateral steps against Israel in the UN during the nine-month period slated for negotiations. The Palestinians demanded that Israel reciprocate with significant confidence-building measures: an indefinite freeze on construction over the 1967 'Green Line' and an additional release of 104 Palestinians imprisoned before the 1993 Oslo Accords. They also demanded that the talks be based on the 1967 lines as the international border. Israel agreed to a four-stage release of the prisoners and significantly to limit settlement construction during the months of negotiation.[15] The sides agreed in advance to discuss all the core issues during the negotiations and that the final accord would end the conflict and the demands of both sides.

On the basis of the agreement to resume talks, Kerry sent a letter of guarantees to both sides in which he declared that the US position was that the borders of the future Palestinian state should be based on the 1967 lines with land swaps.[16] At the same time he sent Israel a letter of guarantees clarifying that the US position was that the borders of the Palestinian state would not be identical to the 1967 lines: border adjustments would be made in accordance with the reality on the ground – implying recognition of the Sharon–Bush letter regarding the large settlement blocs. This letter also made clear the US acceptance of the key Israeli demand to be recognized as a Jewish state.[17]

The USA intended to play an active role in the talks, to oversee their progress, to resolve crises, and to offer bridging proposals if necessary.

From the outset, the Israelis and Palestinians were unable to agree on the agenda for the talks. There were wide gaps between them on all the core issues, as well as considerable scepticism on both sides.[18]

Although Kerry had intended to mediate between the two sides in direct talks in order to reach a detailed final status accord, he had already realized in mid-November 2013 that, in light of the vast disagreements, this goal was not realistic. At this stage the Americans switched to indirect negotiations via proximity talks aimed at a more modest goal: the signing of a framework document by the end of March, outlining negotiations between the two sides that would define the principles for resolving the core issues. Kerry and 'special envoy' Martin Indyk[19] conducted intensive contacts on the document, shuttled between the Israelis and the Palestinians, and tried to bridge the gaps.[20] However, here too, after they reached some understandings with Netanyahu, the Americans discovered (in Kerry's meeting with Abbas in Paris on 19 February) that these terms were very far from what Abbas was ready to accept. The gaps between the sides were too wide, making it impossible to reach agreement on this sort of framework document.[21]

Kerry adopted an even more modest goal in late February 2014: an American document of principles that both sides could accept 'in principle' while expressing reservations about some of its content. The document of principles was designed to enable continuation of the nine months of final status negotiations that were supposed to conclude in April 2014. The Americans understood that, without reaching understandings on the document, it would be very difficult for Netanyahu to carry out the fourth and last round of prisoner releases, which would lead to the collapse of the entire process. Consequently, they began a marathon series of conversations in order to extend the negotiations.[22] However, the gaps between the sides were still too big.[23]

Under intense public pressure, Israel refused to release the fourth group of prisoners on the scheduled date without a Palestinian commitment not to quit the peace talks at the end of April, as well as refrain from resuming unilateral action at the UN. Abbas, on his part, emphasized that, if the prisoners were not released, he would not even consider extending the negotiations and would immediately reactivate Palestinian UN activities. The Palestinians rejected proposed alternatives to the prison release and refused American compromise proposals for continuing the process, preferring 'unilaterally' (for the Palestinians, this was a move from a 'bilateral' to an 'international' framework) to seek acceptance into international institutions.[24]

In June tensions increased rapidly. Three Israeli teenagers were kidnapped and killed, followed by a revenge killing of a Palestinian boy and increased rocket fire from Hamas-controlled Gaza. This led to an Israeli response and the seven-week war in Gaza.

In October 2014, after the Gaza action ended, Kerry tried to promote a new diplomatic initiative as an alternative to the unilateral or 'international' Palestinian efforts at the Security Council. Kerry checked with Netanyahu if he would agree to an initiative that would include resuming negotiations on the borders of the Palestinian state based on the 1967 lines with land swaps. Netanyahu did not reject Kerry's ideas out of hand. At the time the Palestinians were trying to win the support of nine members of the Security Council for their request to define a timetable for ending the Israeli occupation of the West Bank in their quest to establish a state. The proposal was rejected by the Security Council in late December 2014.[25] In early January 2015, the Palestinian authority submitted a request to join twenty-two international conventions, including the Rome Statute of the International Criminal Court (ICC) in the Hague.

Analysis

It is illuminating to use the elements of principled negotiation given in the previous section to pinpoint why conflict resolution failed. This is not to set up a 'straw man' by suggesting that these elements were explicitly endorsed by other negotiators or mediators. It is to use the chief Palestinian negotiator's understanding of what was advocated in the Negotiations Support Unit as a useful lens through which to evaluate the process. We suggest that the deepest reason was that conflict resolution itself was premature. The assumptions on which it is based did not yet apply. The conditions necessary did not yet exist. And the conflict parties were not yet prepared to think and behave as third-party peacemakers wanted. We have seen why to focus on relations *between* conflict parties and to neglect internal differences and debates *within* them is a mistake in attempts to negotiate agreement between complex entities. The Kerry team cannot be said to have ignored this and, indeed, went to considerable lengths to engage security constituencies in Israel, for example. But it is questionable how well informed the mediators were about the ways in which such differential moves were likely to be received reciprocally on the Palestinian side, as commented on below.

We will now consider the elements of principled negotiation in turn, and in the same order as that given in box 8.1.

(i) It became plain early on that the negotiation process itself was not so much part of the solution as part of the problem. Given the asymmetry between the conflict parties, for Israel the process of bilateral negotiation brokered by the United States was essential as the only avenue towards a settlement. For Palestinians, on the contrary, for the same reason the process of bilateral negotiation was almost universally seen to be an instrument of continuing occupation, a mask behind which ever-deeper Israeli colonization of the territories in question could proceed incrementally – as had already been the case for more than twenty years.

(ii) The 'best alternatives to a negotiated agreement' (BATNAs) were entirely different for the two sides, but in both cases they were seen as better than what was offered by the process and likely outcome of the negotiation itself. As possessor – and in light of the catastrophic consequences of Israel's withdrawal from the Gaza strip in 2005 – Israel throughout perceived a better alternative to the risks of withdrawal from Judea and Samaria, namely continuing with the status quo. As challenger, on the other hand, Palestinians had a perceived better alternative to what they saw as the indefinite perpetuation of fruitless bilateral negotiations, namely the 'internationalization' route, already successfully pursued, for example, in securing overwhelming international support for UN General Assembly Resolution (A/RES/67/19) in November 2012.

(iii) Any idea of separating the 'people' from the 'problem' was premature. It was, rather, more a question of understanding – and therefore anticipating and managing – damaging and mutually opposed emotional impacts, such as that over prisoner release, where Palestinian jubilation at the liberation of martyrs compounded Israeli horror at the release of murderers. Much of this was beyond the power of the mediators to alter, such as what the Israeli public regarded as continued incitement by PA officials close to Abbas, as well as in the education system and Palestinian media, against the existence of Israel,[26] and almost universal scepticism among the Palestinian public about the possibility of reaching an accord with the Netanyahu government. But lack of trust was sometimes increased rather than decreased by the way the process was conducted.[27] What were intended as confidence-building measures often had the opposite effect.[28] For example, for Israel the concession on prisoner release meant that talks would resume without freezing settlement construction, which in turn undermined Palestinian support for the negotiations. What was meant to strengthen Abbas ended up weakening him politically. For the Israeli public, the final destructive chord was struck by the reconciliation pact between Fatah and Hamas in late April 2014 and Fatah's agreement to form a unity government with Hamas and Islamic Jihad – despite widely publicized declarations by their leaders that they did not recognize Israel and would not abandon the path of terrorism. In the light of this, and the internal limits on each party, it is hard to see how Kerry could have been expected to separate the people from the problem, especially in such a limited period of time.

(iv) The principled negotiation advice to pass over what the parties said (positions) in order to focus on supposedly more amenable underlying 'interests', which the conflict parties themselves might not yet realize, was again precipitate. Key constituencies within the conflict parties did not welcome 'instructions' about what their own long-term 'best interests' were from outsiders who did not live in the region. As argued below, in intractable conflicts it is best to try to understand what the complex interrelations between the existing positions *are* before attempting to alter them.

(v) The notion of brainstorming options in a search for mutual gain was also not yet possible. Conflict parties evidently were not ready for this. From the outset of the contacts, the gaps between the sides on all the core issues were wide, there was great scepticism on both sides, and their assessment of the likelihood of reaching a final accord within nine months was very low. The situation did not change during the course of the negotiations. The talks conducted under

American leadership between August and December of 2013 between Justice Minister Tzipi Livni and Yitzhak Molcho (Netanyahu's representative) from the Israeli side and Saeb Erekat and Mohammad Shtayyeh from the Palestinian side did not lead to a breakthrough. The two sides focused on presenting their basic positions and, reportedly, did not include the 'give and take' expected in any negotiation.[29] What *was* needed – as indicated below – was rigorous exploration with the conflict parties of the interrelationship between different strategic scenarios.

(vi) The stipulation that outcomes should be seen to be 'legitimate' and 'based on objective or fair standards' begged the main question. For example, the whole nature and application of international law was itself part of what was in dispute (for example, disagreement about the right to self-determination and Geneva IV if this was an occupation, or equal citizens' rights, indigenous rights, and minority rights if it was not).

(vii) To advocate avoiding the 'blame game' in the interest of preserving communication was to overlook a key aspect of the strategic struggle. For example, it was central to Palestinian strategy that, although bilateral negotiation is regarded as an instrument for perpetuating occupation, it must be Israel that is seen to be responsible for its breakdown – otherwise the central Palestinian strategy of internationalization is undermined. Israelis blamed Palestinians for repeatedly refusing a two-state outcome since the UN partition resolution of 29 November 1947. This was, and is, integral to the whole Israeli case.

(viii) The idea that the agreement must be a final settlement – although demanded by Israel[30] – is to overlook the fact that in nearly all intractable asymmetric conflicts this is not the case. For example, in Northern Ireland, the 1998 Good Friday agreement did not end the conflict. Nor did the 2006 St Andrews agreement, which eventually brought in the biggest Unionist party, the DUP. Sinn Fein continues to struggle for a united Ireland, albeit via the route of power sharing, not the armed struggle. Were this not the case, the Republicans would never have entered the peace process in the first place.

(ix) You cannot make peace only between 'moderates'. Israel Beiteinu and Jewish Home – at various times Israeli government coalition partners – were (and are) implacably opposed to what the American mediators were trying to achieve. So were many in Likud – including Netanyahu himself. There are similarly strong constituencies opposed to such a settlement on the Palestinian side. Abbas was weak within his own political camp and, now that nearly ten years had passed since the presidential elections of 2005, lacked legitimacy among the Palestinian public at large. Palestinian society was immersed in a deep political crisis. Hamas fiercely opposed Abbas's diplomatic efforts. In Abbas's own Fatah party there were also reservations about negotiating with the Netanyahu government. Throughout the process many senior Palestinian figures favoured returning to 'unilateral' action at the UN and exerting international pressure on Israel.[31] As noted earlier, the important distinction is between 'extremists of ends', who do not want to give up central values but do not espouse violence, and 'extremists of means', who do.

(x) Finally, in intractable conflicts, third-party mediators are not neutral, impartial or disinterested, however much they may want to describe themselves as such. It is not up to them. Third parties want to change the way conflict parties think and are therefore bound to antagonize central constituencies on both sides – particularly as the peace process goes on, which is what happened in the case of the Kerry initiative. So they too need a strategy in order to 'win'. The mediator's conduct was perceived by the two sides to be asymmetrical, but in opposite directions. From the Palestinian point of view, the stance of the American mediators was widely seen to be compromised by the role of the United States in 'guarding Israel's back' – for example, by supplying weaponry to maintain Israeli military preponderance and through their support in the UN Security Council. Israelis felt that Kerry exerted disproportionately heavy pressure on Israel to accept the framework agreement and that he refrained from investing similar efforts vis-à-vis Abbas.[32] American pressure on the Netanyahu government to moderate its stance was perceived by the Israeli public as unfair and as a misguided effort aimed at pushing Israel towards unacceptable concessions.[33] For example, in order to influence public opinion in Israel, the secretary of state made an exceptional public statement on the alleged danger Israel faced from boycotts and international isolation if it failed to reach an accord and argued that Israel would become an apartheid state if it did not achieve peace. This received extensive publicity in Israel, much of it highly critical.[34]

In summary, as a result of the deep discrepancies and imbalances inherent in the conflict, the US mediator was caught between these conflicting strategic priorities, seen by one party (Palestinians) to be part of the problem in terms of the negotiation *process* and by the other (Israelis) to be initially closer to their opponents in terms of proposed *outcome*. The result was that key moves made by the mediator in order to save the talks had the unintended (but not difficult to predict) effect of ending them. The shift in mid-November 2013, from the aim of securing a final status agreement by direct talks to the lesser aim of signing a framework agreement by indirect negotiation and proximity talks, unsurprisingly confirmed the worst suspicions of most Palestinians: that the United States had reneged and that the process had reverted to previous toothless 'statements of principles', etc., which left the initiative perpetually in the hands of Israel. This was further confirmed in their eyes in late February 2014, when the goal was watered down further to being merely the production of an American document of principles in order to extend the talks beyond April. In parallel with this, the US secretary of state undertook intensive discussions with Israel on the framework document in order to bring what was seen as the more recalcitrant side on board. Israelis may have felt unfairly leaned on by this, but more devastating was the widespread Palestinian conviction that a separate negotiation was being conducted with Israel, that the outcome would be sprung on Palestinians, and that this would trap them into having to accept some form of non-sovereign 'pseudo-state' that would leave Israel in effective permanent control of the whole of Palestine. This was the reason why the second Palestinian negotiator, Dr Mohammad Shtayyeh, resigned permanently in anger in December 2013. American mediators appear *not* to have anticipated the consequent events of February and March 2014, when the PA president summarily rejected the whole package.[35]

This is not to say that the US mediators themselves specifically subscribed to particular conflict resolution elements as listed here. But, in the light of considerations such as the above, it is to say that in a number of instances they can be seen to have underestimated – and misunderstood – the multiple and complex interconnection of factors that was blocking their way. Structural factors, and substantive factors, as well as some factors related to the conduct of the American mediation approach itself, have been identified. Obstacles of this kind are to be expected in severely asymmetric intractable conflicts. They need to be recognized by would-be peacemakers, who consequently from the outset require a sufficiently informed, flexible and comprehensive strategy of their own for anticipating and overcoming them. That the Kerry initiative was relatively deficient in this respect, despite the heroic efforts of the secretary of state himself, is suggested by the striking discrepancy between the initial optimism of some of the leading mediators that a final settlement could be reached within nine months and the almost universal pessimism among the conflict parties that it could not.[36]

What is the alternative? Principled negotiation and strategic negotiation compared

What is the alternative? Faced with the linguistic intractability and radical disagreement characteristic of intense political conflict, the foregoing analysis suggests that it is best to begin not where third parties want conflict parties to be, but where they are. This means switching from principled negotiation (PN) to strategic negotiation (SN). As seen earlier in this book, a strategic negotiation approach promotes strategic engagement within, across and between conflict parties, including third parties – beginning with a focus on collective internal strategic thinking in which conflict parties attempt to determine where they are, where they want to go, and how they get there. Only in this way is it possible to analyse what would need to happen for antagonists to enter negotiations, reach agreement and implement agreement – and for would-be third-party peacemakers to act accordingly. Instead of beginning *between* conflict parties, strategic negotiation looks through a wider lens that relates what goes on *within* them to the regional and global *context* where complex conflicts are now increasingly structured and defined.

Strategic negotiation defines three strategic conditions for the possibility of successful negotiation (see box 8.2). So the first question in an SN approach to intractable conflict is why one or more of the conflict parties would prefer alternatives to a negotiated settlement under one or more of these three conditions. The starting – and ending – point in the investigation is what conflict parties say. This refers not just to leaderships but also to the wider internal and cross-cutting constituencies, particularly among non-unified actors, that are likely to affect overall strategic calculations. (In the case of non-democratic states, yet other considerations apply, which are considered in chapter 9.) Whatever the external prohibitions or inducements, it is in the end the internal debate within conflict parties that is the critical arena. So this provides the first clue for would-be third-party peacemakers: promote

157

Box 8.2 Strategic conditions for successful negotiations

Condition (1) All parties must conclude that entering negotiations is better for them than not entering negotiations.

Condition (2) All parties must conclude that reaching agreement is better for them than not reaching agreement.

Condition (3) All parties must conclude that implementing agreement is better for them than not implementing agreement.

Box 8.3 Strategic scenarios and the Kerry initiative

Scenario (A) An independent Palestinian state as internationally agreed

Scenario (B) Permanent effective Israeli control over the disputed territories

Scenario (C) Indefinite continuation of the status quo – incremental Israeli settlement in the West Bank and international life-support for an otherwise unviable Palestinian Authority

---

and learn from inclusive strategic thinking and strategic debate within the conflict parties.

A good way of seeing the importance of focusing on collective internal strategic thinking in this way is to realize the central role it plays in linking strategic scenarios to the conditions necessary for a revival of principled negotiation. This is especially so if one of the scenarios represents what the third-party peacemakers want as the negotiated outcome. As an illustration, we will revisit the simplified set of scenarios looked at in chapters 5 and 6 (see box 8.3).

Once again, in this abbreviated summary we do not yet take in other scenarios and sub-scenarios. For the sake of clarity at this point, we do not include what is sometimes misleadingly called the 'one-state solution' (for example, the idea of a bi-national or unitary democratic state) as discussed in earlier chapters in the case study. The main choice facing negotiators and general publics during the Kerry talks was between a Palestinian state and no Palestinian state. A 'one-state solution' so far had no serious strategic thinking associated with it. Where we do bring this in is at the end under Plan B below – arguing that this is now exactly what does need serious strategic evaluation – for instance, by third parties wishing to clarify real alternatives for the conflict parties including key constituencies within them (this is scenario (D) in box 5.2, p. 000).

In setting out this analysis we will briefly revisit strategic considerations looked at separately in chapters 5 and 6, but now brought together and seen from the perspective of the would-be third-party peacemaker.

If we take scenario (A) as, roughly, the outcome that the US secretary of state hoped might emerge from the negotiations, what inhibited the conflict parties from negotiating, agreeing and implementing it?

We have seen in chapter 6 that, under condition (1) (entering negotiations), many Palestinians as challengers perceived that they had a better strategic alternative to the *process* of the bilateral negotiation, namely an internationalized route to statehood. So the main question for the third-party mediator here was how this could be overcome. How could Palestinians be persuaded to persist with the bilateral negotiation process?

Under condition (2) (reaching agreement), on the other hand, we have seen in chapter 5 that it is Israelis, as possessors, who see a perpetually better alternative, namely scenario (C). How can third parties help to change these strategic calculations, so that scenario (B) is seen by Israelis to carry greater risks, scenario (A) is seen to carry fewer risks and greater incentives, and scenario (C) is seen to be rapidly running out so that the strategic choice for Israelis is between (A) and (B)? For example, can greater prominence be given to economic and other – political, cultural, and even spiritual – incentives for embracing scenario (A)?

Under condition (2), most Palestinians do not see a better alternative to scenario (A) (so long as it includes provisions on all the issues already adumbrated in UN General Assembly resolutions). But, because they have lost faith in the bilateral 'Oslo' route, they do not expect this any time soon. So in the meantime their focus is on coordinating domestic and international resistance against what they see as the already existing 'apartheid' reality of scenario (B). How can third parties help to convince Palestinians that violent means are counter-productive; that, to be attainable, scenario (A) has to include reassurance that a 'right of return' will not compromise the existing Israeli state; and that the withdrawal from Judea and Samaria will not repeat the Gaza scenario in which evacuated land has, since 2005, consistently been used as a launching pad for rockets?

Finally, under condition (3), implementation, both Israelis and Palestinians would have severe problems if an agreement were actually reached. An Israeli government would find it difficult to survive in the face of fierce resistance from settlers and the political right if an agreement was anything like most international interpretations of scenario (A). For Palestinians, there is the key question of how Hamas leaders would be prevailed upon to accept and assent to implement an agreement to which they are as yet principally and politically opposed. In addition, a weak and divided Palestinian leadership would be hard pressed to survive a strong internal backlash if an agreement was seen to neglect the interests of Palestinians in Israel, Jerusalem, Gaza and the near and far diaspora, such as ensuring 'the right of return'. How can third parties help to alleviate these inhibitions for negotiating parties from the beginning, because from the outset they are blocks to successful negotiation – what greater disincentive for a negotiator could there be than the likelihood that agreement will mean its loss of power?

From a strategic negotiation perspective, all three conditions have to be considered together by US mediators from the start, so that, having entered negotiations, there are already strategies in place in case of both success and failure. In the case of success, it is the period after an agreement that is often the most precarious, as shown after 1993 (Plan A would be to anticipate this). In the case of failure, the danger is that violence will result from disappointed hopes and the consequent strategic vacuum, as happened after 2000 – and seems to be happening again at the time of writing (Plan B would be to fill this vacuum).

On this ongoing basis, we have seen earlier in this case study how further strategic space is opened by including other players (for example, Palestinians in Israel) and other issues (alternatives to the status quo that otherwise do not appear on the radar screen – such as possible confederal arrangements between the State of Israel and a future Palestinian state). Unlikely though some of these may at first appear, imaginative statecraft demands that they be factored in from the start to strategic debate about short-term, medium-term and long-term possibilities and goals. Negotiation is all about weighing up *alternatives*, so it is a possibly fatal impoverishment of negotiation not to argue out all the alternatives that emerge from prior and ongoing sustained strategic engagement.

In chapters 5 and 6 we have also noted the importance of uncovering the deeper levels of heuristic engagement that underpin the whole possibility space for a negotiated accommodation in the first place. We have seen how beneath strategic considerations lie, not subjective 'narratives', but lived realities. How can third parties best understand and handle this explosive dynamic? By recognizing that they do not

160

understand it. For deep reasons to be discussed further in chapter 10, there is no adequate third-party theory of radical disagreement. Third parties – whether mediators or academic experts – do not know more than the protagonists. There is no 'view from nowhere'. Intervening third parties are part of the struggle. They need to realize this. A strategic negotiation (SN) approach is based on humility.

Summing up

We can now sum up the differences between principled negotiation (conflict resolution) and a strategic negotiation approach (conflict engagement) to intractable conflicts, apply this to the 2013–14 Kerry initiative, and ask what would need to happen from a strategic engagement perspective if there were to be an attempt to revive something similar. Box 8.4 lists the differences between principled negotiation (PN) and strategic negotiation (SN) in an admittedly somewhat starkly drawn format. For example, the strategic aim of peacemakers (internal as well as third party) can be said to be to persuade conflicting societies and leaderships that an NA (negotiated agreement) is better than any BA (best alternative) under each of the three strategic conditions listed in box 8.2 (p. 158). This requires sustained strategic engagement before, during and after the negotiation process, in which the focus of SN is to link collective strategic thinking within conflict parties to the wider regional and international strategic context (about which relatively little is said in this book). Chapters 4 through 7 have set out and illustrated the kind of work that needs to be done here. This chapter shows how, in the light of this, prospective peacemakers (internal as well as third party) are then able to understand the complex interplay of comparative perceived strategic advantage and disadvantage of differing scenarios for a range of relevant constituencies. This pinpoints what blocks a desired outcome and suggests what needs to be done, who needs to be influenced, and how this can be best achieved.

At the time of the 2013–14 Kerry initiative, the following were some of the questions asked from a strategic negotiation perspective, based on the understanding that, in intractable asymmetric conflicts, a powerful mediator requires such a strategy from the outset:

- What is the preferred outcome of the negotiations for the US secretary of state? Is it scenario (A)? If so, what is his strategy for attaining this goal? What strategic prerequisites are needed? How can these be brought about?

Box 8.4 Principled negotiation and strategic negotiation compared

(i) Principled negotiation sees the negotiation as an end to the conflict; strategic negotiation sees the negotiation as part of the conflict.

(ii) Principled negotiation assumes symmetry between conflict parties; strategic negotiation sees asymmetry as a major factor to be engaged with.

(iii) Principled negotiation wants to separate the people from the problem; strategic negotiation sees people (the fusion of facts, values, emotions, actions) as part of the problem to be addressed.

(iv) Principled negotiation wants to focus on interests, not positions; strategic negotiation begins from where conflict parties are and takes positions (what conflict parties say, including strategic planning) seriously.

(v) Principled negotiation wants conflict parties to look for mutual gains; strategic negotiation wants conflict parties to think strategically (e.g., evaluate scenarios, etc.).

(vi) Principled negotiation wants agreed outcomes to be based on objective standards; strategic negotiation sees the definition of objective standards as part of the disagreement to be overcome.

(vii) Principled negotiation wants to avoid the 'blame game'; strategic negotiation sees the blame game as integral to the negotiations – and as a possible weapon for third-party peacemakers.

(viii) In principled negotiation, final agreements end the conflict; in strategic negotiation, 'final agreements' in hitherto intractable conflicts usually lead to a 'continuation of the conflict by other means'.

(ix) Principled negotiation sees the removal of extremism as a precondition; in strategic negotiation, the precondition is to separate extremists of ends from extremists of means.

(x) In principled negotiation, third-party peacemakers should be neutral, impartial and disinterested; in strategic negotiation, peacemakers should think and act strategically in order to 'win' (i.e., succeed in transforming internal conflict party evaluations of strategic alternatives so that a successful negotiated outcome is in each case seen to be the least bad option).

- Does he begin from an understanding that the process of negotiation is itself part of the struggle? Does he see asymmetry as a major factor to be overcome?
- How does he propose to surmount the Israeli perception that at the moment scenario (C) carries fewer strategic risks (and

continues to offer more strategic opportunities) than scenario (A) – whatever the long-term difficulties may be if scenario (C) is internationally seen progressively to approximate towards scenario (B) – including the additional perception that agreement to scenario (A) may be fatal for the incumbent government?

- How does he propose to overcome the Palestinian identification of the bilateral negotiation process, and the US role in it, with the continuing status quo that the talks are meant to end and the subsequent Palestinian preference for 'internationalizing' the peace process as the preferred alternative?
- How can he reduce internal opposition to the negotiation process/ outcome in Israel and among Palestinians – or at least ensure that steps taken by the mediator are not misrepresented in harmful ways within those constituencies?
- What negative and positive inducements is he able to deploy? Is he prepared to use the 'blame game' as a means of putting pressure on the conflict parties? Is he prepared to bring in other third parties to increase pressure – for example, from the Quartet or the Arab League?
- If negotiations succeed, what preparations has he made to underpin the dangerous and long period of implementation? How can he encourage Hamas's collaboration and willingness to implement an agreement when signed?
- If negotiations fail, what is his Plan B? Can the secretary of state communicate Plan B to the conflict parties straight away – together with a strong sense that it will be carried out – in order to be able to use it as a tool to add leverage to Plan A?

It is questions such as these that are identified as critical from a strategic negotiation perspective and will apply whatever form a follow-up to Kerry may, or may not, take. In fact, we could sum up the whole approach as an attempt to bring out into the open the 'strategic struggle between the Plan Bs'. What *alternatives* are envisaged by the embattled parties (including the mediator) to the mediator's preferred Plan A, which is for the negotiation to end in an agreed settlement? At the moment neither Israel nor the Palestinians have publicly clarified, thought through, or argued out what the alternatives are. Nor, crucially, have third parties. European governments, for example, continually repeat that a negotiated two-state 'solution' is the only way of bringing the conflict to an end. For years we have been told that there is now only a six-month window of opportunity and that we are in the 'last chance saloon'. But, to my knowledge, no European

163

government has spelt out what the alternative is in case there is no Palestinian state.[37] Until that is made clear and conveyed to the conflicting parties, and they perceive that this alternative (Plan B) is both imminent and worse than the process/outcome of a negotiated two-state settlement (Plan A), there is little substance to the idea of a 'mutually hurting stalemate', 'way out' or 'mutually enticing opportunity', as will be argued in chapter 9. So let us have not less radical disagreement, but more. Let us bring into the open the internal debates and the inclusive strategic thinking about possible futures of conflict parties and third parties alike. Let us, on this ongoing basis, actively promote strategic engagement across and between all those involved, so that the short-term, medium-term and long-term implications are for the first time properly argued out. Let policy-making be informed by this process so that standards of decision-making are improved. Let words die rather than people. Let the battle of the Plan Bs begin.

Conclusion

Promotion of strategic engagement does not guarantee success in negotiation when conflict resolution fails. But windows of opportunity continually open and close. Strategic engagement enables us to recognize these opportunities and blockages early enough and to determine how best to respond. Sails are kept unfurled to catch any gusts of wind that may be blowing. The sails may not catch enough wind to propel the boat forward in a preferred direction. But one thing is certain. If sails are not raised there will be no progress, however many winds are blowing. Without sails permanently hoisted in this way, it will be much more likely to be an ongoing story of mistiming and missed opportunity.

Part III

Implications

Does the argument presented in Part I and illustrated in Part II also apply elsewhere? The final part of the book looks at practical implications in general, at wider theoretical implications – and at the unavoidable challenge of having to live with radical disagreement as far as we can see into the future.

9

OTHER PHASES, OTHER LEVELS, OTHER CONFLICTS

What are the wider implications of a turn to conflict engagement when so far conflict resolution does not work? In this chapter we are marking out the domain of what I call *extended conflict resolution*. Extended conflict resolution is made up of *strategic dialogue* (SD), *strategic problem-solving* (SPS) and *strategic negotiation* (SN). SD, SPS and SN are prior to the dialogic, problem-solving and negotiation approaches in classic conflict resolution discussed in chapter 3. Their prime strategic function is to address the *preconditions* without which dialogue for mutual understanding (DMU), interactive problem-solving (IPS) and principled negotiation (PN) are not possible (see figure 9.1).

Strategic dialogue (SD) explores agonistic dialogue in order to identify what blocks dialogue for mutual understanding (DMU).

Strategic problem-solving (SPS), using the information from strategic dialogue, promotes strategic thinking within and across conflict parties, and by third parties, with a view to learning what is required for there to be interactive problem-solving (IPS) in the first place. Strategic problem-solving clarifies what the problem is.

Strategic negotiation (SN), in the light of strategic dialogue and strategic problem-solving, is focused on the preconditions required to make principled negotiation (PN) possible. It links strategic thinking within conflict parties to the wider strategic context (regional, international) that structures the scope for negotiations, and informs third parties accordingly. It helps to clarify what is needed to promote 'ripeness'.

Extended conflict resolution links *conflict resolution* to *strategic studies* in a way that mutually informs – and mutually changes – both. Conflict resolution takes on, but adapts, some of the

CONFLICT ENGAGEMENT	—>		CONFLICT RESOLUTION
Starts where conflict parties are			Starts where third parties want conflict parties to be

Heuristic engagement

| Takes radical disagreement seriously Explores agonistic dialogue | **strategic dialogue (SD)** | —> | **dialogue for mutual understanding (DMU)** | Ignores radical disagreement |

Strategic engagement

| Promotes strategic thinking within, across and between conflict parties and by third parties | **strategic problem-solving (SPS)** | —> | **interactive problem-solving (IPS)** | Promotes cooperative thinking |

| Shares the aim of conflict resolution, but links to strategic studies and engages existing political reality, including threat power | **strategic negotiation (SN)** | —> | **principled negotiation (PN)** | Does not link to strategic studies and wants from the outset to transform existing political reality and reject threat power |

| INTRACTABILITY | —> | | TRACTABILITY |

Figure 9.1   Extended conflict resolution

methodology of strategic studies. Strategic studies takes on the normative aim of conflict resolution – to reduce levels of violence in international politics.

Other phases and other levels

The Israeli–Palestinian conflict is a major ongoing intractable conflict at the top end of the spectrum of conflict. Do conclusions reached about conflict engagement in the case study also apply in other phases (prevention, mitigation, post-war peacebuilding) and at other levels? There is space here for only a brief answer to these questions.

Other phases

The main opportunity to apply a heuristic and strategic engagement approach to *preventing* escalation towards violence is provided by the long lead-times that there are in the build-up of many of these conflicts. We noted this above in relation to Ted Gurr's work on 'minorities at risk'. Prevention includes both reducing the *likelihood* of violent conflict by addressing preconditions (root causes and structural 'fragility') and also halting or reversing the *process* of escalation in individual cases once conflict parties have formed. In Sri Lanka it took some fifteen years for clear manifestations of Tamil dissatisfaction to escalate to all-out war. In Afghanistan there was a similarly long gestation period before the Taliban became an active militarized force. Even Boko Haram in Nigeria began as a peaceful protest movement up to the time of the death of its first leader. In his analysis of 'preconditions' for protracted social conflict and the 'process mechanics' that may or may not lead to war, we have also seen how, in relation to the latter, Edward Azar places his emphasis on the interlocking factors of the 'actions and strategies' of possessors, the 'actions and strategies' of challengers, and the escalatory/de-escalatory 'built-in mechanisms of conflict' that result between them. It is evident that ongoing heuristic and strategic analysis of the kind illustrated in the case study might enhance understanding of these processes and, in this way, help to guide efforts to manage, settle and transform them before war breaks out.

In *mitigating* violence once it has broken out, the distinction between *extremists of ends* and *extremists of means* is important. We have seen how extremists of ends are uncompromising in their pursuit of strategic goals. But the key question is whether these ends are pursued violently or non-violently. Extremists of means use violence to attain their goals. A central aim in conflict resolution, therefore, is to separate extremists of ends from extremists of means. This lies at the heart of most peace processes. Will challengers give up violent resistance and enter a political process? Will possessors give up violent suppression and share power? For example, in most conflicts, 'terror' is a *tactic* – a means to an end rather than an end in itself. So the aim is to persuade conflict parties using, or likely to use, terror tactics – and those who support them – that their strategic goals would be better served by non-violent means. This is where a strategic engagement approach can be powerful – as shown in the case study in relation to the Palestine Strategy Group's concept of 'smart resistance'. It is only where terror is not just a means to an end but also

169

part of the end itself, as in the case of Islamic State, that a strategic engagement approach cannot work. The parallel with Hitler here leads some to call the violent ideology of al-Qaeda, Boko Haram, al-Shabaab and Islamic State 'Islamo-fascism'. This will be discussed further in the conclusion.

In *post-war peacebuilding*, the main reason why strategic engagement can still be helpful is because in many complex transnational conflicts peace agreements are not the end of the conflict. I call this *Clausewitz in reverse* – my term for the fact that, in hitherto intractable conflicts, the political struggle often continues after the war into the subsequent peace – the settlement transmutes military conflict into continuing non-military conflict. Indeed, if it did not, there would in many cases not be a peace agreement at all. So, in these cases, heuristic and strategic engagement need to be extended into the 'post-war' phase during the long – and often dangerous – transition period.

In fact, Clausewitz himself (the author of *On War* who accompanied Napoleon on his Russian campaign in 1812), with his usual perspicacity, was well aware of this – in the sentence immediately following his famous observation that war is 'a continuation of political intercourse, with the addition of other means', he adds that the 'main lines along which military events progress, and to which they are restricted, are political lines that continue throughout the war into the subsequent peace.'[1] There are many examples of deliberate ambiguities in the wording of peace agreements that enable rival leaders to claim victory in this way. This is the 'discursively paradoxical reality' referred to in relation to the 1998 Good Friday agreement in Northern Ireland, for example, by Laura Filardo-Llamas:

> [I]t can be claimed that the ambiguity of the language of the Agreement has allowed the creation of a discursively paradoxical reality which manifested through manifold nuances of discourse, which lie, in turn, at the heart of the success of the peace process as we know it today.[2]

Navigating the depths and eddies of 'discursively paradoxical reality' is just what heuristic and strategic engagement is able to do.

Other levels

Do the conclusions reached in the case study also apply at other levels? For example, could this approach be used as an extra string to the bow in some of the most obdurate cases in family, neighbourhood or community mediation, or in the various kinds of alternative dispute resolution, or in some restorative justice settings? This is too large a terrain to enter here. But I have discussed this – and in some cases tried it out – in several seminars and workshops with experts and practitioners in those fields with promising results. This is a topic to be pursued elsewhere.

It is worth remembering in this regard that the promotion of strategic engagement as illustrated in Part II in itself does much to enhance the involvement of wider civil society and democratic processes at other levels. We have seen how collective strategic thinking helps to strengthen the voice of civil society within conflict parties, across and between conflict parties, and in relation to third parties. For example, civil societies gain access, hitherto denied, to inform and influence contextual strategic thinking and decision-making at wider regional and international levels. Those who are most affected by decisions at these levels at last begin to have a say in them.

We now turn to 'other conflicts' and consider the added scope for extended conflict resolution that strategic dialogue, strategic problem-solving and strategic negotiation give.

Strategic dialogue

We have seen that the aim of strategic dialogue (SD) is to explore agonistic dialogue in order to identify what blocks dialogue for mutual understanding (DMU). Strategic dialogue does not set aside the radical disagreements that constitute the discursive dimension of the conflict but, on the contrary, forefronts them in order first to acknowledge and understand what stands in the way of conflict resolution before trying to deal with it. Let us look at the application to two – admittedly very large-scale – types of dialogue currently being promoted in various parts of the world.

National dialogue

National dialogues are 'inclusive extra-constitutional decision-making mechanisms' that aim to embrace all national stakeholders in an effort (a) to address 'the root causes of constitutional failures' and (b) to 'provide space and instruments for reconciliation' in complex conflict environments.[3] National dialogues are usually formally mandated, as in the cases of South Africa (the National Peace Accord structures), Nepal (both the Ministry for Peace and Reconstruction and Nepal Transitions to Peace), Lebanon (the Common Space Initiative) and

171

Yemen (the National Dialogue Conference). Sometimes they can be informally initiated – as in the case of the 2013 Social Forum in the Basque Country, which aimed to make up for deficiences in the formal 2006 peace process.[4]

In the remarkable attempt at national dialogue in Burma (Myanmar), for example, the challenge is to reconcile and integrate a large number of combatants who have been locked in bitter fighting for more than fifty years. This is a good example of what, on the face of it, looks like a much more complicated case than that of Israel–Palestine, given the number and diversity of the main players. Can a strategic engagement approach help here?

In 2011, President Thein Sein surprised many by declaring at his inauguration that his main aim was to rebuild national unity. An idea of the ambition of the enterprise can be gauged from the elaborate 'Panglong II Roadmap', signed in April 2013 by seventeen armed ethnic groups and including the proposed Panglong Union Conference with its envisaged 900 participants – 300 each from government/army, democratic forces, and opposition – in an effort to include all major stakeholders in the process.[5] In a further move to support the process of reconciliation, in October 2012 the government of Myanmar established the Myanmar Peace Centre (MPC) to provide an active agency for negotiating with ethnic insurgent groups. The MPC's mandate involved 'deep engagement in the process of political dialogue with the insurgent groups as well as peace building activities to consolidate on-going efforts'.[6] Critics point out that, following sixty years of ethnic civil wars, Myanmar has neither a culture of peace nor robust infrastructures supporting peace and reconciliation below the level of the MPC. But the victory of Aung San Suu Kyi's National League of Democracy (NLD) party in the national elections of November 2015 may galvanize the process.

The main point here, as in similar cases elsewhere, is that, in a highly complex situation with multiple conflict parties, many of whom are internally divided between political leaderships and military militia, the capacity of collective strategic thinking by identity groups to help overcome internal divisions in the interest of strategic unity, and the possibilities subsequently opened up for cross-group strategic engagement, is evident. Inevitable setbacks are more likely to be anticipated and understood. In the end the long-term success of the national dialogue is likely to depend on it. Beyond this lie even more complex challenges in the case of 'disintegrated war zones' where a plethora of competing militia, maintained by what Alex de

Waal calls the 'business model' where allegiance is bought and sold in the 'political marketplace', cannot be said to represent coherent identity groups at all (see note 2 in the Conclusion).

Dialogue of civilizations

2001, the UN 'year of the dialogue of civilizations', was also the year of the attack on the Pentagon and the World Trade Center in the United States. Such are the contradictions inherent in the idea of world cultural solidarity at a time of continuing transnational conflict. This applies both to Gadamerian 'hermeneutical' dialogue that seeks a 'fusion of horizons', as discussed in chapter 3, and to the different idea that there already is a shared 'global ethic' which underlies all religions ('all religions in the end teach the same thing') – for example, Hans Küng's non-Gadamerian conception of inter-religious dialogue, as exemplified in his 1993 Parliament of the World's Religions: 'there is already a consensus among the religions which can be the basis for a global ethic – a minimum fundamental consensus concerning binding values, irrevocable standards, and fundamental moral attitudes.'[7]

In both cases, aspirations for a 'dialogue of civilizations' can be seen to be premature unless there is first a readiness to engage with the differences that stand in the way. In his influential book *The Ethics of Disagreement in Islam*, for example, Taha Jabir al'Alwani, having argued that there can be no radical disagreement within Islam ('dogmatism, discord and violent disagreement [ikhtilaf] within the Muslim Ummah has no place in the authentic teachings of Islam'), makes it plain that this does not extend to radical disagreement between Islam and non-Islamic beliefs:

> No one should jump to the conclusion, however, that our keenness to preserve the brotherhood and solidarity of Muslims implies any negligence of the fundamental Islamic beliefs, which are not open to any speculation or compromise. The determination to confront the enemies of the Ummah will prevent us from joining hands with those who do not have any affinity with Islam.[8]

Despite what al'Alwani says, however, these differences clearly do extend to ferocious sectarian struggles within each faith community – and also within the various sects themselves. Indeed, fully in line with the central argument in this book, it is the outcome of strategic battles and fierce radical disagreement *within* Islam that will largely determine the scope for wider accommodation *beyond* it.

For Gadamer:

> The human solidarity that I envisage is not a global uniformity but unity in diversity . . . Such unity-in-diversity has to be extended to the whole world – to include Japan, China, India, and also Muslim cultures. Every culture, every people has something distinctive to offer for the solidarity and welfare of humanity.[9]

But this book suggests that it is only by first acknowledging, understanding and addressing *radical disagreement* (which goes beyond the Gadamerian concept of mere 'prejudice') that visionary dialogical hopes for *mutual accommodation*, such as those of Gadamer himself, can be fulfilled.

Strategic problem-solving

With strategic problem-solving we reach the core approach advocated in this book. Just as, in conflict resolution, *interactive problem-solving* connects *dialogue for mutual understanding* to *negotiation for political accommodation*, so, in extended conflict resolution, *strategic problem-solving* connects *strategic dialogue* to *strategic negotiation*.

Strategic problem-solving (SPS) uses the information from strategic dialogue, looked at above, to focus on the *preconditions* required for interactive problem-solving (IPS) to be possible. For example, in the Israeli–Palestinian conflict there is widespread support by leading interactive problem-solving exponents for the idea of some variant on 'two states, one homeland' as the solution, because only this can satisfy the underlying basic human needs whose frustration is seen to be the deep driver of the conflict. But so far this gains little traction. The task of SPS is to understand why.

Does this also apply to other conflicts? I think that it does. In the Middle East and North Africa (MENA), for example, we have seen in chapter 2 that at the core of the complex patterns of transnational conflict lies a general crisis in the state system in the region. That is why a traditional state-centric approach, as has been the norm in classic strategic studies, is no longer adequate. For example, the Arab League – created in a previous era and still limited almost exclusively to traditional diplomatic practices – needs enhanced capacity at all levels and across all sectors. In addition to overcoming its own internal divisions, in order to play an effective role in creating any future peace system in the region it needs not only to be able to reach up to the United States and Russia at international level, or Iran and Turkey at regional level, but above all also to the overlapping and warring identity groups at sub-state level. All these levels need to be integrated within the parameters of what in conflict resolution is called 'contingency' (fitting appropriate responses to the differing aspects and phases of the conflict in question) and 'complementarity' (coordinating the actions of different agents insofar as this is possible), as noted in chapter 1.

It is worth briefly illustrating this in relation to the much neglected topic of the strategic interest of the Shia minority in Syria and the Sunni minority in Iraq. This has been fundamental in creating the gaps in the state system that insurgents such as Islamic State have been able to exploit.

For instance, since the time of Bashar al-Assad's father, the Alawite Shia minority in Syria (about 12 per cent of the population) has been the political and military power base of the regime. A 'transition to democracy', therefore, means that power for the first time passes to the Sunni majority. So a failure to answer the strategic question of how the interests and needs of the Alawite minority (and the other minorities) can be safeguarded in those conditions lies behind the ferocity with which the regime and its Alawite supporters have resisted this transition. Until these fears are allayed, there can be no peace process in Syria. Alawite needs – and the needs of other minorities such as the Syrian Kurds – must somehow be accommodated within any constitutional arrangements capable of preserving Syria as a state, if that is a desirable and possible outcome. So the promotion of prior and continuous collective strategic thinking within the Alawite minority, and its consequent feeding into wider regional strategic engagement, can be seen as one example of a strategic engagement approach that has been missing from the outset – with fatal consequences. It has been, and at the time of writing largely remains, a major 'strategy gap'.[10]

This replicates a mirror-image strategy gap in Iraq, where the invading forces in 2003 sought to topple Saddam Hussein's regime while neglecting the implications of the fact that the regime was based on the support of the Sunni minority. This strategic neglect resulted, first, in the immediate emergence in Sunni areas of the forerunner of Islamic State in 2003 (al-Qaida in Iraq, AQI), which was only defeated by major US military action on the ground supported by the 'Anbar awakening' of Sunni tribal leaders, reassured that their security would be protected in the new Iraq against Shia militias backed by Iran. The subsequent (re)emergence of what eventually renamed itself Islamic State (IS), announced by the unexpected seizure of Mosul on 10 June 2014, came when, in a repeat performance, the highly partisan Shia-based government in Iraq of Nouri al-Maliki had clearly betrayed that promise. A strategic engagement approach would from the start have promoted collective strategic thinking within the Sunni minority in order to identify what was needed to prevent Sunnis (including former leaders dismissed in 2003) from preferring a *jihadist* takeover to the depredations of Shia militias. This, too, is still a damaging 'strategy gap' at the time of writing.

To end the fighting and build a post-war regional peace system that can fill the gaps that terrorist groups exploit will require at least as high a standard of strategic problem-solving, creative imagination and international statecraft as was displayed at world level in 1945.

A formal start has been made to link *strategic studies* and *conflict resolution* in the region through a joint project organized by the leading Egyptian strategic think tank, the Regional Center for Strategic Studies (RCSS) in Cairo and the Oxford Research Group (ORG). Two workshops have been held in Cairo in 2015 and 2016, looking, respectively, at an analysis and mapping of the current situation ('where are we?') and at the strategic requirements for an integrative peace in the region ('where do we want to go?'). The intention in the next stage is to consider the strategic question 'how do we get there?' Each workshop has produced a publication. The first (2015) was called *The Management of Complex Conflicts in the Middle East*, was published in Arabic, and has been made available for analysis to Egyptian ministries, military academies such as the Nasser Academy, Arab embassies in Cairo, and foreign ministries in the Gulf. The second (2016) is (at the moment perhaps provisionally) called *Resolving Conflicts in the Middle East: An Integrative Perspective*. It is hoped that this may become the first journal explicitly to link strategic studies and conflict resolution in the Middle East and, in this way, reflect the conclusion of the second workshop that 'a *strategic problem-solving approach* that combines strategic studies and conflict resolution is the best way ahead' (Ramsbotham 2016).[11]

Strategic negotiation

Chapter 8 in the case study has already shown how principled negotiation in the Israel–Palestine conflict needs to be supplemented by a broader strategic negotiation approach in intractable conflicts. Here we make one or two further comments and then consider some implications for the idea of 'ripeness'.

Violent conflicts, peace agreements and international law

One of the best studies of negotiation and mediation efforts in the post-Cold War world is Christine Bell's *On the Law of Peace*.[12] In her book she analyses 646 documents 'which could lay claim to the name peace agreements' signed between 1990 and 2007, addressing 102 conflicts in 85 jurisdictions. Her definition of peace agreements is that they are 'documents produced after discussion with some or all of the conflict's protagonists, that address militarily violent conflict with a view to ending it'.[13] Christine Bell's main argument is that this ongoing flood of agreements makes up a rapidly evolving 'law of peace' in which 'peace agreements assert their own legalization, and force changes in international law's core doctrines.'[14] Drawing explicitly on my idea of 'Clausewitz in reverse', she sees the myriad aspects of 'hybrid self-determination' and 'constructive ambiguity' reflected in these documents as ultimately derived from the attempt to 'translate the conflict from violent to non-violent forms, rather than resolve it'. In order to achieve this, competing ideologies, interests and identity groups have to be permanently accommodated by the adaptation of existing power structures in a wide variety of different ways. This forces innovatory forms of 'disaggregated' and 'dislocated' power arrangements that progressively redefine the nature of the state itself. Bell concludes that 'international law appears to be moving towards underwriting a more complex and ambiguous mix of representative and participative democracy linked to a more fluid concept of statehood with fuzzy sovereignty.'[15]

Nina Caspersen challenges the extent to which 'liberal values' have tempered traditional conceptions of sovereignty in the post-Cold War era.[16] But she also argues that more emphasis should be placed in peace agreements on intra-communal dynamics and political contestation within conflict parties (particularly separatist movements) than has been accorded in the past. This may help to temper the tendency of peace agreements to reflect unduly the interests and perspectives of the negotiating elites with the result that post-settlement politics often fail to address the underlying grievances of non-dominant groups sufficiently. Secret elite talks may for good reason be the norm in peace processes, but, as Caspersen argues, there is no reason why additional measures that broaden the process may not be undertaken in parallel. This links to an argument that 'legitimacy' is a more important component of 'security sector reform' than is often realized.

In their different ways, therefore, both these analyses suggest that prior and ongoing collective strategic thinking by identity groups

> **Box 9.1   Contributing elements in the 9 January 2005 Comprehensive Peace Agreement in Sudan**
>
> Twenty-three contributory agreements made since 10 April 1995 are included in the Sudan/Southern Sudan Comprehensive Peace Agreement. These cover:
>
> - agreements between the government of Sudan (GoS) and different rebel factions (e.g., Sudan People's Liberation Movement (SPLM), United Democratic Salvation Front (Sudan) (UDSF))
> - different sub-conflicts (e.g., Southern Kordofan/Nuba Mountains conflict, Abyei conflict)
> - different issues/aspects (e.g., humanitarian, security, government structures, wealth sharing, power sharing)
> - different phases (e.g., cessation of hostilities, capacity building and joint planning, interim arrangements during negotiations, implementation arrangements).

and subsequent strategic engagement, as advocated in this book, might usefully inform efforts to bring violent conflicts to an end and consolidate an ensuing peace. Box 9.1 gives the example of the 2005 Comprehensive Peace Agreement in Sudan to show how, even in highly dispersed and complex war zones, eventual peace agreements are built out of smaller interim agreements that include sub-factions, sub-conflicts, sub-issues and sub-phases. A strategic negotiation approach based on illuminating these aspects is, therefore, likely to be helpful.

Ripeness revisited

William Zartman's 'ripeness theory' tries to specify when conflicts are 'ripe for resolution' and conflict parties are ready to negotiate. But, without clear independent criteria, the process can be circular:

> This, however, points to a more general problem with the concept of a ripe moment. It is very difficult to assess if it exists in a particular conflict. If negotiations and the resulting agreement were successful, observers will tend to conclude that the conflict was indeed ripe for resolution; if they failed, then the conflict was clearly not ripe.[17]

Can a strategic negotiation approach help to provide these independent criteria? This section is abbreviated from a longer joint article written with Amira Schiff.[18]

Ripeness theory has, rightly, been highly influential both with academics and among practitioners.[19] It focuses on 'push' and 'pull' factors:

> Ripeness theory is intended to explain why, and therefore when, parties to a conflict are susceptible to their own or other efforts to turn the conflict towards resolution through negotiation. The concept of a ripe moment centres on the parties' perception of a Mutually Hurting Stalemate (MHS) and a Way Out. The MHS provides the push to begin negotiations; the Way Out provides the pull into a negotiated solution. Once the negotiations have begun, the pressure of the MHS needs to be maintained and the Way Out transformed by the parties into a resolving formula that provides a Mutually Enticing Opportunity (MEO) for agreement.[20]

In a joint report with Alvaro de Soto, Zartman builds on this by summarizing five steps that mediators need to take in order to initiate the process:

> This toolkit lays out the steps mediators can take to recognize ripeness themselves, to foster the parties' perception of ripeness, and to ripen the conflict. Step 1 describes how the mediator should assess whether a mutually hurting stalemate exists and, if it does, how painful it is. Step 2 focuses on assessing the parties' perception of a way out . . . Step 3 presents measures the mediator can take to induce parties' perception of a stalemate and a way out. Step 4 explains how to enhance objective conditions for ripeness, creating a stalemate and the pain associated with it as a basis for further efforts to encourage the perception of the new facts. If ripening is not possible, a mediator should take step 5, which involves the mediator positioning so that the parties recognize that they can turn to the mediator for help when the situation eventually becomes ripe.[21]

Can a strategic negotiation (SN) approach help to inform this? Unlike ripeness theory, which originally focused on entering into negotiations, we have seen in chapter 8 how SN sees the need to engage all five stages of the negotiation process from the outset:

- when negotiation first becomes a possibility;
- at pre-negotiation stage;
- during negotiations;
- at implementation stage in case agreement is reached;
- at post-negotiation stage in case there is no agreement.

Let us look at each of these five phases in turn.

First, at a *preliminary stage*, before even pre-negotiation is possible, a strategic negotiation approach can help to provide a framework for assessing how best to recognize and promote a 'mutually hurting stalemate' and perceptions of a 'way out'.

In ripeness theory (steps 1 and 2), mediators assess these through a combination of 'objective' and 'subjective' indicators while recognizing that, in the end, it is the subjective components that are the decisive ones.[22] Subjective indicators include evaluation of the meaning behind official statements and assessment of unofficial statements in the public media. A 'way out', for example, is 'primarily subjective and depends on each parties' perception of the other parties' intentions',[23] so the 'perfect indicator would read something like "[w]e think our opponent is willing to join us in looking for a solution".'[24]

It is evident from the example given in chapter 8 that a strategic negotiation approach can supplement this through prior insights from inclusive strategic thinking within conflict parties and strategic engagement across and between them. This is neither purely 'objective' nor purely 'subjective'. It is focused on the *comparative strategic evaluation* of cost, risk and benefit in relation to the different futures that in the end determine whether the status quo is seen to be better or worse than a particular negotiated alternative. And this can be ascertained independently. This can help to guide mediators in Zartman's and de Soto's steps 3 and 4 above.

Second, at *pre-negotiation stage*, when conflict parties have in one way or another indicated readiness to enter negotiations, the clear relevance of a strategic negotiation approach can be seen by noting the 'pre-negotiation functions' listed by Zartman and de Soto that need to be 'established or decided upon before actual negotiations can be initiated':[25]

- identification of the parties necessary to a settlement as well as identification of spoilers to be isolated;
- identification of the issues to be resolved and separation of issues not resolvable in the conflict;
- identification of alternatives to the current conflict course and to a negotiated agreement;
- establishment of contacts and bridges between the parties;
- clarification of costs and risks involved in seeking settlement;
- establishment of requitement (assurance of reciprocity) between the parties;
- assurance of support for a settlement policy within each party's domestic constituency.

A strategic negotiation approach can illuminate all of these.

Third, at the *negotiation stage* itself, the emphasis in the extension of ripeness theory, as sought by Zartman, is still on a continuing mutually hurting stalemate so that negotiating parties do not decide to pull out. But the main focus switches to converting the mutually perceived 'way out' into a shared 'formula for resolution', and thus a mutually enticing opportunity (MEO).[26] Ripeness theory sees a mutually enticing opportunity (the main 'pull' factor) as a shared achievement of the conflict parties and mediator within the negotiating process itself – in line with conflict resolution thinking.

What a strategic negotiation approach can add here is a more concrete indication of how particular negotiation moves are perceived by constituencies within the conflict parties – and how this plays out within the wider pattern of their evolving strategic priorities. For example, in relation to the damaging wider Palestinian responses to shifts in the third-party US mediation approach during the Kerry talks, chapter 8 showed the key importance of a capacity to monitor this. The crucial point is that a strategic negotiation approach adds the required precision to the fruitful principled negotiation idea of the 'best alternative to a negotiated agreement' (BATNA) – particularly if the outcome favoured by the mediators is included as well – as is logically implied in Zartman and de Soto's steps 3 and 4.

Fourth, *in case of agreement in the negotiations*, a strategic negotiation approach stresses the key significance of implementation from the beginning – for example, in decisions whether to enter negotiations in the first place – and cannot therefore be deferred, as can happen in principled negotiation. Leaders will not enter negotiations if it seems likely in advance that implementation will lead to loss of power. We have already noted how the post-agreement phase is often the most dangerous.

Fifth, and finally, *in case the talks break down without agreement*, again a strategic negotiation approach is useful. The role that the mediator can continue to play after breakdown will depend on what happened during the previous talks. To the extent that mediators have earlier acted as suggested under steps 3 and 4 in the Zartman/ de Soto 'toolkit' (in step 4 actually promoting a hurting stalemate, perhaps using economic or even military means, albeit short of direct intervention), it may no longer be possible just to 'position' for future availability (step 5). Even short of this, as noted in chapter 3 and illustrated in chapter 8, a strategic negotiation approach recognizes why would-be third-party peacemakers in severe asymmetric conflicts should not expect to be seen as neutral, impartial or disinterested but, rather, as likely to offend more and more constituencies as

181

negotiations progress. Above all, a strategic negotiation approach shows why the mediator's strategy must from the beginning include a Plan B in case negotiation fails. A Plan B is needed to fill the strategy vacuum that may otherwise be filled by frustration and violence if negotiations fail. But, as seen in chapter 8, Plan B is also needed from the beginning in order to persuade conflict parties that the alternative to Plan A (to reaching agreement) will be worse – which is again how it informs ripeness theory.

Perhaps the key point in all this is that, without a strategic negotiation approach, ripeness theory lacks clear independent criteria for distinguishing when increasing 'hurt' (as advocated in de Soto's and Zartman's step 4) will be likely to push a conflict party towards negotiation and when it may have the opposite effect. For example, in the case study in chapter 8, to increase boycott, divestment and sanctions (BDS) on Israel may persuade Israeli decision-makers to behave as third parties want. But it may have the opposite effect of intensifying a 'siege mentality' in Israel and reinforcing a sense of isolation and determination not to be reliant on international security guarantees. Which is it likely to be? This can be determined only with reference to the ongoing strategic thinking promoted in SN, where the focus is precisely on how factors such as this impact on prevailing patterns of Israeli cost–benefit strategic analysis.[27]

Conclusion

Chapter 8 suggested why the US president's attempt to mediate an end to the Israeli–Palestinian conflict in 2013–14 was premature. But this chapter shows why his subsequent announcement in November 2015 that, during the remaining year of his presidency, there was no more that could be done was premature (although at the time of writing in May 2016 it is still possible that he might make a final effort in his last few months just as president Clinton did in 2000 – perhaps linked to a renewal of US military aid to Israel). There is always more work to be done. This applies particularly during periods of maximum intractability. Indeed, that is when such initiatives are needed most.

We have reached the end of the main argument about conflict resolution in this book. In chapter 10 we move beyond conflict resolution to follow through the second and third stages of heuristic engagement: What is happening when conflicting discourses clash with each other in intractable conflicts? And how adequate are third-party descriptions and explanations of this?

10

EXPLORING AGONISTIC DIALOGUE

Having completed the main argument in the book about strategic engagement and conflict resolution, it remains to pick up the threads of what I am calling 'heuristic engagement' – taking the phenomenon of radical disagreement itself seriously.

In chapters 5 and 6 we looked at examples of the *first level* of heuristic engagement – exploring what conflict parties are saying individually in the context of radical disagreement. We saw how this gives deep insight into what underlies collective strategic thinking and shows clearly why, so far, conflict resolution does not work. The first part of this chapter generalizes this result by summarizing what I call 'the moments of radical disagreeing'.

It then remains, in the light of this, to try to understand the *second* and *third levels* of heuristic engagement – what is being said in the radical disagreement as a whole, and how adequately third parties encompass it. This is where, in my experience, an unexplored continent in conflict studies – one that lies at the very heart of linguistic intractability – finally begins to come into view.

Here are two examples of radical disagreement to make these distinctions clear.

In the first example, the opening speaker is Leonard Cheshire, an observer at the dropping of the Nagasaki bomb on 9 August 1945, and the second speaker is John Finnis, an Oxford professor and the author of what is, in my view, the best book on the ethics of nuclear deterrence:[1]

l(A) 'I hold that it was not morally wrong to bomb Hiroshima and Nagasaki. And the reason why I say this is that the only fore-seeable alternative was the all-out invasion of Japan. Given the

Japanese military mind at the time, that would have involved a fight to the last man, total war across the whole of Japan, in which, not hundreds of thousands, but millions would have died.'

(B) 'As to Hiroshima and Nagasaki, the dropping of the two atomic bombs on those two cities was indeed morally wrong. In fact, as one can plainly see from the records of those who made the decision, neither the motive nor the intention was to attack military targets. The intention was simply to cause maximum damage in largely civilian areas – which it did. Even if Leonard Cheshire is right, and this was the only way in which the war could have been ended short of a much more costly invasion of Japan, it was clearly morally wrong and should certainly not have been done.'|[2]

In the second example, the opening speaker is the Republican governor of South Dakota, Mike Rounds, and the second speaker is his chief Democrat opponent, Steve Hildebrand:

|(A) 'Abortion is murder. God creates human life and it is blasphemous for any of God's creatures to take it away. It is an unforgivable sin. The State of South Dakota is right to ban it by law.'

(B) 'They've gone too far. They're essentially saying that if your daughter gets raped, she has no choice but to have the criminal's baby. This is entirely inhumane and morally deeply wrong. It is un-Christian. It must be immediately reversed.'|[3]

In these examples, what conflict parties say individually (the first level of heuristic engagement) appears inside the separate sets of inverted commas. But the resulting radical disagreement itself (the second level of heuristic engagement) is what is contained within the bar lines as a whole. And the third level of heuristic engagement is what third parties in turn say about this.

This chapter is based on several years' work – since the original research for my 1987 book *Choices* – spent analysing radical disagreements with conflict parties. Although the treatment here is highly compressed, I hope that enough is included to convey the broad significance of this strangely neglected line of enquiry in conflict studies.

What conflict parties say individually in agonistic dialogue: the anatomy of radical disagreeing

Radical disagreement consists largely of a sequence of distinctions that conflict parties make in the process of agonistic dialogue. These comprise what I call 'the moments of radical disagreeing'. What follows is generalized from many simulations conducted in recent years with groups from all over the world. Agonistic dialogue moves at lightning and unpredictable speed, so it is hard to pin it down. In consequence, somewhat analogously to William Harvey's attempt to study the motions of the heart in his analysis of the circulation of the blood, the methodology is to slow down the bewildering pace of radical disagreement so that underlying structures can be discerned. There is no claim that this is what happens every time, or even most times, or that it happens in the order given here. But, despite different cultural locations, in my experience broad patterns of this kind recur. These are experiments that others can test out for themselves.

The moment of recommendation

Radical disagreeing begins with thwarted action. If conflict parties had the power, they would simply impose the outcome they want. But, frustrated, the moment of recommendation moves between imperative mode – 'do this!' (or 'do not do this!') – to hortatory and suasive mode – 'this must be done!', 'this should be done!'. The ethical is built into radical disagreement from the start. And so is the emotion that goes with it. Conversely, when passions rise in intense human conflict – as they almost invariably do – there is already radical disagreement. Radical disagreement begins with emotion. The two are inseparable.

The moment of justification

Under the moment of justification, the radical disagreement is developed in answer to the question *why* this should or should not be done. The response ('because . . .') in nearly every case points directly at how things are, as in the two examples given above: 'the reason why I say this is . . .'; 'in fact as one can plainly see . . .'. The pointing is immediate and usually unreflective. In its first appearance, the moment of justification does not mention words like 'fact', 'real' or 'true'. It is much quicker and more unqualified than that. It is purely ostensive: 'look – that is why – you can see for yourself'.

The moment of alignment

Under the moment of alignment, conflict parties are asked to respond to the other's recommendation and justification. Very often, initial justifications miss each other entirely – as here:

185

|(A) 'Drop the bomb, because it will shorten the war and save millions
      of lives.'
(B)   'Do not drop the bomb, because thousands of innocent people
      will be killed.'|

If each is then asked to respond to the other, arguments usually line up
accordingly, even if there is no logical reason why they should, as here:

|(A) 'Drop the bomb because it will shorten the war and save millions
      of lives.'
(B)   'The war would have ended anyway.'|

|(B) 'Do not drop the bomb because thousands of innocent people
      will be killed.'
(A)   'Conventional fire-bombing killed more people.'|

It is unusual, in my experience, for protagonists to argue, as John
Finnis does above, that, even if the other is right and this was 'the
only way in which the war could have been ended short of a much
more costly invasion of Japan', it was still 'clearly morally wrong and
should certainly not have been done'.

The moment of alignment is repeated throughout as the main way
of developing and exploring agonistic dialogues – in the richness of
what pours out there are nearly always innumerable issues raised that
are as yet unaddressed. The ramification of radical disagreements
under recurrent applications of the moment of alignment is rapid,
unpredictable, and varies from case to case.

The moment of refutation

Under the moment of refutation, what the other says is dismissed. It is
factually untrue, ethically wrong, logically irrational. What the other
says is seen against a background. It is the background – how things
are (what is pointed at under the moment of justification; the world
in which our recommendation should be enacted) – that dictates as
much. And now the whole language of 'fact/delusion', 'truth/false-
hood', 'justice/injustice', 'right/wrong', 'knowledge/error' – the world
of distinctions out of which radical disagreement is constructed –
springs into being, and is as immediately plunged into the vortex.

The moment of explanation

Under the moment of explanation, the question arises *why* the other
persists in arguing the unarguable. This is quite easy to test. In answer

to the question 'why do you say this?' under the moment of justification, as seen above, the usual response is to point to how things are in the world. In answer to the question 'why does the other say this?' under the moment of explanation, however, the usual response is to refer to the ignorance, ulterior motives, unconscious conditioning or ethical shortcomings of the other. What the other says is explained – away.

This is the first appearance of what, at the *third level* of heuristic engagement (third-party description and explanation), becomes a general third-party account of the whole phenomenon of radical disagreement in terms of underlying 'explanation' in general. But at its first appearance, under the moment of explanation, it applies only to what the other says. I think that this is of great significance in understanding why third-level accounts do not engage with what first- (and second-)level exploration shows. We return to this below.

The moment of explanation perpetually hovers over agonistic dialogue and threatens to end it. Why continue to converse with someone whose verbal behaviour is explained by deeper internal and external causes, and who is evidently already conditioned to believe what is untenable? If the other is sincere, it is the sincerity described by Jonathan Swift as the state of self-assurance that comes from one who is blissfully self-deceived. We can recognize the beginning of the slide that may eventually lead to mutual dehumanization.

The moment of description

Under the moment of description, conflict parties sometimes include themselves in third-party description of radical disagreement in terms of a mirror reflexivity: 'I know that this is my perspective on things and you have yours, but . . .'. As we have seen, this is often a key moment for conflict resolution, which wants to ignore what has gone before in the internal economy of radical disagreeing and begin at this point with mutual recognition of reflexivity, contingency and equivalence.

This is also the moment when social scientific explanation fully enters the scene. In its first entry, under the moment of explanation, as seen above, critical explanation applied only to the other. Now, under the moment of description, the explanation applies generally. I think that this late appearance of social scientific explanation in the phenomenology of radical disagreement is linked to the fact that what has gone before is not picked up on its radar screen. As demonstrated in chapters 5 and 6, this includes the almost instantaneous prior fusion of fact, value, emotion and action that is generated under the

187

first five moments of radical disagreeing (recommendation, justification, alignment, refutation, explanation). This happens before social scientific, psychological or philosophical expert third-party explanation enters the scene under the moment of description. Palestinian outrage at the enormity of the injustice of the *Nakba* fuels Palestinian strategy from the outset. This precedes any subsequent third-party attempts to describe and explain the resulting radical disagreement.

But in ongoing radical disagreement the moment of description does not play the role that either conflict resolution or social science has written for it. In the crucible of agonistic dialogue the moment of description has a different – indeed, almost an opposite – function. 'I know that this is my perspective on things and you have yours, but . . .' – and it is what follows the 'but' that signifies. The symmetric and neutral language adopted under the moment of description is indeed indistinguishable from third-party description in general. But this does not affect the nature of what follows 'but' when radical disagreement is resumed.

So what is the function of the moment of description in ongoing radical disagreement? Repeated experience suggests that the function of acknowledging symmetry at one level is to preserve asymmetry at another – deeper – level. The moment of description enables conflict parties to switch levels and, having acknowledged equivalence, then safely set it aside. The world the conflict parties refer to under the moment of description contains both their perspective and that of their opponent. So disputants establish in this way that, in the continuing radical disagreement, they are *not* merely referring to their own references. They are referring to the world that contains both. And *that* is the world that now continues to justify their recommendations and refute the other's arguments. With 'but' they can once again look out on the world through clear glass – and act accordingly.

Here is an example where the speaker repeatedly oscillates in the struggle to accommodate this function – but clearly ends up with an untrammelled field of action:

> Is the US closer to truth and human dignity than the Taliban or Saddam Hussein? Hell yes. Understanding and dialogue with the cultures of the Middle East does not require us to abdicate our moral arguments for democracy, liberty and human rights, or our critique of nations that oppose those values in word and deed. I recognize the subjectivity of my own values. I happily acknowledge that many other value-systems can be just as 'true' as my own (I put 'true' in quotes because I'm not really comfortable calling any value system 'true' or 'false'). That said, my subjective values tell me in no uncertain terms that the values of the

United States, flawed though they may be, are better than the values of reactionary Islamic extremists. Every public execution in Iran, every mass grave unearthed in Iraq, and every story of oppression in the Taliban's Afghanistan reinforces these values. I unapologetically believe that democracy is a better form of values than fascism.[4]

The moment of revision

Under the moment of revision, conflict parties are prepared to change their minds. They may adjust their arguments under the impact of agonistic dialogue. In many cases they produce arguments they had not thought about before.

The moment of revision is the second moment that conflict resolution aims for. In conflict resolution, the encouragement of a translation of aggressive statements about the world into reflexive descriptions of our own perceptions, as seen under the moment of description above, prepares the way for mutual accommodation and transformation under the moment of revision. In many cases this does, indeed, happen. But, in the case of intractable conflicts and ongoing radical disagreement, it does not. In agonistic dialogue, the moment of revision is found to play a different role, and one that is akin to the moment of description.

At one end of the spectrum is reluctant admission of minor quali-fication accompanied by vigorous reassertion of the original case. Confidence, emotional intensity and intransigence may wax and wane while core positions remain unchanged. Here the function of the moment of revision, when under pressure, is to readjust the periph-ery of the 'web of belief' that surrounds these positions. Discredited arguments are dropped and others are taken up. The purpose is not to reconsider and change the core but to protect and sustain it.[5]

At the other end of the spectrum – as it were leapfrogging the part of the spectrum that conflict resolution wants to occupy – lies radical conversion. On the road to Damascus, scales fall from our eyes. We see with blazing clarity that the other is right after all. And now we argue in reverse, but with intensified zeal. The blindness of our erst-while companions is all the more plain to us, because we, too, used to be like that.

The moment of exploration

Under the moment of exploration, heuristic engagement (the explo-ration of agonistic dialogue) reaches a point where conflict parties discover that beneath their original argument lie even deeper disagreements. Instead of discovering that apparent disagreement covers underlying agreement, the opposite happens. For example, in the radical disagreement between Leonard Cheshire and John Finnis recorded above, although both speakers were devout Catholics, it was discovered that beneath the quarrel about the use of nuclear weapons was more general ethical disagreement between a *consequentialist* ethic (Cheshire) and a *deontological* ethic (Finnis).[6]

The moment of action

Under the moment of action, the time for deliberation is over. There is no further time for prevarication. Either the bomb is dropped or it is not dropped. Either the baby is born or it is not born. Either the state is created or it is not created. One way or another, either through action or through inaction, the decision is made. Under the either–or pressure of decision in intense political conflict, indeterminate alternatives collapse into the crude yes–no of radical disagreement. Those who have the power, act. Under the moment of action – often to our horror – the full enormity of what the other says is shown in what the other does. And we, too, discover what we think by what we find that we have done.

Exploring the resulting radical disagreement: what happens when discourses clash?

Having traced the moments of radical disagreeing in what conflict parties say individually (what is contained between inverted commas), we can now explore the resulting radical disagreement itself (what is contained between bar lines). We move on to the *second level* of heuristic engagement. What is happening in the clash of discourses that constitutes linguistic intractability?

This, in my experience, is an almost undiscovered country in conflict studies. Because most analysts drastically underrate the nature and significance of radical disagreement, there is no incentive to look in that direction. But there is also a more profound reason – the nature of radical disagreement itself and the difficulty of conveying what is found if the attempt at exploration is made. Third-party analysis (including this book) is *monological*, but radical disagreement is *polylogical*. This will be spelt out at the end of the chapter.

There is no room in this book to do justice to such a large theme. Readers can find more in my book *Transforming Violent Conflict* (2010). But an idea of the extent of the topic can be given by briefly addressing three questions: *What are radical disagreements about? How far do they reach?* And *how deep do they go?*

What are radical disagreements about?

Exploration of radical disagreement shows that the disagreement extends to what is at issue: radical disagreement is about what it is about. There is space to give only one example.

What is the Israeli–Palestinian conflict about? Here is a characteristic response:

> *The core of the Israeli–Palestinian conflict is the claim of two peoples to the same piece of land.*[7]

This seems unexceptionable. There may be 'two opposed formulations' given by the conflict parties, but, in stating these, 'both actually confirm the basic definition above':

> stripped of the advocacy of their own answers, both agree that this is a question of conflicting claims to the same territory.

The 'objective core' of the conflict is distinguished from the 'subjective formulations' that surround – and obscure – it. Radical disagreement is then usually identified with the latter. But in radical disagreement this description is found not to be separate from what is at issue in it. Who are the 'two peoples'? What is 'the same piece of land'? Answers to these questions are already part of what is disputed.

Here is another example, looked at earlier in this book:

|(A) 'There are two nations on this sub-continent. This is the underlying fact that must shape the future creation of Pakistan. Only the truly Islamic platform of the Muslim League is acceptable to the Muslim nation.'

(B) 'Geography and mountains and the sea fashioned India as she is, and no human agency can change that shape or come in the way of her final destiny. Once present passions subside, the false doctrine of two nations will be discredited and discarded by all.'|

The first speaker is Jinnah, the second is Nehru, on the eve of the momentous partition of India in 1947. Reference to |two nations| appears in what both speakers say. But is the reference to a 'fact' or to a 'false doctrine'? Is |the same territory| what is referred to as 'this sub-continent' or 'India'? Benedict Anderson famously describes nations as 'imagined communities'.[8] This is an informative third-party description. But neither of the conflict parties is saying this in the radical disagreement. They are not saying that Pakistan and India are both 'imagined communities'. That they are not saying this is what makes it a radical disagreement. They are trying to *distinguish* what is merely an imagined community from what is not. That is the verbal battle. They are engaged in a life-and-death struggle to *define* and *name* 'two nations' and 'the same territory'. Whoever succeeds, wins. A radical disagreement is about what it is about.

So can radical disagreement be reduced to misunderstanding? There are plenty of analysts who think that it can. Here is an account by the seventeenth-century English philosopher John Locke:

> I was once in a Meeting of very learned and ingenious Physicians, where by chance there arose a Question, whether any Liquor passed through the Filaments of the Nerves. The Debate having been managed a good while, by a variety of Arguments on both sides, I (who had been used to suspect, that the greatest part of Disputes were more about the signification of Words, than a real difference in the Conceptions of Things) desired that before they went any further in this Dispute, they would first examine, and establish amongst them, what the word *Liquor* signified. [When they did this they found that] the signification of that Word, was not so settled and certain, as they had all imagined; but that each of them made it a sign of a different complex *Idea*.[9]

Something similar can be found in some 'cultural' readings of radical disagreement. Plenty of work has been done on cultural variation in conflict resolution, with different analysts seeing cultural differences reaching more or less deeply into the exchanges.[10] Edward Hall distinguished high-context communication cultures (Arabic, Chinese), where information is transmitted through context and comparatively little through verbal messages, from low-context communication cultures (German, English), where most of the information is transmitted through explicit linguistic codes.[11] Subject–predicate grammar encourages logical dichotomies (true/false, right/wrong, etc.) in a way that other grammars do not.

Here the archbishop of Canterbury wants to transmute radical disagreement into different understandings of word use:

> Faced with the disbeliefs of another discourse, each of the three participants in the Abrahamic conversation [Judaism, Christianity, Islam] should be prompted to ask whether the God of the other's disbelief is or

is not the God they themselves believe in. If the answer were a simple yes, dialogue might be a great deal more difficult than it is; the reality of dialogue suggests that we do not in fact have to do with a simple 'atheism' in respect of the other's models of God.[12]

But the idea that radical disagreement is simply a result of misunderstanding does not hold up in general. There may be such cases (for instance, the famous mistranslation of Khrushchev's 1956 'we will bury you' speech). But more often, to the extent that cultural misunderstandings are cleared up, to that extent, the starker the radical disagreement is found to be. Some of the most bitter radical disagreements are not *between* cultures but *within* them.

In genuine misunderstanding, the bar lines are empty. There is not enough in common for there to be radical disagreement. This is one of the *limits* to radical disagreement (at the other limit there is too much in common – the bar lines disappear). A more frequent experience in radical disagreement, though, is that the question of misunderstanding is itself found to be part of what is at issue. Conflict parties often say that whoever does not agree with them must, therefore, have misunderstood them. And then this, too (the same/different distinction), becomes part of what is at issue:

|(A) 'You have misunderstood me.'
 (B) 'I have understood you all too well – you are wrong.'|

How far do radical disagreements reach?

In radical disagreements, under repeated applications of the moment of alignment, conflict parties continually reach out for the decisive argument. In this way, more and more of what had been background is brought into the foreground – and is found to be already involved. A radical disagreement about the upbringing of children becomes a radical disagreement about God. A radical disagreement about dropping the bomb becomes a radical disagreement about the foundations of ethics. A radical disagreement about wages becomes a radical disagreement about capitalism. A radical disagreement about a piece of territory becomes a radical disagreement about history and religion. It is rather as if, when someone has fallen through the ice, ladders are brought to rescue the person struggling in the water, and the ladders fall in too.

But what is the background? Is it what Gadamer called our 'horizon'? So is a radical disagreement a 'clash of horizons'? It is often said that in our social and intellectual relationships we cannot get outside our own culture or language or 'lifeworld'. For Jürgen Habermas: 'Communicative actors are always moving within the horizon of their lifeworld: they cannot step outside of it.'[13] We are told that there is no external 'skyhook' or 'view from nowhere' or escape from our *habitus*.[14] But what does this mean in the context of radical disagreement? We have space for one concrete example.

In the radical disagreement between Marxism and Thatcherism, does each try to include the other in its horizon of comprehension? So is this a coexistence – or battle – of ideologies (horizons)? No. Neither party is saying anything like this. To suppose as much is to invoke a 'view from nowhere' within which equivalent horizons can be conceptually juxtaposed. But this is to miss the murderous war of annihilation being waged, which includes the very notion and application of the whole idea of 'ideology' (horizon):

|(A) 'In our capitalist society, the dominant bloc exercises economic and political domination over the working class and other intermediate strata of the population ... The authority element in political leadership, as in leadership in other domains, is thus determined by class relations. Why, then, have political leaders affected solidarity with 'the people'? ... This form of 'solidarity' functions as a strategy of containment: it represents a concession to the strength of the working class and its allies on the one hand, but constitutes a veil of equality beneath which the real inequalities of capitalist society can carry on, on the other ... This is the relationship which, I shall suggest, exists right across Thatcherite discourse.'[15]

(B) 'I believe that government should be very strong to do those things which only government can do. And at that point you have to say 'over to people'. People are inventive and creative, so you expect PEOPLE to create thriving industries, thriving services ... I wouldn't call this populist. I would say that many of the things which I've said strike a chord in the hearts of ordinary people. Why? Because they're British, because their character IS independent, because they DON'T like to be shoved around, because they ARE prepared to take responsibility, because they DO expect to be loyal to their friends and loyal allies – that's why you call it populist. I say it strikes a chord in the hearts of people. I know, because it struck a chord in my heart many, many years ago.'[16]|

In this radical disagreement, the first speaker, Nigel Fairclough, in a well-known and influential book, explicitly denies that Marxism is an 'ideology'. Critical discourse analysis scrutinizes texts and their processes of production in relation to the *reality* of the social conditions that generate them (for example, the class struggle). Thatcherism, on the other hand, *is* an ideology, because it is a discursive veil whose purpose is to fool the working class and conceal the reality of continuing inequality – and those who benefit from it. Margaret Thatcher, conversely, the second speaker, explicitly attacks Marxism as, precisely, an ideology – and one that is 'ideologically, politically and morally bankrupt' (1980 Conservative Party Conference). In contrast, she vigorously denies that there is a 'populist' ideology called 'Thatcherism'. She just calls a spade a spade. And the British people respond, because she is attuned to, and shares, what they feel.

Who will prevail? The verbal fight is to define what is mere ideology in order to eliminate it. It is to include what the other says not within another ideology, but within the world, which, under the moment of refutation, is what can be seen to expose its subterfuge and delusion. So the very notion of coexisting 'horizons' – and the idea of a horizon itself – is already existentially compromised in the verbal struggle. The fight is to annihilate the other. And, with the elimination of the other, horizons disappear, too. A radical disagreement is a prior involvement of the background invoked, which includes everything that is appealed to in the ongoing contest. A radical disagreement reaches as far as the eye can see.

How deep do radical disagreements go?

How deep does radical disagreement go? As deep as the distinctions invoked by conflict parties in the process of agonistic dialogue. We have seen above how it is under the moment of refutation that the 'world of distinctions out of which radical disagreement itself is constructed' springs into being. And it is these very distinctions – 'truth/opinion' 'fact/value', 'real/delusory', 'just/unjust', 'right/wrong', 'form/content', 'subject/object', 'same/different' – that are thereby found to be integrally involved. It is the distinction between these distinctions and what they do/do not distinguish that is already at issue.

There is no room to demonstrate this further here. My *Transforming Violent Conflict* offers a survey of examples. For instance, if I am involved in a radical disagreement, *my* opinion is a *true* opinion. A true opinion is my opinion. But, in the resulting radical disagreement, it is the invoked distinction |truth|/|opinion| that is itself already found to be existentially compromised.

195

Is there a theory of radical disagreement?

We now turn to the *third level* of heuristic engagement by asking how adequate third-party expert accounts of radical disagreement are. This means testing *theories* and *philosophies* of radical disagreements against *examples*. As seen in chapter 3, it is ultimately on these accounts that the theory behind communicative conflict resolution itself rests. For many years I have been searching for an adequate third-party account that can ground conflict resolution work. Is there a theory of radical disagreement?

In the search I have used three *adequacy tests*:

1. Does the theory offer a satisfactory account of radical disagreements in which it is not itself directly involved?
2. Does the theory offer a satisfactory account of its own involvement in radical theoretical disagreements?
3. Does the theory offer a satisfactory account of its own involvement in radical political disagreements?

In my article 'Is there a theory of radical disagreement?'[17] I apply the adequacy tests to twelve candidate theories (or clusters of theories) (see box 10.1). I will not repeat this here. Instead, we will begin with an *example* of radical disagreement, consider some brief third-party *descriptions*, and look at one illustration of applying the first

Box 10.1 Putative theories of radical disagreement reviewed

1 Realist theory
2 Marxist theory
3 Habermasian critical theory
4 Foucauldian theory
5 Gadamerian hermeneutic theory
6 Levinasian theory
7 Informal reasoning theory
8 Psycho-social constructionist theory
9 Anthropological theory
10 Radical feminist theory
11 Post-structural theory
12 Complex systems theory

adequacy test. We will then conclude with brief instances of applying the second and third adequacy tests.

An example

Kenize Mourad travelled through Israel, Gaza and the West Bank in 2002 at the height of the Al-Aqsa Intifada, and at exactly the time the Arab Peace Initiative was being launched. She spent months interviewing 'ordinary Palestinians and Israelis'. Here is an instance of radical disagreement recorded by Mourad involving the mother of the first female Palestinian suicide bomber and the Israeli sister of a bomb victim: the two younger women were both twenty-seven.

I(A) '[My daughter] had joined the Red Cross as a nurse and there she saw the worst. She witnessed atrocious things in Nablus, Jenin, Ramallah – women and children killed when they broke the curfew to go and buy food, wounded people dying without her being able to help. Three times when she had tried to go to people, she had been shot with rubber bullets. She had seen women give birth in front of checkpoints and lose their baby and sick people dying because they could not get to hospital. She told me how she had pleaded in vain with soldiers to let ambulances through . . . Every night she would come home exhausted and stressed and tell us everything she had seen. She was more and more outraged by what the Israelis were doing to civilians and by the world's indifference. But she never talked to me about the suicide bombings.'

(B) 'Arafat is no different from Hitler – you can't negotiate with him. Why doesn't the world understand that? How can the world not see that we have nothing but this country? Where can we go? It is the only place we Jews have. The Palestinians want to force us to leave . . . How can you compare Sharon and Arafat? . . . Perhaps you think I hate Arabs? Not at all. There are two Arab women in the firm where I work. I don't have any problem with them, even since my sister died. I have nothing against Palestinians or Israeli Arabs. I will never hate them. It's Arafat that I hate. He exploits his people and doesn't give them any means of educating themselves. All he can do is teach them how to kill . . . You think the Israelis are just as much to blame. You don't understand. You put us on the same level, but it's false. We are not the same. Our soldiers are not there to kill. It's a war and they are defending themselves; sometimes there's an accident, that's all. The Palestinians want a bloodbath. They don't care if they die or if they see their children dying. You can't compare us and you don't have the right to do that.'[18]

197

This is an example of radical disagreement but not of agonistic dialogue, because the speakers are not directly addressing each other. The author's third-party account is that her purpose in the interviews was to let 'ordinary Palestinians and Israelis tell their stories' and that the resulting radical disagreement was a manipulated misunderstanding:

> During my time there, I was filled with the sense that every encounter was weighted down by a terrible misunderstanding. Manipulated by extremists at either end, most of the people whom I interviewed were convinced that the other side wanted to annihilate them.[19]

This third-party description is illuminating in its own terms. But, for reasons seen above, it is not an adequate account of what is recorded between the bar lines. It is not what either of the speakers is saying. In each case, in the radical disagreement, under the moment of justification, the reference is not reflexive (to a story) but ostensive (to how things are). And, conversely, under the moments of refutation and explanation, what the other says and does (the behaviour of Israeli soldiers, the violent actions of Palestinians) is both condemned and accounted for in terms of what *causes* such unacceptable speech and behaviour. Kenize Mourad's third-party account assumes *reflexivity* and *equivalence*. The speakers, in their different ways, reject reflexivity and equivalence. That is what makes it a radical disagreement.

In his excellent analysis of the Israel–Palestine conflict, Alan Dowty says that to listen to each side separately is to find both sides' arguments 'utterly compelling':

> But of course one cannot consider the two claims in isolation from each other: there is only one Palestine. The most common response, probably, is to pronounce that if one side is right, then the other must be wrong; the rights and wrongs must match each other, like the wins and losses in a zero-sum game. But life seldom mimics a zero-sum game. These are clashes of right with right, in which history offers no easy answer about which right is superior to the other.[20]

Dowty's recommendations are admirable. But I do not think that the phrase 'clashes of right against right' is yet an adequate description of the radical disagreement, because it is not what either party is saying.

Some other third-party accounts

Something similar can be found in other, apparently equally uncontroversial, third-party descriptions of radical disagreements, such as the following.

In Northern Ireland the 'uncompromising mantras' uttered by the embattled communities are expressions of 'conflicting perceptions' in which 'the only solution is utter capitulation by one side or the other, as they see it.'[21]

In Kashmir 'fundamentalist beliefs' and 'hardened attitudes' lead to violence, where all sides in the conflict 'speak their own truth' and spill the blood of 'those of the opposite persuasion'.[22]

In Kosovo, the Albanians and Serbs 'not only live in segmented territories, but in segmented realities and segmented time, claiming the monopoly of victim status.'[23]

In Jerusalem, 'Arabs and Jews inhabit different mental worlds, informed by fundamentally different ideological axioms, infected with profound collective suspicions of each other and infused with a mutual dread that has repeatedly exploded into hate-filled aggression.'[24]

All of these offer valuable insights into the conflicts in question. But they are not adequate accounts of what lies at the heart of linguistic intractability. In each case, the third-party description assumes *reflexivity* and *equivalence*. The disagreements are described as coexisting and equivalent 'fundamentalist beliefs', 'conflicting perceptions', 'hardened attitudes', 'segmented realities', 'mental worlds' and 'ideological axioms'. But we have seen earlier in this chapter why, in the drastically restricted space of the war of words, there is no room for this. That is not what the conflict parties are saying. The verbal battle is not a generalized interchange between coexisting beliefs, perceptions, attitudes, truths, realities, mental worlds or ideologies, but a struggle to identify and eliminate *mistaken* beliefs, perceptions, truths and versions of reality by pointing at *how things are* – and to act accordingly. This applies as much to sophisticated theorists engaged in radical disagreement as to anyone else. That one army destroys another army in the war of weapons shows the sense in which, in the war of words, beliefs do not coexist either.

Here is an example of how the editors of a special issue of a (social and political) philosophy journal on 'disagreement and difference' define disagreement: 'First, not all forms of diversity entail conflict; disagreement does ... Second, disagreement does not encompass every form of conflict but only conflicts of a particular sort: conflicts of belief.'[25] This is also innocuous. The term 'conflicts of belief' once again assumes reflexivity and equivalence. But a radical disagreement is not a mere coexistence of subjectivities within some supposed neutral 'third space'. It is a life-and-death struggle to occupy the whole of discursive space.

Application of the first adequacy test – Michel Foucault and Kosovo

In her outstanding study of the way in which 'myths and truths started a war' in Kosovo, Julie Mertus gathers a remarkable collection of antagonistic Serb and Albanian testimonies. Here is a rich store of raw material for exploring, and trying to understand, the linguistic intractability at the heart of the conflict. Mertus could have gained deep insights into the conflict by taking the radical disagreement seriously and exploring it with the conflict parties. But she did not do this. Why not?

For Mertus, the leaders on both sides knew that much of this was politically motivated propaganda. At the level of the 'general population', in contrast, confined as they were within their own communities, it was more a case of 'hidden transcripts of anger, aggression and disguised discourses of dignity', where neither would 'understand each other's transcripts' even if they could gain access.[26] So, because she identifies radical disagreement at one level with superficial propaganda, and at another level with mutual misunderstanding, Mertus has no interest in exploring the radical disagreement itself further.

Beneath this is her theory that: 'for those who are interested in understanding and predicting behaviour, what matters is not what is *factually true* but what people believe to be "Truth".' Here Mertus explicitly invokes Michel Foucault in her use of inverted commas and capital letters for 'Truth'. Each society has its own 'regime of truth' and the 'opposite of a Truth is not necessarily a lie, rather it is a competing Truth linked to an alternative self-image.'[27] It is this theory of verbal disputes as competing 'Truths' that are functional for and private to communities, and are to be understood as contingent productions of power, that renders pointless any idea of taking the radical disagreement itself seriously.

It is worth noting that Mertus does not apply this to her own verbal battle with Serb officials. When she set out on her research, her original aim was to study not competing Kosovo Albanian and Serb 'Truths' but the factual truth about alleged Serb atrocities. She was then sidetracked into the former when the wide disparity between those accounts became apparent to her. But she did not forget her first intention. On Serb atrocities she is clear that there had indeed been 'years of gross human rights abuses against Albanians by Serbian officials'. This was not just a 'Truth' for Mertus but a factual truth:

I was right about the abuse.[28]

In her radical disagreement with the Serbs, Mertus no longer talks about 'Truths' but about truth. This is an example of applying the third adequacy test, which asks whether the theory in question 'offers a satisfactory account of its own involvement in radical political disagreements'. Here it does not.[29]

This is not a criticism of Foucault, because he never claimed to offer a theory of radical disagreement in the first place, whether in his early 'archaeological' research, in his 'genealogical' homage to Nietzsche, or in his later reinterpretation of his work in terms of 'problematization'.[30] To plunge for a moment into the difficult language of Foucault, his aim was to trace the subtle ways in which intricate eddies of power/knowledge precipitate forms of reification, subjection and exclusion. Things that appear ineluctable happen to have evolved like that and can therefore evolve differently in future. Foucault's concern was to subvert rigid categories – including the crude dialectic of disagreement that reproduces what it opposes in oversimplification and violence – in the interest of emancipation. The solvent for the normalizing deceptions of domination is micro-analysis and hyper-dispersal, not confrontation. Nothing could be further from the mutual refutation and brutal either–or of radical disagreement.

Returning to Mertus – and in simpler language – consequent upon her *descriptions* and *explanations* come her conflict resolution *prescriptions* for what should be done. Her suggestions are similar to those recommended in *Israeli and Palestinian Narratives of Conflict*, discussed at the beginning of Part II, although she is one of the few who recognizes the limits to dialogue for mutual understanding in times of maximum intractability:

> Allowing competing Truths to float through the air in the same space, unjudged and unquestioned, can be a revolutionary act. The Truths may always exist. But the very telling can provoke self-reflection and dismantle the link between Truths and the degrading of an oppositional 'other'. The telling may narrow the gap between Truths, creating a common bridge toward something else. Yet sometimes the divisions between people are too great, the fear too intense, the desire of some to maintain or gain power too overwhelming. The mere telling is not enough to stem conflict. Thus we cannot stop after the story-telling. We must have the will to think of bold, even drastic interventions to change the status quo into a more peaceful something else.[31]

But, because Mertus interprets what is said in terms of 'Truths' rather than truth, she leaves her examples 'floating' separately, and 'unjudged', and sees no point either in promoting their dynamic engagement or in exploring the resulting radical disagreement that lies at the heart of the linguistic intractability. She does not recognize radical disagreement as distinct from what she has already – brilliantly – exposed. So there is no further linguistic recourse after the limits of 'story-telling' are reached. The rest is non-verbal intervention, or linguistic therapy – or just 'something else'.

Application of the second and third adequacy tests

As an example of the application of the second adequacy test (Does the theory offer a satisfactory account of its own involvement in radical theoretical disagreements?), here is Michael Kelly's conclusion after studying the intense theoretical disputes between Habermas and Gadamer – both influential theorists in conflict resolution. On the Habermas–Gadamer disagreement, Kelly comments:

> The debate between Hans-Georg Gadamer and Jürgen Habermas had a rather ironic feature in that its path and conclusion seemed to contradict their notions of philosophical discourse. The path did not conform to Habermas's notion of communicative action oriented to understanding, because Habermas's interest in the dialogue was admittedly to establish his differences with Gadamer and, as a result, his action in the debate was more instrumental than communicative; and the conclusion did not conform to Gadamer's notion of a dialogue that culminates in a fusion of horizons, for the two participants were farther apart at the end of the dialogue than they had been at the start.[32]

I suggest that this is not just a 'rather ironic feature' of a specific example of theoretical radical disagreement but a feature of radical disagreement in general. The fact that, in agonistic dialogue, participants find that they are 'farther apart at the end of the dialogue than they had been at the start' is what exploration of radical disagreement with conflict parties repeatedly shows.

Turning to the third adequacy test (Does the theory offer a satisfactory account of its own involvement in radical political disagreements?), Jacques Derrida has also been influential in dismissing radical disagreement as a clumsy eruption of conflicting binaries. He was concerned to expose their prior equivocated self-erasure in the very notion of iteration at the heart of 'writing'. He carried this over into his own ironic and self-concealing exchanges with both John Searle and Hans-Georg Gadamer.

But none of this affected the straightforward language Derrida used when he was himself involved in direct political struggle and radical disagreement. Here, for example, he scornfully refutes Francis Fukuyama's 'end of history' thesis, fiercely rejects the US-led reordering of global priorities after 1989, and calls for the setting up of a 'new International':

> For it must be cried out, at a time when some have the audacity to neo-evangelize in the name of the ideal of a liberal democracy that has finally realized itself as the ideal of human history: never have violence, inequality, exclusion, famine, and thus economic oppression affected as many human beings in the history of the earth and of humanity.[33]

I think that even in this short passage we can detect the moment of recommendation (advocacy for the setting up of a new International), the moment of justification (reference to the scale of violence, inequality, exclusion and economic oppression in the world), the moment of alignment (confronting Francis Fukuyama's 'end of history' argument), the moment of refutation (the dismissal of its 'audacity' as a transparently mendacious 'neo-evangelizing' tract) and the moment of explanation (the reason why Fukuyama and others extol the 'ideal of liberal democracy' is to perpetuate the reordering of global priorities post-1989 in the interest of hegemons, foremost among whom is the USA). The fusion of fact, value, emotion and action is also manifest. Here, therefore, under the intense pressure of urgent political choice, is an example of the breaking out of the first level of heuristic engagement that Derrida's own theory had tried to deconstruct in advance.

Conclusion

Exploration of radical disagreement by, and with, conflict parties regularly shows that they are not closer, but much further apart than was realized. Radical disagreements are found to be about what they are about. Radical disagreements reach as far as the eye can see. Radical disagreements go as deep as the distinctions invoked in the process of radical disagreeing. Testing third-party expert accounts shows that there is no adequate theory or philosophy of radical disagreement.[34] Far from being 'all too familiar', radical disagreement is perhaps the least familiar aspect of intense and enduring political conflict.

CONCLUSION:
LIVING WITH RADICAL
DISAGREEMENT

It is notoriously difficult to predict the future in human affairs. Given the increasing pace and complexity of change, forward projection is hazardous over quite short spans of time. Few can guess what will happen even ten years ahead when there are sudden discontinuities. How many in 1919 foresaw the Wall Street Crash? Or in 1929 the outbreak of the Second World War? Or in 1979 the collapse of the Soviet Union? Or one year before the 2011 Arab revolutions the disintegration of the entire regional system? Perhaps the only thing that can be safely predicted is that commentators will later read back into their accounts of the past the *post hoc* knowledge that was so conspicuously absent before.

But there is another, much broader, prediction that can be made with some confidence. As far ahead as we can see, human life on earth will be conflictual. And at the heart of our most virulent and intractable conflicts will be the linguistic intractability that blocks all attempts at conflict resolution. Human beings do not struggle in silence. The only reason there was no radical disagreement in H. G. Wells's *War of the Worlds* was because one of the protagonists was non-human.

So, in contrast to classic conflict resolution, this book puts the phenomenon of radical disagreement at the centre of its focus. Far from being a *terminus* to dialogue, radical disagreement is seen as an *opportunity* to engage with struggles that are otherwise inaccessible. This opens up a new frontier in conflict studies. *Heuristic engagement* discloses a largely unexplored continent. This is the submerged Atlantis on which so many conflict resolution enterprises founder. *Strategic engagement* shows how to adapt practice accordingly if we want to navigate these unfamiliar waters.

But the frontiers of failure are never ending. No sooner is one challenge confronted than another appears. As we move forwards, 'hills peep o'er hills, and Alps on Alps arise'.[1] What when conflict parties prefer to repeat familiar scripts than undergo the discomfort of strenuous strategic engagement? Or powerful players are able to ignore the position of others (opponents and third parties) and have strategic reasons *not* to engage with them? Or possessors and challengers in asymmetric conflicts are controlled by intransigent leaders who crush the possibility of collective internal strategic thinking? Or, in disintegrated war zones, conflict parties are too disaggregated to sustain coherent strategic thought and action?[2] From the examples looked at in this book, we are very aware that overcoming these obstacles requires patience, insight and determination.

Beyond this again lie even greater challenges, where extended conflict resolution itself fails. What when the promotion of heuristic and strategic engagement leads to greater emphasis on more violent means rather than less? What when the distinction between extremism of ends and extremism of means breaks down and it is no longer possible to separate them, because violence and terror become an end as well as a means – as in the case of Hitler's Germany or Islamic State? Or when it is impossible to apply 'Clausewitz in reverse' and continue the hitherto violent conflict by other means, because the fundamental aim of the perpetrator is in itself violent – for example, the physical elimination of opposed identity groups? We have reached the extreme boundary of possibility for conflict resolution, where it is confronted by opponents of its own fundamental principles and values who refuse even to countenance strategic alternatives to violence.

In response to the events of September 2001, Bikhu Parekh rejected the US government's militaristic and 'punitive' reaction, which he saw as counter-productive and morally equivalent to the terrorism it purported to oppose. Instead he advocated 'intercultural dialogue' between Western and non-Western (in this case, particularly Muslim) societies with a view to uncovering the deeper sources of grievance and perceived injustice behind the attack:

> The point of the dialogue is to deepen mutual understanding, to expand sympathy and imagination, to exchange not only arguments but also sensibilities, to take a critical look at oneself, to build up mutual trust, and to arrive at a more just and balanced view of both the contentious issues and the world in general.[3]

This conflict resolution response is admirable, often successful, and, in terms of a broad response to conditions which breed violence and terrorism, no doubt wise. But is it always appropriate? Here is an example where outrage is expressed at the murder of the Rev. Julie Nicholson's daughter, Jenny, by Mohammad Siddique Khan on the Edgware train in London on 7 July 2005:

> There are few human words that can adequately express what we feel about people who indiscriminately carry out apparent acts of senseless violence against innocent civilian populations and, unbelievably, do so in the name of God. Such delusion, such evil, is impossible for us to begin to comprehend.

Julie Nicholson herself eventually gave up her own ministry because she could not forgive the perpetrator:

> No parent should reasonably expect to outlive their children. I rage that a human being could choose to take another human being's life. I rage that someone should do this in the name of a God. I find that utterly offensive. We have heard a lot in the media about things causing certain groups of people offence and I would say that I am hugely offended that someone should take my daughter in the name of a religion or a God.[4]

For Julie Nicholson, the prime purpose of any 'dialogue' with those perpetrating and justifying such acts in this way would not be to 'expand sympathy and imagination' or to 'take a critical look at oneself', but to expose their unimaginable inhumanity and the outrageous travesty of their spurious attribution to God.

A conflict engagement approach, as advocated in this book, does not expect to be 'above the fray'. It knows that, in cases like this, it is itself involved in the struggles it is attempting to influence. It, too, needs a strategy in order to win. In the war of weapons Hitler's armies are defeated, and Raqqa and Mosul have to be retaken from Islamic State. But what is the equivalent in the war of words?

Here is the reason given by the editor for republishing an English translation of Hitler's *Mein Kampf* in 1991:

> *Mein Kampf* is lengthy, dull, bombastic, repetitious and extremely badly written. As a historical picture of Hitler's life up to the time he wrote it, it is also quite unreliable. Most of its statements of fact and the entire tenor of the argument in the autobiographical passages are demonstrably untrue. Why then revive *Mein Kampf*? Firstly, it is an introduction to the mind and methods of Adolf Hitler. It is a mind at once concise and repetitive, a mishmash of *idées reçus* and insights, a second-rate mind of immense power, the mind of a man whose early death would have made Europe a safer place to live in for all its citizens. The second reason for its study is that we may know and recognise

the arguments of the enemies of democracy in our midst. 'Oh that my enemy had written a book', said Job. Hitler did. It was there for people to read. Despite the omissions from the first British edition, bits of it were circulated to the British cabinet and made available through the British pamphlet press. *Mein Kampf* is not in any sense the work of a civilised man who thought peace a desirable or normal state of international relations. It does not only raise the historical question of why its British readers did not recognise this and know that in Hitler they faced an implacable enemy. It faces us in the post-Cold War era with a similar question. Are there enemies of peace in power in the world today? Are we trying to recognise them?[5]

This is an argument for a reprint after Hitler's defeat and death. But what would exponents of a conflict engagement approach have done in 1925/6 when *Mein Kampf* first appeared, knowing that it might help to propel its author to power a few years later? Would they have followed conflict resolution principles in aiming to 'deepen mutual understanding' and tried to promote acceptance of 'the validity of competing narratives'? Or followed Voltaire in disagreeing with what Hitler said but 'defending to the death his right to say it'? Or acted on Jefferson's advice to rely on truth to dispel error, because 'truth is great and will prevail if left to herself'? Or would they, rather, have done everything in their power not just to 'refute Hitler in the open court of public opinion' but to ensure that his discourse never reached its intended audience at all?

As far ahead as we can see, we will have to live with intense political conflicts, and with the linguistic intractability and radical disagreements that go with them. We live in an agonistic world. This book suggests that we know far less about radical disagreement than we think we do, and that taking radical disagreement seriously, trying to understand it, and learning how to adapt accordingly, will be not the least of our tasks if we want future generations to flourish – or even to survive.

NOTES

1 King ([1963] 1992), pp. 533–4.
2 Coser (1956); Coleman (1957).
3 Schelling (1960); Rapoport and Chammah (1965).
4 Burton (1968, 1969, 1972, 1990a).
5 Quoted Kerman (1974), p. 83.
6 Rapoport (1960) p. 441; original emphasis.
7 For this paragraph and the previous paragraph I am indebted to my colleague Tom Woodhouse, who did the original research into this topic for chapter 2 of *Contemporary Conflict Resolution* (Miall, Ramsbotham and Woodhouse 1999).
8 *Journal of Conflict Resolution*, 1/1 (1957): 1.
9 *Journal of Conflict Resolution*, 27/1 (1973): 5.
10 Karl Popper's well-known test for the empirical content of hypotheses is whether they are falsifiable. If they are not, as scientific theories they are devoid of content (1959). So scientific advance depends on searching for 'failure'. In the same vein, Thomas Kuhn (1962) argued that scientific revolutions take the form of paradigm shifts as a result of anomalies in the old paradigm. It can thus be said that the old paradigm (for example, the Ptolemaic world system) deserves the credit for identifying its own 'failure' and therefore generating the new paradigm (for example, the Copernican system). And so on.
11 Polemology is the study of struggle and war; eirenics is the study of conditions for peace. Both are required in conflict resolution.
12 Deutsch (1949, 1973).
13 Galtung (1976, 1996).
14 Burton (1997), p. 38; see also Burton (1987, 1990b).
15 Summed up in Kelman (1996) and Mitchell and Banks (1996).
16 E.g., Boulding (1977) vs. Galtung (1987).
17 Osgood (1962); Axelrod (1984).
18 Barber (1984); Susskind and Cruikshank (1987); Floyer Acland (1995); Dukes (1996).

19 Azar (1990); Azar and Burton (1986); Carnegie Commission (1997).
20 Boulding (1976, 1990).
21 Fisher and Keashly (1991).
22 Anderson (1996).
23 Salem (1993, 1997).

CHAPTER 2 CONFLICT RESOLUTION AND ITS ENEMIES

1 Given the size of the topic and the limited space available, the coverage in this chapter is selective but, I hope, gives a representative idea of the overall nature of current analysis and discussion. For a fuller treatment, see the fourth edition of *Contemporary Conflict Resolution* (Ramsbotham, Woodhouse and Miall 2016), particularly chapters 3 and 4.
2 The title of the book is taken from US President Abraham Lincoln's first inaugural address.
3 Pinker (2011), p. xxi.
4 Pinker (2002), p. 336.
5 Produced by Andrew Mack and his colleagues at the School for International Studies, Simon Fraser University, Vancouver: Mack et al. (2014).
6 Ibid., p. 3.
7 Pinker and Mack (2014).
8 Holsti (1991).
9 United Nations Charter, Preamble.
10 Pettersson and Wallensteen (2015).
11 IEP (2015).
12 *Global Terrorism Database* (2015).
13 *Global Burden of Armed Violence* (2015).
14 OECD (2014).
15 IPS (2014), p. 4.
16 IEP (2015).
17 UNHCR (2015).
18 IEP (2015), pp. 82–90, 65.
19 Mead (2014) pp. 1, 3.
20 Ikenberry (2014), pp. 80–1.
21 Suganami (1996).
22 Kriesberg, Northrop and Thorson (1989).
23 Mayer (2009).
24 Coleman (2011).
25 Mitchell (2014).
26 Mouffe (1999).
27 Little (2014).

CHAPTER 3 WHY CONFLICT RESOLUTION FAILS

1 Howard (1984), p. 22.
2 For example, according to Simon Sebag Montefiore in his book *Young Stalin*, Stalin's propaganda ('a lie always has a stronger effect than the truth: the main thing is to obtain one's objective') concealed a deeper and more

significant level of sincerity: 'Ultimately Stalin was a devout Marxist of "semi-Islamic fervour" allowing no friend or family to stand between him and his mission' (Montefiore 2007, p. 230).

3 Fisher and Ury (1981), p. x; original emphasis.

4 Deutsch (2000), p. 31. The greatest living exponent of interactive problem-solving is Herbert Kelman (1996, 2011, 2016, 2017 forthcoming).

5 Dialogue approaches reviewed in Bojer and McKay (2006) include Appreciative Enquiry, Change Lab, Deep Democracy, Future Search, Open Space, Scenario Planning, Sustained Dialogue, World Café, Bohmian Dialogue, Corrymeela Community, Israeli–Palestinian School of Peace (Neve Shalom/Wahat El Salam) and Learning Journeys (Montfleur process).

6 Bojer and McKay (2006), p. 10; Bohm (1996).

7 Fisher (1997), p. 121.

8 Galtung (2004), p. 38.

9 Ibid., p. 57.

10 Ibid., p. 80.

11 Jabri (1996), p. 165.

12 Lederach (2005), p. 53.

13 Saunders (1999), p. 60.

14 Rothman (1992), p. 170.

15 See Ronald Fisher (1997), pp. 163–4.

16 See Ramsbotham (2016 forthcoming).

17 Broome (1993), p. 104.

18 Taylor (2002), p. 287.

19 www.Islamic-world.net/war/Islamic-world_position.htm (2003; no longer available).

20 Fisher, Kopelman and Schneider (1996), pp. 143–4.

21 Ibid., pp. 20, 28.

22 Ibid., p. 39.

23 Ibid., p. 40.

24 Quoted in Schofield (1996), pp. 291ff.

25 Rothman (1992), p. 171.

26 Ibid., p. 19.

27 Ropers (2008), pp. 11–41.

28 Ibid., p. 17.

CHAPTER 4 PROMOTING STRATEGIC ENGAGEMENT

1 Ramsbotham (2010), p. 254.

2 This is not quite the same as Chantal Mouffe's idea of agonism. In Mouffe's conception of *agonistic pluralism*, the raw antagonism and violence characteristic of human society in general (the 'political') is domesticated and tamed within the democratic *agon* so that 'enemies' become 'adversaries', who thereby gain a respect for each other as well as for the democratic 'rules of the game' that define the space of democratic 'politics' (1999, p. 755). Whereas what I call *agonistic dialogue* is precisely verbal exchange between enemies, it still includes the antagonistic. Agonistic dialogue is the dialogue of intense political struggle in general without trying to distinguish yet between domesticated and undomesticated varieties. Ibid., pp. 745–58.

3 Deutsch (2000), pp. 32, 35.
4 Freedman (2013), p. xi.
5 Ibid., p. x.
6 Theory of change emerged in the 1990s at the Aspen Institute (USA) and was exemplified in Weiss et al. (1995).
7 Boulding (1990).
8 Nye (2004).
9 Palestine Strategy Group (2008).
10 Bashir (2009).
11 Zalzberg (2009), pp. 2, 9.

PART II CASE STUDY

1 Excerpts from Rotberg (2006), pp. 1–17.
2 Rouhana (2006), p. 118.
3 Ibid., p. 116.
4 Ibid., p. 127.
5 Bar-On (2006), p. 153.
6 Rouhana (2006), p. 128.
7 Ibid., p. 125.
8 Bar-On (2006), p. 148.
9 Nadim Rouhana is a professor at the Fletcher School, Tufts University, and formerly the Henry Hart Rice Professor of Conflict Analysis and Resolution at George Mason University. Mordechai Bar-On, a historian and former Israel Defense Forces Chief Education Officer, was for many years a leader of the Peace Now movement. In this case they are also colleagues in a joint project.
10 Rouhana (2006), p. 133.
11 Bar-On (2006), pp. 147–8, 167–8.
12 Rotberg (2006), p. 8.
Israeli Strategic Forum (ISF), Palestine Strategy Group (PSG), Palestinian Citizens of Israel Group (PCIG)
In the first phase, funded by the European Union, the directors of the Oxford Research Group project were Gabrielle Rifkind (director of the ORG Middle East programme) and Ahmed Badawi; the Palestine Strategy Group was formed and guided by Husam Zomlot and facilitated by Ahmed Badawi; the Israeli Strategic Forum, co-sponsored by Tzav Pius, was led by Avner Haramati, Mario Schejtman, Baruch Oveda and Ofer Zalzberg, with workshop methodology devised and conducted by Adam Kahane assisted by Shay Ben Yosef and Tova Averbuch. The second phase, funded by the Norwegian and UK governments, was managed by Refqa abu-Remaileh for ORG; the Israeli Strategic Forum was facilitated and run by Moty Crystal (director of NEST Consulting), Orit Gal (the Complexity Hub) and Amira Dotan; and the Palestine Strategy Group was directed by Khaled Hroub, with Husam Zomlot and Hani Masri as co-directors, in partnership with Badael in Ramallah. In the third phase, funded by the Norwegian government and the United States Institute for Peace, the Israeli Strategic Forum was directed by Chris Langdon and Gabrielle Rifkind and managed by Sharri Plonsky for ORG, and by the Van Leer Institute, Jerusalem, under the direction of Anat Lapidot-Firilla and Yoni Mendel, managed by Eran Hakim and facilitated by Michael Sternberg;

the Palestine Strategy Group was managed for ORG by Sara Hassan and directed by Husam Zomlot, in partnership with Mazarat, Ramallah, directed by Hani Masri, co-directed by Khalil Shaheen, Palthink in Gaza, directed by Omar Shaban, and with advice from Sam Bahour and Bashir Bashir. The Palestinian Citizens of Israel Group was directed by Refqa abu-Remaila and Marzuq Halabi, with advice from Bashir Bashir and in partnership with the I-lam Media Center for Arab Palestinians in Israel, director Amal Jamal. The Strategic Thinking for Citizens project was directed by Refqa abu-Remaileh and facilitated by Marzuq Halabi and Anat Reisman-Levi. Gabrielle Rifkind has been director of ORG's Middle East programme throughout. Oliver Ramsbotham has been chair of ORG for most of this period and consultant on strategic thinking throughout. Tony Klug has been Middle East consultant throughout. In the fourth phase of this enterprise, beginning in 2016, Refqa abu-Remaileh has been the overall director of the project.

Chapter 5 Strategic Thinking for Possessors

1 Wistrich (1991).
2 Schlaim (2000), p. 20.
3 Ibid., p. 35.
4 Meir (1975), p. 226, quoted in Dowty (2012), p. 72.
5 Goldmann (1969), pp. 289–90, quoted in Schlaim (2000), p. 40.
6 This had been originally triggered by the signing on 17 April 1963 of a pro-visional constitution for an Arab Federation between Egypt, Syria and Iraq: 'Ben-Gurion's personal reaction to the Arab Federation was one of deep, almost irrational, anxiety' (Schlaim 2000, pp. 213–14; Schlaim 2009).
7 Schlaim (2000), p. 239. Rabin had been chief of operations of the Palmach (commandos) during the War of Independence and had been made chief of staff of the Israel Defense Forces (IDF) in 1964. He oversaw Israel's victory in the Six-Day War.
8 Laqueur and Rubin (2008), p. 99, quoted in Dowty (2012), p. 116.
9 Dowty (2012), p.117.
10 Schama (2013).
11 Sand (2009).
12 'From the beginning (whether in biblical or archaeological version), Jews were made in hill country. In Hebrew, emigrating to Israel is still *aliyah*, a going up. Jerusalem was unimaginable on the low fluvial plain. Rivers were murky with temptation; the sea was even worse ...' (Schama 2013, pp. 3–4). It is the 'West Bank' – Judea and Samaria – that constitutes the heart of the ancient 'land of Israel', not the coastal plain where Tel Aviv has been built.
13 Ross (2004), pp.767, 756–7.
14 See, for example, *A Brief History of Palestine* (forthcoming) by Mohammad Shtayyeh for a recent very different reading, including an alternative account to that given in the rest of this chapter.
15 Schlaim (2009), pp. 35–6.
16 Pappe (2012), p. 276.
17 Hamas Charter (1988).
18 See, for example, Thiessen and Darweish (forthcoming), which analyses

212

current 'dialogue and encounter initiatives' and opposition to them by advocates of 'more confrontational forms of conflict resolution' in the current circumstances. See also Ifat Maoz's thorough survey 'Does contact work in protracted asymmetrical conflict?' (2011), where she assesses the 'coexistence model', the 'joint projects model' and the 'narrative-story-telling model'.

19 Zalzberg (2009).

20 This was the Israeli response to the attempted infiltration by six boats in the 'Gaza Freedom Flotilla' organized by Free Gaza Movement and Turkish Foundation for Human Rights and Freedoms and Humanitarian Relief (IHH). The flotilla was carrying humanitarian aid and construction materials with a view to breaking the Israeli blockade. Ten activists were killed, including eight Turkish nationals and one Turkish American. Ten commandos were wounded, one seriously.

21 As argued, for example, by Bronwen Maddox (2014) and by the editors of *The Economist* (2014).

22 Arab Peace Initiative (2002).

23 For example, Arab governments who officially 'sign up' to the Arab Peace Initiative but at the same time continue to advocate the eradication of Israel.

24 For some time now opinion polls have suggested that some 80 per cent of Israeli Jews still think that 'the Palestinians have not accepted the existence of the State of Israel and would destroy it if they could' (Israel Democracy Institute, 2010, quoted in Dowty 2012, p. 252); and 67 per cent of Palestinians believe that an armed uprising would 'serve their national interests better than negotiations with Israel' (Israel Democracy Institute, *The Times*, 16 December 2015).

CHAPTER 6 STRATEGIC THINKING FOR CHALLENGERS

1 Bahour (2008).

2 Bashir (2009).

3 Zack Beauchamp, 'It's over: why the Palestinians are finally giving up on Obama and the US peace process', 22 January 2015, www.vox.com/2015/1/22/7324107/Palestinian-abbas-peace-process. See also Turner and Hussein (2015), p. 424, n. 15: 'A former member of the PLO Negotiation Support Unit told Turner in an interview that Saeb Erekat often referred to the options outlined in the PSG paper *Regaining the Initiative*.'

4 This proposal was first drafted by Tony Klug and Sam Bahour. As noted in the preface, this is now planned as a major initiative focused on 5 June 2017, the anniversary of the Israeli takeover, in line with the new two-track Palestinian strategy: 'a Palestinian-led international campaign ... leveraging support across the globe to pressure the Israeli government into making its choice by the proposed deadline: ending the occupation, or equal treatment of all subjects under its control until a political solution is found' (Bahour 2016).

5 Rouhana (2006), p. 133.

6 Palestine Strategy Group (2008), p. 16.

7 Ibid., p. 15.

8 Today UNWRA estimates Palestinian refugee numbers at nearly 5 million, of whom 1.5 million live in UNRWA camps. According to a 2003 survey, only 10 per cent would live in Israel if given the chance. Most would accept citizenship elsewhere and/or compensation.
9 The quotations come from the Quartet 'Road Map', specifically endorsed in United Nations Security Council Resolution 1515.
10 Palestine National Council, Political Communiqué and Declaration of Independence, A/43/827-S/20278.
11 PSG (2008), p. 16.
12 Palestine Strategy Group (2008), p. 8.
13 YNet News, 28 January 2011, quoted in Dowty (2012), p. 220.

CHAPTER 7 STRATEGIC ENGAGEMENT WITHIN, ACROSS AND BETWEEN CONFLICT PARTIES

1 See, for example, the analysis by Ben-Porat (2008). The experience of the ISF demonstrates this. Its membership – some of whom were settlers – included many passionate supporters of a Palestinian state, a single bi-national state, and other variations such as 'two states, one homeland'. For example, with reference to the Palestinian-led campaign to force an Israeli choice by 5 June 2017 between the two stark alternatives of ending occupation or equal treatment for all throughout mandate Palestine, this is now paralleled by an Israeli-led campaign to do the same (Schnell and Bar-Tal 2016).
2 Presentation at the Harvard Middle East Seminar 'New Visions and Strategies for an Israel–Palestinian Peace', 17 September 2015.
3 Ravid (2015). Immediately after the election Netanyahu tried to row back from this – for reasons seen in chapter 8 below.
4 Netanyahu's coalition includes the Likud, Jewish Home, Shas, Torah Judaism and Kulanu parties (61 seats). In June 2016 Yisrael Beiteinu (6 seats) also joined the coalition.
5 Lintl (2015).
6 *The Times of Israel*, 5 October 2015.
7 The Israeli Labor Party resolution *A Comprehensive Diplomatic-Security Plan* can be found, together with commentary, in Ofer Zalzberg (2016), pp. 6–7.
8 The discussion was held under the aegis of the Harvard Middle East Seminar 'New Visions and Strategies for an Israel-Palestinian Peace', 17 September 2015.
9 See Rouhana (1997); Ghanem (2001); International Crisis Group (2004); Pappé (2011); International Crisis Group (2012).
10 Rouhana (1989), p. 55; Smooha and Peretz (1982).
11 In particular, the National Committee of the Heads of Arab Local Councils (NCALC), the sole non-partisan organization representing the Palestinian minority, formed the main constituent in the Follow-Up Committee.
12 The four documents were issued by the Adalah (Justice) Center, the Mada Al-Karmel Center, the Musawa (equality) Center, and the National Committee of the Heads of Arab Local Councils.
13 Palestinian Citizens of Israel Group (2015), pp. 3–4, 1, 6.
14 Ibid., p. 1.

15 Ibid., p. 7.
16 Ibid., pp. 8, 7.
17 Ibid., p. 27.
18 Ibid., p. 28.
19 Ibid., p. 11.
20 Ibid., pp. 8–10.
21 Ibid., p. 20.
22 Ibid., p. 15.
23 Ibid., p. 21.
24 At the moment only Druze Arabs serve in the Israel Defense Forces.
25 Palestinian Citizens of Israel Group (2015), p. 17.
26 Ibid., p. 25.
27 Ibid., p. 26.
28 Ibid., pp. 9–10.
29 Ibid., pp. 9, 30.
30 Ibid., p. 9.
31 Ibid., p. 16.
32 Ibid., p. 29.
33 Israeli Strategic Forum (2015), pp. 5, 6.
34 Ibid., p. 7.
35 Ibid., p. 17.
36 I owe this information to Alan Dowty.
37 Israeli Strategic Forum (2015), pp. 18, 19.
38 Ibid., p. 20.
39 Ibid., p. 19.
40 Ibid., p. 17.
41 Borchard (2015).
42 Beneath this again lie even deeper cultural complexities that cannot be explored here: for example, just as Mizrahi Jews are on the whole more at home with Arab music and culture, so among some Arab Israelis there is the emergence of 'Arabrabiya' – a 'distinct Palestinian Israeli dialect of Arabic intertwined with Hebrew words' (Pappe 2011, p. 275).
43 'Strategic Thinking for Citizens'. This project, funded in October 2014 by the US Institute for Peace, was initiated by Refqa abu-Remaileh and facilitated by Marzuq Halabi and Anat Reisman-Levy.

CHAPTER 8 THE KERRY INITIATIVE AND THE ROLE OF THIRD PARTIES

1 Ramsbotham and Schiff (forthcoming).
2 Erekat (2008, 2015).
3 In addition to Fisher and Ury (1981), Erekat cites Fisher and Brown (1988), Fisher and Sharp (1988), Fisher, Ury and Bruce (1991 – the second edition of *Getting to Yes*), and Fisher, Kopelman and Schneider (1996).
4 Erekat cites the unpublished 'Negotiation training workshop notes' (2007) used by John Murray (advisor to the Negotiations Support Unit) and Terry Barnett (co-founder of the Crisis Management Program and Crisis Management Group of the Harvard Negotiations Project) in the Palestinian Negotiations Affairs Department, Ramallah. The Negotiations Support Unit was later renamed the Palestine Negotiations Support Project.

5 Erekat (2015).
6 Murray and Barnett (2007), quoted in Erekat (2015), p. 11.
7 Murray and Barnett (2007), quoted ibid., pp. 13, 26.
8 Fisher et al. (1994) p. 39.
9 Murray and Barnett (2007), quoted in Erekat (2015), p. 11.
10 Murray and Barnett (2007), quoted ibid., p. 12.
11 Murray and Barnett (2007), quoted ibid., pp. 13, 20.
12 Murray and Barnett (2007), quoted ibid., p. 22.
13 Murray and Barnett (2007), quoted ibid., p. 26.
14 Schiff (2015).
15 Birnbaum and Tibon (2014).
16 Ibid.
17 Ravid (2013).
18 Ibid.; Birnbaum and Tibon (2014).
19 A former US ambassador to Israel, Martin Indyk, was appointed to serve as special envoy for the peace process, responsible for facilitating the talks on behalf of the American administration.
20 Ravid (2014c).
21 Ravid (2014a); Ravid and Khoury (2014).
22 Brom (2014).
23 Birnbaum and Tibon (2014).
24 Ibid.; Yadlin (2014).
25 Ravid and Khoury (2014); Tibon (2014).
26 Yaar and Hermann (2014a).
27 Birnbaum and Tibon (2014).
28 Brom (2014); Yadlin (2014).
29 Birnbaum and Tibon (2014); Ravid (2014c).
30 Israel's position is that no further claims should be advanced following the signing of a peace agreement. Israel's concern is that, if the peace will not be permanent but rather an interim agreement, the Palestinians would be able to use their state to pursue further conflict with Israel.
31 Birnbaum and Tibon (2014); Halevi (2014).
32 Ravid (2014c).
33 Yaar and Hermann (2014b).
34 Ibid.; Ravid (2014b).
35 Friedman (2014).
36 Birnbaum and Tibon (2014).
37 Perhaps France has come nearest to proposing a Plan B. This proposes an alternative route to a Palestinian state rather than an alternative to a Palestinian state. It would involve a regional context for negotiations, with the possibility of independent French recognition of Palestine if negotiations failed. For example, on his state visit to Egypt in April 2016, President Hollande, together with President Sisi, announced that 'in the forefront' of 'our joint efforts' to find settlements for the regional crisis 'is the drive to revive Palestinian–Israeli negotiations with a view to implementing the two-state solution and the establishment of a Palestinian state with East Jerusalem as its capital.' *Egyptian Gazette*, 18 April 2016, p. 1.

CHAPTER 9 OTHER PHASES, OTHER LEVELS, OTHER CONFLICTS

1 Clausewitz ([1832] 1976), p. 70.
2 Filardo-Llamas (2008).
3 Siebert (2014), p. 37.
4 For national dialogue in general, see Collén (2014).
5 Yawnghwe (2014), p. 49.
6 Ganesan (2014), p. 131.
7 Küng and and Kuschel (1993), p. 18.
8 Al'Alwani (1997), p. 17.
9 Pantham (1992), p. 132, quoted in Petito (2011), p. 14.
10 See, for example, the April 2016 Alawite document *Declaration of an Identity Reform*, which draws a distinction (a) between Alawite beliefs and majority Shia doctrines and (b) between the long-term strategic needs of the Alawite minority and the short-term internal interests of the Assad regime, on the one hand, and the external interests of Iran, on the other. This is vital information for planning possible future constitutional arrangements to preserve/reconstruct the Syrian state (available on the internet in translation in a number of versions; see Wyatt 2016).
11 Sara Hasan, who initiated the project and is managing it for the Oxford Research Group. See also Ramsbotham (2016) Strategic studies, conflict resolution and prevailing patterns of transnational conflict, in Arabic in the workshop proceedings and in English on the Oxford Research Group Website.
12 Bell (2008).
13 Ibid., p. 53. Of these, 91 per cent were 'intrastate', covering issues ranging from ceasefires to new constitutional arrangements for how power will be held and exercised. According to the United Nations, some 50 per cent of civil wars have terminated in peace agreements since 1990 (Wallensteen and Sollenberg 2007). Bell comments that this is 'more than in the previous two centuries combined, where only one in five resulted in negotiated settlement', and that 'this figure is supported by empirical research' (Bell 2007, p. 27). So there has been an unprecedented torrent of legally significant agreements, which is something to set against the perhaps more gloomy 'statistics of deadly quarrels' discussed in chapter 3.
14 Ibid., p. 22.
15 Ibid., p. 236.
16 Caspersen (2017 forthcoming).
17 Ibid.
18 Ramsbotham and Schiff (2016 forthcoming).
19 Zartman (2000, 2008).
20 Zartman (2008), p. 232.
21 Zartman and de Soto (2010), p. 7.
22 Zartman (2008), p. 233.
23 Zartman and de Soto (2010), p. 23.
24 Ibid., p. 26.
25 Ibid., pp. 41–2.
26 Zartman (2008), p. 232.
27 Something similar applies to Dan Pruitt's 'readiness theory', although there is no space to develop this here. See Ramsbotham, Woodhouse and Miall (2016) pp. 211–12; Schiff (2015).

CHAPTER 10 EXPLORING AGONISTIC DIALOGUE

1 Cheshire (1985); Finnis, Boyle and Grisez (1987).
2 Ramsbotham (1987), pp.197, 232.
3 *USA Today*, 7 March 2006.
4 Matt Roth-Cline (2004) 'Half measures', The Armchair Philosopher, online source (no longer available).
5 On the idea of the 'web of belief', in which belief systems are likened to spider webs with some beliefs central to our conceptions of the world and some more peripheral, so that we are more ready to give up or adapt the latter than the former, see Quine and Ullian (1970).
6 In a consequentialist ethic, (roughly) things are right or wrong because of their consequences (i.e., if more people are saved by bombing than not bombing, then do it). In a deontological ethic, things are right or wrong in themselves (i.e., do not deliberately kill innocent people). A classic comparison here is between the ethical systems of Jeremy Bentham and Immanuel Kant.
7 Dowty (2012), p. 4; original emphasis.
8 Anderson (1991).
9 Locke ([1690] 1975), III.ix.16.
10 Augsburger (1992); Cohen (1991); Gulliver (1979). See Ramsbotham, Woodhouse and Miall (2016), ch. 15. Kevin Avruch was the first to emphasize the centrality of the topic of culture for conflict resolution, and he continues to be the foremost analyst of it; see Avruch (1998) and Avruch (2012).
11 Hall (1976), p. 91.
12 Williams (2004), p. 5.
13 Habermas (1987), p. 126.
14 See Rorty (1988); Nagel (1986); Bourdieu (1984).
15 Fairclough (1989), pp. 194–5.
16 Margaret Thatcher, BBC Radio 3 interview, 13 December 1985, quoted in Fairclough (1989), pp. 174–5; repunctuated, capitalization in the original.
17 Ramsbotham (2013).
18 Mourad (2004), pp. 76, 80.
19 Ibid., p. 2.
20 Dowty (2012), p. 258.
21 Ryder and Kearney (2001), p. 365.
22 Schofield (1996), p. 121.
23 Nicolić (2003), p. 54.
24 Wasserstrom (2001), p. xi.
25 Jones and Caney (2003), p. 154.
26 Mertus (1999), p. 10.
27 Ibid., pp. 9–10.
28 Ibid., p. 9.
29 Foucault (1980), p. 377.
30 For more on this, see Ramsbotham (2010), pp. 146–7.
31 Mertus (1999), p. 4.
32 Kelly (1995), p. 139.
33 Derrida (1994), p. 85.
34 The fact that there is no adequate philosophy of radical disagreement has far-reaching implications, I think, that extend beyond the scope of this book. At its heart lies the fact that the monological cannot finally encompass the poly-

logical. In demonstrating this, heuristic engagement can be a useful corrective to the *reductionism* inherent in realist theory, the *didacticism* that haunts critical theory, and the *relativism* that pervades post-structuralism (despite protests to the contrary). For example, see the application of Dominick LaCapra's notion of 'empathic unsettlement' (Capra 2001) in Bashir Bashir's and Amos Goldberg's groundbreaking 'Deliberating the Holocaust and the Nakba: disruptive empathy and binationalism in Israel/Palestine' (2014). This echoes themes in Gadamer's 'hermeneutic dialogue' as discussed earlier in this book. See also Boaz Hameiri et al. (2014) 'Paradoxical thinking as a new avenue of intervention to promote peace', which echoes themes in dilemmatic communication as also discussed earlier.

Conclusion

1 Alexander Pope, *An Essay on Criticism* (1711), lines 231–2.
2 For example, in his study of *The Real Politics of the Horn of Africa: Money, War and the Business of Power* (2016), Alex de Waal contrasts 'Schmittian conflicts', between organized conflict parties over sovereignty and power, and 'Hobbesian conflicts', made up of a bewildering array of shifting localized struggles and alliances in poor and ill-governed countries fuelled by exports, aid funds, and Western military assistance and peacekeeping payments. In this 'business model', allegiance is bought piecemeal in the 'political market-place'. There is little or no connection between power-brokers and identifiable local 'identity groups', so a limit is reached to the scope for promoting 'collective strategic thinking' as a basis for wider strategic engagement as advocated in this book. Overcoming this fragmentation in countries such as Sudan, Somalia and Eritrea, therefore, means somehow reaching down beneath this self-perpetuating 'marketplace of violence' to the underlying social groupings in whose name much of the violence is rhetorically carried out. However difficult, this is the process required if the erosion of institutions of government is to be reversed and post-war state-building is again to become possible.
3 Parekh (2002), p. 274.
4 *Guardian*, 4 September 2005.
5 Watt ([1964] 1991), pp. xi–lxi (omissions not marked).

REFERENCES

al'Alwani, Taha (1997) *The Ethics of Disagreement in Islam*, trans. A. Hamid. Herndon, VA: International Institute of Islamic Thought.

Albin, Cecilia (1997) Negotiating intractable conflicts: on the future of Jerusalem, *Cooperation and Conflict*, 32(1): 29–77.

Althusser, Louis (1971) Ideology and ideological state apparatuses (notes towards an investigation), in *Lenin and Philosophy, and Other Essays*, trans. B. Brewster. London: New Left Books.

Anderson, Benedict (1991) *Imagined Communities: Reflections on the Origin and Spread of Nationalism*. 2nd edn, London: Verso.

Anderson, Mary (1999) *Do No Harm: How Aid Can Support Peace – or War*. Boulder, CO: Lynne Rienner.

Arab Peace Initiative (2002) www.al-bab.com/arab/docs/league/peace02.htm.

Augsburger, David (1992) *Conflict Mediation across Cultures*. Louiseville, KY: Westminster/John Knox Press.

Avruch, Kevin (1998) *Culture and Conflict Resolution*. Washington, DC: US Institute of Peace Press.

Avruch, Kevin (2012) *Context and Pretext in Conflict Resolution: Conflict, Identity, Power and Practice*. Boulder, CO: Paradigm.

Axelrod, Robert (1984) *The Evolution of Cooperation*. New York: Basic Books.

Azar, Edward (1990) *The Management of Protracted Social Conflict: Theory and Cases*. Aldershot: Dartmouth.

Azar, Edward, and Burton, John (1986) *International Conflict Resolution: Theory and Practice*. Brighton: Wheatsheaf.

Bahour, Sam (2008) Reference report on the Regaining the Initiative project, unpublished MS.

Bahour, Sam (2016) *Asynchronous and Inseparable Struggles for Rights and a Political End-Game*. Palestinian Center for Policy and Survey Research (PSR), www.pcpsr.org/sites/default/files/Sam%20Bahour%20print%20English. pdf

Bahour, Sam, and Klug, Tony (2015) Israel can't have it both ways: recognize Palestine or grant equal rights, Tikkun 30(4): 26 www.tikkun.org/nextgen/israel-cant-have-it-both-ways-recognize-palestine-or-grant-equal-rights.

Barber, Benjamin (1984) *Strong Democracy*. Berkeley: University of California Press.

Bar-On, Mordechai (2006) Conflicting narratives or narratives of a conflict?, in Robert Rotberg (ed.), *Israeli and Palestinian Narratives of Conflict: History's Double Helix*. Bloomington, IN: Indiana University Press, pp. 142–73.

Bashir, Bashir (2009) Reference report on the Regaining the Initiative project, unpublished MS.

Bashir, Bashir, and Goldberg, Amos (2014) Deliberating the Holocaust and the Nakba: disruptive empathy and binationalism in Israel/Palestine, *Journal of Holocaust Studies*, 16(1): 77–99.

Bell, Christine (2008) *On the Law of Peace: Peace Agreements and the Lex Pacificatoria*. Oxford: Oxford University Press.

Ben-Porat, Guy (2008) Israeli society, in Guy Ben-Porat, Yagil Levy, Shlomo Mizrahi, Arye Naor and Erez Tzfadia, *Israel since 1980*. Cambridge: Cambridge University Press, pp. 9–41.

Bieber, Florian, and Daskalovski, Židas (eds) (2003) *Understanding the War in Kosovo*. London: Frank Cass.

Birnbaum, Ben, and Tibon, Amir (2014) The explosive, inside story of how John Kerry built an Israel–Palestine peace plan – and watched it crumble, *New Republic*, 20 July 20, www.newrepublic.com/article/118751/how-israel-palestine-peace-deal-died.

Bohm, David (1996) *On Dialogue*, ed. L. Nicol. London: Routledge.

Bojer, Marianne, and McKay, Elaine (2006) *Mapping Dialogue*, http://portals.wi.wur.nl/files/docs/msp/Mapping%20Dialogue.pdf.

Booth, Ken, and Dunne, Tim (eds) (2002) *Worlds in Collision: Terror and World Order*. Basingstoke: Palgrave Macmillan.

Borchard, Michael (2015) Waking up with Bibi: how stable is the Israeli government? *Orient: German Journal for Politics, Economics and Culture of the Middle East*, 56(3): 36–41.

Boulding, Elise (1976) *The Underside of History: A View of Women through Time*. Boulder, CO: Westview Press.

Boulding, Elise (1990) *Building a Global Civic Culture: Education for an Interdependent World*. Syracuse, NY: Syracuse University Press.

Boulding, Kenneth (1977) Twelve friendly quarrels with Johan Galtung, *Journal of Peace Research*, 14(1): 75–86.

Boulding, Kenneth (1990) *Three Faces of Power*. London: Sage.

Bourdieu, Pierre (1984) *Distinction: A Social Critique of the Judgement of Taste*. Cambridge, MA: Harvard University Press.

Brinton, Crane (1938) *The Anatomy of Revolution*. New York: W. W. Norton.

Brom, Shlomo (2014) The American principles document: the negotiations with Israel and the Palestinians, *INSS*, no. 515, 9 February, http://heb.inss.org.il/index.aspx?id=4354&articleid=6593 [in Hebrew].

Broome, Benjamin (1993) Managing differences in conflict resolution: the role of relational empathy, in Denis Sandole and Hugo van der Merwe (eds), *Conflict Resolution Theory and Practice: Integration and Application*. Manchester: Manchester University Press, pp. 97–111.

Burr, Vivien (1995) *An Introduction to Social Constructionism*. London: Routledge.

Burton, John (1968) *Systems, States, Diplomacy and Rules*. London: Macmillan.

Burton, John (1969) *Conflict and Communication: The Use of Controlled Communication in International Relations*. London: Macmillan.

Burton, John (1972) *World Society*. London: Macmillan.

Burton, John (1987) *Resolving Deep-Rooted Conflict: A Handbook*. Lanham, MD: University Press of America.

Burton, John (1990a) *Conflict, Resolution and Prevention*. London: Macmillan.

Burton, John (1990b) *Conflict: Human Needs Theory*. London: Macmillan.

Burton, John (1997) *Violence Explained*. Manchester: Manchester University Press.

Carnegie Commission on Preventing Deadly Conflict (1997) *Preventing Deadly Conflict*. Washington, DC: Carnegie Corporation of New York.

Caspersen, Nina (2017 forthcoming) *Peace Agreements: Finding Solutions to Intra-State Conflicts*. Cambridge: Polity.

Cheshire, Leonard (1985) *The Light of Many Suns*. London: Methuen.

Clausewitz, Carl von ([1832] 1976) *On War*, trans. and ed. Michael Howard and Peter Paret. Princeton, NJ: Princeton University Press.

Cohen, Raymond (1991) *Negotiating across Cultures: Communication Obstacles in International Diplomacy*. Washington, DC: United States Institute of Peace Press.

Coleman, James (1957) *Community Conflict*. New York: Free Press.

Collén, Charlotta (ed.) (2014) *National Dialogue and Internal Mediation Processes: Perspectives on Theory and Practice*. Helsinki: Ministry for Foreign Affairs of Finland.

Coleman, Peter (2011) *The Five Percent: Finding Solutions to Seemingly Impossible Conflicts*. Philadelphia: Public Affairs.

Coser, Lewis (1956) *The Functions of Social Conflict*. New York: Free Press.

Cristal, Moty, and Gal, Orit (2010) Israeli Strategic Forum workshop presentation, Haifa.

Dallmayr, Fred (2002) Dialogue of civilizations: a hermeneutical perspective, in *Dialogue among Civilizations: Some Exemplary Voices*. New York: Palgrave, pp. 17–30.

Davidson, Donald (1984) On the very idea of a conceptual scheme, in *Inquiries into Truth and Interpretation*. Oxford: Clarendon Press, pp. 183–98.

de Waal, Alex (2016) *The Real Politics of the Horn of Africa: Money, War and the Business of Power*. Cambridge: Polity.

Derrida, Jacques (1994) *Spectres of Marx: The State of the Debt, the Work of Mourning, and the New International*, trans. P. Kamuf. London: Routledge.

Deutsch, Morton (1949) A theory of cooperation and conflict, *Human Relations*, 2: 129–52.

Deutsch, Morton (1973) *The Resolution of Conflicts: Constructive and Destructive Processes*. New Haven, CT: Yale University Press.

Deutsch, Morton (2000) Cooperation and competition, in Morton Deutsch and Peter Coleman (eds), *The Handbook of Conflict Resolution: Theory and Practice*. San Francisco: Jossey-Bass, pp. 21–40.

Dowty, Alan (2012) *Israel/Palestine*. 3rd edn, Cambridge: Polity.

Dukes, Frank (1996) *Resolving Public Conflict: Transforming Community and Governance*. Manchester: Manchester University Press.

The Economist (2014) Winning the battle, losing the war, 2 August, p. 7.

Erekat, Saeb (2008) *Life is Negotiations*. Nablus: An-Najah National University.

Erekat, Saeb (2015) *Imam Ali Bin Abi Taleb and Negotiations*. Bradford: University of Bradford, Division of Peace Studies.

222

Fairclough, Nigel (1989) *Language and Power*. Harlow: Longman.

Filardo-Llamas, Laura (2008) Legitimizing through language: political discourse worlds in Northern Ireland after the 1998 agreement, *Peace and Conflict Studies*, 15(1): 77–94.

Finnis, John, Boyle, Joseph M., and Grisez, Germain (1987) *Nuclear Deterrence, Morality and Realism*. Oxford: Clarendon Press.

Fisher, Roger, and Brown, Scott (1988) *Getting Together: Building Relationships as We Negotiate*. New York: Penguin.

Fisher, Roger, and Sharp, Alan (1988) *Getting it Done: How to Lead When You Are Not in Charge*. New York: Harper.

Fisher, Roger, Kopelman, Elizabeth, and Schneider, Andrea (1994) *Beyond Machiavelli: Tools for Coping with Conflict*. Cambridge, MA: Harvard University Press.

Fisher, Roger, Ury, William, and Patton, Bruce (1991) *Getting to Yes: Negotiating Agreement without Giving In*. 2nd edn, Boston: Houghton-Mifflin.

Fisher, Ronald (1997) *Interactive Conflict Resolution*. Syracuse, NY: Syracuse University Press.

Fisher, Ronald, and Keashly, Loraleigh (1991) The potential complementarity of mediation and consultation within a contingency model of third party intervention, *Journal of Peace Research*, 28(1): 29–42.

Floyer Acland, Andrew (1995) *Resolving Disputes without Going to Court*. London: Century Business Books.

Follett, Mary Parker (1942) *Dynamic Administration: The Collected Papers of Mary Parker Follett*. New York: Harper.

Foucault, Michel (1980) *Power/Knowledge: Selected Interviews and Other Writings*. New York: Pantheon.

Freedman, Laurence (2013) *Strategy: A History*. Oxford: Oxford University Press.

Friedman, Uri (2014) Martin Indyk explains the collapse of the Middle East peace process, *The Atlantic*, 3 July, www.theatlantic.com/international/print/2014/07/indyk-netanyahu-and-abbas-loathe-each-other/373922.

Gadamer, Hans-Georg (1975) *Truth and Method*. London: Sheed & Ward.

Galtung, Johan (1976) Three approaches to peace: peacekeeping, peacemaking and peacebuilding, in *Essays in Peace Research*, Vol. 2: *Peace, War and Defence*. Copenhagen: Christian Ejlers, pp. 282–304.

Galtung, Johan (1987) Only one friendly quarrel with Kenneth Boulding, *Journal of Peace Research*, 24(2): 119–203.

Galtung, Johan (1996) *Peace by Peaceful Means: Peace and Conflict, Development and Civilization*. Oslo: PRIO.

Galtung, Johan (2004) *Transcend and Transform*. London: Pluto Press.

Ganesan, N. (2014) The Myanmar Peace Center: its origins, activities, and aspirations, *Asia Journal of Peacebuilding*, 2(1): 127–41.

Ghanem, As'ad (2001) *The Palestinian-Arab Minority in Israel 1948–2000: A Political Study*. New York: SUNY Press.

Global Burden of Armed Violence (GBAV) (2015) Geneva Declaration Secretariat.

Global Terrorism Database (GTD) (2015) www.start.umd.edu/gtd.

Goldmann, Nahum (1969) *The Autobiography of Nahum Goldmann: Sixty Years of Jewish Life*. New York: Holt, Reinhart & Winston.

Gulliver, P. (1979) *Disputes and Negotiations: A Cross-Cultural Perspective*. New York: Academic Press.

Gurr, Ted (2000) *Peoples versus States: Minorities at Risk in the New Century.* Washington, DC: US Institute of Peace Press.

Habermas, Jürgen (1986) *The Theory of Communicative Action*, Vol. 1: *Reason and the Rationalization of Society*, trans. T. McCarthy. Cambridge: Polity.

Habermas, Jürgen (1987) *The Theory of Communicative Action*, Vol. 2: *The Critique of Functionalist Reason*, trans. T. McCarthy, Cambridge: Polity.

Halevi, Jonathan (2014) The crisis in the peace talks was pre-planned by the Palestinians, *Jerusalem Center for Public Affairs*, 10 April, http://jcpa.org/article/crisis-peace-talks/.

Hall, Edward (1976) *Beyond Culture.* New York: Doubleday.

Hameiri, Boaz, Porat, Ron, Bar-Tal, Daniel, Bieler, Atara, and Halperin, Eran (2014) Paradoxical thinking as a new avenue of intervention to promote peace, *Proceedings of the National Academy of Sciences*, 111(3), www.pnas.org/content/111/30/10996.full.

Hand, Sean (ed.) (1989) *The Levinas Reader.* Oxford: Blackwell.

Holsti, Kalevi (1991) *Peace and War: Armed Conflicts and International Order 1648–1989.* Cambridge: Cambridge University Press.

Howard, Michael (1984) *The Causes of Wars.* Cambridge, MA: Harvard University Press.

Hutchby, Ian, and Wooffitt, Robin (1998) *Conversation Analysis.* Cambridge: Polity.

IEP (Institute for Economics and Peace) (2014) *Global Peace Index 2014: Measuring Peace and Assessing Country Risk*, http://economicsandpeace.org/wp-content/uploads/2015/06/2014-Global-Peace-Index-REPORT_0-1.pdf.

IEP (Institute for Economics and Peace) (2015) *Global Peace Index 2015: Measuring Peace, its Causes and its Economic Value*, http://economicsandpeace.org/wp-content/uploads/2015/06/Global-Peace-Index-Report-2015_0.pdf.

Ikenberry, John (2014) The illusion of geopolitics: the enduring power of the liberal order, *Foreign Affairs*, May/June.

International Crisis Group (2004) Identity crisis: Israel and its Arab citizens, *Middle East Report*, no. 25, 4 March.

International Crisis Group (2012) Back to basics: Israel's Arab minority and the Israeli–Palestinian conflict, *Middle East Report*, no. 119, 14 March.

Irigaray, Luce ([1977] 1985) *This Sex Which Is Not One.* Ithaca, NY: Cornell University Press.

Israeli Strategic Forum (ISF) (2015) Is there a path to a more equal Israel? (Unpublished).

Issacharov, Avi, and Amir, Tibon (2014) The meeting between Livni and Erekat looks like a battlefield, 3 April, http://news.walla.co.il/item/2735012 [in Hebrew].

Jabri, Vivienne (1996) *Discourses on Violence: Conflict Analysis Reconsidered.* Manchester: Manchester University Press.

Jones, Peter, and Caney, Simon (2003) Introduction: disagreement and difference, *Disagreement and Difference*, special issue of the *Critical Review of International Social and Political Philosophy*, 6(3): 1–11.

Kalyvas, Stathis (2006) *The Logic of Violence in Civil War.* Cambridge: Cambridge University Press.

Karmi, Ghada (2015) *Return: A Palestinian Memoir.* London: Verso.

Kelly, Michael (1995) The Gadamer/Habermas debate revisited: the question of ethics, in David Rasmussen (ed.), *Universalism vs. Communitarianism: Contemporary Debates in Ethics*. Cambridge, MA: MIT Press.

Kelman, Herb (1996) The interactive problem-solving approach, in C. Crocker and F. Hampson (eds), *Managing Global Chaos: Sources of and Responses to International Conflict*. Washington, DC: US Institute of Peace Press, pp. 500–20.

Kelman, Herbert (2011) A one-country/two-state solution for the Israeli–Palestinian conflict, *Middle East Policy Journal*, 18(1): 27–41.

Kelman, Herbert (2016) *Resolving Deep-Rooted Conflicts: Essays on the Theory and Practice of Interactive Problem Solving*, ed. Wilfried Graf and Werner Wintersteiner. London: Routledge.

Kelman, Herbert (2017 forthcoming) *The Israeli–Palestinian Conflict: From Mutual Negation to Reconciliation*, ed. Philip Mattar and Neil Capan. London: Routledge.

Kerman, Cynthia (1974) *Creative Tension: The Life and Thought of Kenneth Boulding*. Ann Arbor: University of Michigan Press.

King, Martin Luther ([1963] 1992) Lincoln memorial address, in Walter Safire (ed.), *Lend Me Your Ears: Great Speeches in History*. New York: W. W. Norton, pp. 533–4.

King, Sallie (2000) A global ethic in the light of comparative religious ethics, in Sumner B. Twiss and Bruce Grelle (eds), *Explorations in Global Ethics: Comparative Religious Ethics and Interreligious Dialogue*. Boulder, CO: Westview Press.

Körppen, Daniela, Schmelze, Beatrix, and Wils, Oliver (eds) (2008) *A Systematic Approach to Conflict Transformation: Exploring Strengths and Limitations*. Berlin: Berghof Research Center for Constructive Conflict Management.

Kriesberg, Louis, Northrop, Terrel, and Thorson, Stuart (1989) *Intractable Conflicts and their Transformations*. Syracuse, NY: Syracuse University Press.

Kuhn, Thomas (1962) *The Structure of Scientific Revolutions*. Chicago: University of Chicago Press.

Küng, Hans (1996) *Yes to a Global Ethic*. New York: Continuum.

Küng, Hans, and Kuschel, Karl-Josef (eds) (1993) *A Global Ethic: The Declaration of the Parliament of the World's Religions*. New York: Continuum.

LaCapra, Dominick (2001) *Writing History, Writing Trauma*. Baltimore: Johns Hopkins University Press.

Laqueur, Walter, and Rubin, Barry (eds) *The Israel–Arab Reader: A Documentary History of the Middle East Conflict*. 7th edn, London: Penguin.

Lederach, John-Paul (2005) *The Moral Imagination: The Art and Soul of Building Peace*. Oxford: Oxford University Press.

Levinas, Emanuel (1998) *Entre Nous: On Thinking-of-the-Other*, trans. M. Smith and B. Harshav. London: Athlone Press.

Lewin, Kurt (1948) *Resolving Social Conflicts*. New York: Harper.

Lintl, Peter (2015) Understanding coalition formation in Israel: party positions and cleavages in light of the 2015 election, *Orient: German Journal for Politics, Economics and Culture of the Middle East*, 56(3): 27–35.

Little, Adrian (2014) *Enduring Conflict: Challenging the Signature of Peace and Democracy*. London: Bloomsbury.

Locke, John ([1690] 1975) *An Essay Concerning Human Understanding*. Oxford: Oxford University Press.

Macdonell, Diane (1986) *Theories of Discourse*. Oxford: Blackwell.

Mack, Andrew, et al. (2014) *Human Security Report 2013: The Decline of Global Violence: Evidence, Explanation and Contestation.* Vancouver: Human Security Press.

Maddox, Bronwen (2014) Israel – drifting towards disaster? *Prospect Magazine,* July, pp. 25–33.

Malpas, Jeff, Arnswald, Ulrich, and Kertsche, Jens (eds) (2002) *Gadamer's Century: Essays in Honor of Hans-Georg Gadamer.* Cambridge, MA: MIT Press.

Maoz, Ifat (2011) Does contact work in protracted asymmetrical conflict? Appraising 20 years of reconciliation-aimed encounters between Israeli Jews and Palestinians, *Journal of Peace Research,* 48(1): 115–25.

Mayer, Bernard (2009) *Staying with Conflicts: A Strategic Approach to Ongoing Disputes.* San Francisco: Jossey-Bass.

Mead, Walter Russell (2014) The return of geopolitics: the revenge of the revisionist powers, *Foreign Affairs,* May/June.

Meir, Golda (1975) *My Life.* New York: Putnam.

Mertus, Julie (1999) *Kosovo: How Myths and Truths Started a War.* Berkeley: University of California Press.

Misgeld, Dieter, and Nicholson, Graeme (1992) *Hans-Georg Gadamer on Education, Poetry and History: Applied Hermeneutics,* trans. Lawrence Schmidt and Monica Reuss. Albany, NY: SUNY Press.

Mitchell, Chris (2014) *The Anatomy of Intractable Conflict.* London: Palgrave.

Mitchell, Chris, and Banks, Michael (1996) *Handbook of Conflict Resolution: The Analytical Problem-Solving Approach.* London: Pinter/Cassell.

Mitrany, David (1943) *A Working Peace System: An Argument for the Functional Development of International Organization.* New York: Oxford University Press.

Moi, Toril (ed.) (1986) *The Kristeva Reader.* Oxford: Blackwell.

Montefiore, Simon (2007) *Young Stalin.* London: Weidenfeld & Nicolson.

Morgenthau, Hans ([1948] 1973) *Politics among Nations: The Struggle for Power and Peace.* New York: Knopf.

Morris, Benny (1987) *The Birth of the Palestinian Refugee Problem 1947–1949.* Cambridge: Cambridge University Press.

Mouffe, Chantal (1999) Deliberative democracy or agonistic pluralism, *Social Research,* 66(3): 745–58.

Mourad, Kenize (2004) *Our Sacred Land: Voices from the Palestine–Israeli Conflict.* Oxford: Oneworld.

Murray, John, and Barnett, Terry (2007) Negotiation training workshop, Paper disseminated at a training workshop held by the Negotiation Affairs Department, Ramallah.

Nagel, Thomas (1986) *The View from Nowhere.* Oxford: Oxford University Press.

Nicolić, Lazar (2003) Ethnic prejudices and discriminations: the case of Kosovo, in Florian Bieber and Židas Daskalovski (eds), *Understanding the War in Kosovo.* London: Frank Cass, pp. 51–75.

Nietzsche, Friedrich (1974) *The Gay Science,* trans. W. Kaufmann. New York: Vintage.

Nye, Joseph (2004) *Soft Power: The Means to Success in World Politics.* New York: Public Affairs.

OCHA (United Nations Office for the Coordination of Humanitarian Affairs)

(2015) *Fragmented Lives: Humanitarian Overview 2014*, www.ochaopt.org/documents/annual_humanitarian_overview_2014_english_final.pdf.

OECD DAC (Organization for Economic Cooperation and Development Development Assistance Committee) (2014) *Fragile States 2013: Resource Flows and Trends in a Shifting* World. Paris: OECD.

Osgood, Charles (1962) *An Alternative to War or Surrender*. Urbana: University of Illinois Press.

Palestine Strategy Group (PSG) (2008) *Regaining the Initiative: Palestinian Strategic Options to End Israeli Occupation*, www.palestinestrategygroup.ps/wp-content/uploads/2015/09/Report-2008.pdf.

Palestine Strategy Group (PSG) (2015) *A Post Oslo Strategy: Parameters, Policy Implications, Actions*, www.palestinestrategygroup.ps/wp-content/uploads/2015/09/A-POST-OSLO-STRATEGY-REPORT-2014-15.pdf.

Palestinian Citizens of Israel Group (PCIG) (2015) Strategic thinking for Palestinian Arabs in the State of Israel (unpublished).

Pantham, Thomas (1992) Some dimensions of universality of the philosophical hermeneutics: a conversation with Hans-Georg Gadamer, *Journal of Indian Council of Philosophical Research*, 9: 132.

Pappé, Ilan (2011) *The Forgotten Palestinians: A History of the Palestinians in Israel*. New Haven, CT: Yale University Press.

Pappé, Ilan (2012) *The Idea of Israel: A History of Power and Knowledge*. London: Verso.

Parekh, Bikhu (2002) Terrorism or intercultural dialogue?, in Ken Booth and Tim Dunne (eds), *Worlds in Collision: Terror and World Order*. Basingstoke: Palgrave Macmillan.

Petito, Fabio (2011) In defence of dialogue of civilisations: with a brief illustration of the diverging agreement between Edward Said and Louis Massignon, *Millennium: Journal of International Studies*, 39(3): 759–79.

Pettersson, Therése, and Wallensteen, Peter (2015) Armed conflicts, 1946–2014, *Journal of Peace Research*, 52(4): 536–50.

Pinker, Steven (2002) *The Blank Slate*. London: Penguin.

Pinker, Steven (2011) *The Better Angels of Our Nature: Why Violence Has Declined*. New York: Viking Books.

Pinker, Steven, and Mack, Andrew (2014) The world is not falling apart, 22 December, www.slate.com/articles/news_and_politics/foreigners/2014/12/the_world_is_not_falling_apart_the_trend_lines_reveal_an_increasingly_peaceful.html.

Popper, Karl (1959). *The Logic of Scientific Discovery*. New York: Basic Books.

Priest, Graham (2002) *Beyond the Limits of Thought*. Oxford: Clarendon Press.

Pruitt, Dan (2007) Readiness theory and the Northern Ireland conflict, *American Behavioural Scientist*, 50(11): 1520–41.

Quine, Willard, and Ullian, J. S. (1970) *The Web of Belief*. New York: Random House.

Ramsbotham, Oliver (1987) *Choices: Nuclear and Non-Nuclear Defence Options*. London: Brassey's.

Ramsbotham, Oliver (2010) *Transforming Violent Conflict: Radical Disagreement, Dialogue and Survival*. London: Routledge.

Ramsbotham, Oliver (2013) Is there a theory of radical disagreement?, *International Journal of Conflict Engagement and Resolution*, 1(1): 56–82.

Ramsbotham, Oliver (2016) Strategic studies, conflict resolution and prevailing patterns of transnational conflict, available on the Oxford Research Group website, www.oxfordresearchgroup.org.uk

Ramsbotham, Oliver (forthcoming) Hans-Georg Gadamer, hermeneutic dialogue and conflict resolution, in *Dialogue Theories II*. London: Dialogue Society.

Ramsbotham, Oliver, and Schiff, Amira (forthcoming) Principled negotiation, strategic negotiation and the Kerry initiative.

Ramsbotham, Oliver, Woodhouse, Tom, and Miall, Hugh (2011) *Contemporary Conflict Resolution*. 3rd edn, Cambridge: Polity.

Rapoport, Anatol (1960) *Fights, Games and Debates*. Ann Arbor: University of Michigan Press.

Rapoport, Anatol, and Chammah, Albert (1965) *The Prisoner's Dilemma: A Study in Conflict and Cooperation*. Ann Arbor: University of Michigan Press.

Ravid, Barak (2013) All you wanted to know about the resumption of the Israeli–Palestinian negotiations, *Haaretz*, 5 August, www.haaretz.co.il/news/whatis/.premium-1.2089027 [in Hebrew].

Ravid, Barak (2014a) US is pessimistic about achieving a framework agreement by the end of the month, *Haaretz*, 3 March, www.haaretz.co.il/news/politics/.premium-1.2257349 [in Hebrew].

Ravid, Barak (2014b) Kerry in a closed conversation: without peace, Israel is liable to become an apartheid state, *Haaretz*, 28 April, www.haaretz.co.il/news/politics/1.2306672 [in Hebrew].

Ravid, Barak (2014c) Netanyahu's flexibility, the Americans' mistake, *Haaretz*, 5 July, www.haaretz.co.il/israel-peace-convention/1.2359763 [in Hebrew].

Ravid, Barak (2015) Netanyahu: If I'm elected, there will be no Palestinian state, *Haaretz*, 16 March, http://tinyurl.com/12znpr2.

Ravid, Barak, and Khoury, Jack (2014) Kerry to meet with Abbas today in effort to prevent breakdown of negotiations, *Haaretz*, 24 March, www.haaretz.co.il/news/politics/1.2279728 [in Hebrew].

Richardson, Lewis Fry (1960) *Statistics of Deadly Quarrels*. Pittsburgh: Boxwood Press.

Richmond, Oliver (2008) *Peace in International Relations*. London: Routledge.

Ropers, Norbert (2008) Systemic conflict transformation: reflections on the conflict and peace process in Sri Lanka, in Körppen, Daniela, Schmelze, Beatrix, and Wils, Oliver (eds), *A Systematic Approach to Conflict Transformation: Exploring Strengths and Limitations*. Berlin: Berghof Research Center for Constructive Conflict Management, pp.11–41.

Rorty, Richard (1988) *Contingency, Irony and Solidarity*. Cambridge: Cambridge University Press.

Ross, Dennis (2004) *The Missing Peace: The Inside Story of the Fight for Middle East Peace*. New York: Farrar, Straus & Giroux.

Ross, Dennis (2015) Stop giving Palestinians a pass, *New York Times*, 4 January, www.nytimes.com/2015/01/05/opinion/stop-giving-palestinians-a-pass.html?_r=0.

Rotberg, Robert (ed.) (2006) *Israeli and Palestinian Narratives of Conflict: History's Double Helix*. Bloomington: Indiana University Press.

Rothman, Jay (1992) *From Confrontation to Cooperation: Resolving Ethnic and Regional Conflict*. Newbury Park, CA: Sage.

Rouhana, Nadim (1989) The political transformation of the Palestinians in Israel: from acquiescence to challenge, *Journal of Palestine Studies*, 18(3): 34–55.

Rouhana, Nadim (1997) *Palestinian Citizens in an Ethnic Jewish State: Identities in Conflict*. New Haven, CT: Yale University Press.

Rouhana, Nadim (2006) Zionism's encounter with the Palestinians: the dynamics of force, fear and extremism, in Robert Rotberg (ed.) *Israeli and Palestinian Narratives of Conflict*. Bloomington: Indiana University Press, pp. 115–41.

Ryder, Chris, and Kearney, Vincent (2001) *Drumcree: The Orange Order's Last Stand*. London: Methuen.

Safire, Walter (ed.) (1992) *Lend Me Your Ears: Great Speeches in History*. New York: W. W. Norton.

Salem, Paul (1993) In theory: a critique of Western conflict resolution from a non-Western perspective, *Negotiation Journal*, 9(4): 361–9.

Salem, Paul (ed.) (1997) *Conflict Resolution in the Arab World: Selected Essays*. New York: American University of Beirut.

Sand, Shlomo (2009) *The Invention of the Jewish People*. London: Verso.

Sandole, Dennis, and Van der Merwe, Hugo (eds) *Conflict Resolution Theory and Practice: Integration and Application*. Manchester: Manchester University Press.

Saunders, Harold (1999) *A Public Peace Process: Sustained Dialogue to Transform Racial and Ethnic Conflict*. New York: Palgrave.

Schama, Simon (2013) *The Story of the Jews: Finding the Words, 1000 BCE – 1492 CE*. London: Bodley Head.

Schelling, Thomas (1960) *The Strategy of Conflict*. Cambridge, MA: Harvard University Press.

Schiff, Amira (2014) On success and failure: readiness theory and the Aceh and Sri Lanka peace processes, *International Negotiation*, 19(1): 89–126.

Schiff, Amira (2015) Lessons from the Kerry peace initiative: the need for a constructive approach, *Peace and Conflict Studies*, 22(2): 160–76.

Schlaim, Avi (2000) *The Iron Wall: Israel and the Arab World*. New York: W. W. Norton.

Schlaim, Avi (2009) *Israel and Palestine: Reappraisals, Revisions, Refutations*. London: Verso.

Schnell, Izhak, and Bar-Tal, Daniel (2016) After 50 years: save Irael, stop the occupation, *Palestine–Israel Jounral*, 21(3), www.pij.org/details.php?id=1690.

Schofield, Victoria (1996) *Kashmir in the Crossfire*. London: I. B. Tauris.

Shapcott, Richard (2001) *Justice, Community and Dialogue in International Relations*. Cambridge: Cambridge University Press.

Shtayyeh, Muhammad (forthcoming) *A Brief History of Palestine*.

Siebert, Hannes (2014) National dialogue and legitimate change, in *Legitimacy and Peace Processes: From Coercion to Consent, Accord*, no. 25: 36–9.

Smooha, Sammy, and Peretz, Don (1982) The Arabs in Israel, *Journal of Conflict Resolution*, 26(3): 451–84.

Sorokin, Pitirim (1937) *Social and Cultural Dynamics*, 4 vols. New York: American Book Company.

Suganami, Hidemi (1996) *On the Causes of War*. Oxford: Clarendon Press.

Susskind, Lawrence (1987) *Breaking the Impasse: Consensual Approaches to Resolving Public Disputes*. New York: Basic Books.

Taylor, Charles (2002) Understanding the other: a Gadamerian view on conceptual schemes, in Jeff Malpas, Ulrich Arnswald and Jens Kertsche (eds), *Gadamer's Century: Essays in Honor of Hans-Georg Gadamer*. Cambridge, MA: MIT Press, pp. 279–98.

Thiessen, Chuck, and Darweish, Marwan (forthcoming) Conflict resolution and asymmetric conflicts: competing perceptions of planned contact interventions between Jewish Israelis and Palestinians.

Tibon, Amir (2014) The UN Security Council rejected the Palestinian proposal, *Walla News*, 31 December, http://news.walla.co.il/item/2815391 [in Hebrew].

Turner, Mandy, and Hussein, Cherine (2015) Israel–Palestine after Oslo: mapping transformations and alternatives in a time of deepening crisis, *Conflict, Security and Development*, 15(5): 415–24.

Twiss, Sumner B., and Grelle, Bruce (eds) (2000) *Explorations in Global Ethics: Comparative Religious Ethics and Interreligious Dialogue*. Boulder, CO: Westview Press.

UNHCR (2015) *Global Trends 2014: World at War*. New York: United Nations, www.unhcr.org/558193896.html.

United Nations (1945) United Nations Charter, Preamble, www.un.org/en/sections/un-charter/preamble/index.html.

Von Neumann, John, and Morgenstern, Oskar (1944) *Theory of Games and Economic Behavior*. Princeton, NJ: Princeton University Press.

Wallensteen, Peter, and Sollenberg, Margareta (2007) Armed conflicts, conflict termination and peace agreements, *Journal of Peace Research*, 34(3): 339–58.

Wasserstrom, Bernard (2001) *Divided Jerusalem: The Struggle for the Holy City*. London: Profile Books.

Watt, D. Cameron ([1964] 1991) Introduction to Adolf Hitler, *Mein Kampf*, trans. R. Manheim. London: Pimlico.

Weiss, Carol, Connell, James, Kubisch, Anne, and Schorr, Lisbeth (eds) (1995) *New Approaches to Evaluating Comprehensive Community Initiatives*. Washington, DC: Aspen Institute.

Williams, Rowan (2004) *Analysing Atheism: Unbelief and the World of Faith*. London: Lambeth Palace Press Office.

Wistrich, Robert (1991) *Antisemitism: The Longest Hatred*. Berlin: Schocken.

Woodhouse, Tom (1999) *International Conflict Resolution: Some Critiques and a Response*, Working Paper 1. University of Bradford, Centre for Conflict Resolution.

Woodrow, Peter (2006) Advancing practice in conflict analysis and strategy development: interim progress report, Draft paper, Reflecting on Peace Practice Project, http://cdacollaborative.org/publication/advancing-practice-in-conflict-analysis-and-strategy-development-interim-progress-report/.

Wright, Quincy (1942) *A Study of War*. Chicago: University of Chicago Press.

Wyatt, Caroline (2016) Syrian Alawites distance themselves from Assad, www bbc.co.uk/news/world-middle-east-35941679.

Yaar, Ephraim, and Hermann, Tamar (2014a) *The Peace Index: January 2014*, www.peaceindex.org/indexMonthEng.aspx?num=273&monthname=January.

Yaar, Ephraim, and Hermann, Tamar (2014b) Peace Index column, February 2014, www.idi.org.il/media/3091381/Peace_Index_February_2014-Eng.pdf.

Yadlin, Amos (2014) Focus on the essence, not on the process, *Maariv Online*, 6 August, www.maariv.co.il/landedpages/printarticle.aspx?id=441893 [in Hebrew].

Yawnghwe, Harn (2014) Burma – national dialogue: armed groups, contested legitimacy and political transition, in *Legitimacy and Peace Processes: From Coercion to Consent, Accord*, no. 25, pp. 44–9.

Zartman, William (2000) The hurting stalemate and beyond, in Paul C. Stern and

REFERENCES

Daniel Druckman (eds), *Conflict Resolution after the Cold War*. Washington, DC: National Academy Press, pp. 225–50.

Zartman, William (2008) Ripeness revisited: the push and pull of conflict management, in William Zartman (ed.), *Essays on Theory and Practice*. New York: Routledge, pp. 232–44.

Zartman, William, and de Soto, Álvaro (2010) *Timing Mediation Initiatives*. Washington, DC: United States Institute of Peace Press.

Zalzberg, Ofer (2009) Report on the 'Time is Ripe Project' (unpublished).

Zalzberg, Ofer (2016) *The Israeli Labor Party's 'Separation Plan': Making Peace with the Palestinians by Focusing on the Israelis*. Berlin: Friedrich Ebert Stiftung, http://library.fes.de/pdf-files/iez/12487-20160418.pdf.

INDEX